COMECON

INTEGRATION PROBLEMS OF THE PLANNED ECONOMIES

MICHAEL KASER

Lecturer in Soviet Economics, University of Oxford
Fellow of St Antony's College

Second Edition

Issued under the auspices of the
Royal Institute of International Affairs

OXFORD UNIVERSITY PRESS

LONDON NEW YORK TORONTO

1967

Oxford University Press, Ely House, London W.1
GLASGOW NEW YORK TORONTO MELBOURNE WELLINGTON
CAPE TOWN SALISBURY IBADAN NAIROBI LUSAKA ADDIS ABABA
BOMBAY CALCUTTA MADRAS KARACHI LAHORE DACCA
KUALA LUMPUR HONG KONG TOKYO

Printed in Great Britain by
The Broadwater Press Ltd,
Welwyn Garden City,
Hertfordshire

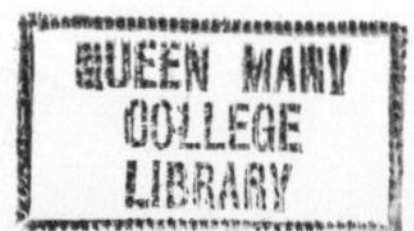

CONTENTS

NOTE TO SECOND EDITION

This edition carries the narrative to February 1967, but recent documentation has also permitted substantial expansion of the book and a closer analysis of the trading relationships underlying the economic evolution of eastern Europe.

ACKNOWLEDGEMENTS

THE author wishes to thank Mr E. F. Jackson, Director of the Oxford University Institute of Economics and Statistics, and Dr A. Zauberman, of the London School of Economics, for many valuable suggestions and the benefit of illuminating discussion. The study owes its origin to Mr Andrew Shonfield and Mrs Jane Degras of the Royal Institute of International Affairs: their constructive advice in its development is warmly acknowledged. Miss Hermia Oliver's unstinting editorial help gave the book its final form.

M. K.

I
INTRODUCTION

THE division of this study into two aspects of Comecon—history and current problems—is designed to follow the two chief lines of interest for western readers. The dispute over Comecon's future, made frankly public in 1964, was politically centred on a new Rumanian nationalism in the context of the Soviet clash with China. The economics of the dispute are, however, rooted in the origins of the organization: more, it has shown up with startling clarity how unsuited are the criteria used by the centrally-planned states of eastern Europe for a rational allocation of resources.

When the members of an economic union are sovereign nations, their separate interests will make explicit the conflict of advantage which decision-makers within any one centralist state may pass over. This is now as true of Comecon as of any other present international group. The principle of sovereignty was entrenched in Comecon's founding declaration of 1949, when Soviet leadership was undisputed, but since 1956—the year of the assertions of Hungarian and Polish nationality—the autonomy of members as such has become a reality. In 1958 Bulgaria, and in 1963 Rumania, made Comecon the testing-ground for particular demonstrations of independence, but, more generally, the shortcomings of the organization in setting up international programmes have exposed the crucial problem of national planning—the selection of economic priorities.

The capitalist economies automate such choice, both within and among themselves, by the equilibrium of prices formed in a market, the disposal of factors of production being directed by the outlay of consumers, whose incomes arise from the ownership of those factors. The many imperfections of the market-price mechanism are not, of course, the subject of the present study, but they underlie current trends in western international integration—the European Common Market, the free-trade areas in Europe and Latin America, the United Nations Conference on Trade and Development.

The western efforts are being pursued in the light of massive official documentation and intensive independent analysis: Comecon, on the other hand, has revealed no more than the barest minimum about itself.[1] It seemed appropriate, therefore, to take particular care to state the facts of Comecon's evolution. The institutional history which constitutes Part I can be shown in perspective only by unravelling the conditions under which the organization was established, and by illustrating its early life. The dilemmas of its middle years must, partly at least, be assessed on a view of its first. It was set up as an extension of reforms of domestic planning in the USSR, at a time when the eastern European states were being remoulded to a specific Soviet model. The supranational proposals of 1962, which precipitated Comecon's political crisis, also originated in Moscow, but at a time when the classic Soviet economic mechanism was under sharp attack, not only in eastern Europe, but—within the twin debates on Liberman's profit motives and Nemchinov's mathematics—in the USSR itself. It is nevertheless a paradox, explicable in political rather than economic terms, that the opposition to Comecon's adoption of traditional central planning was fired by Rumania, whose economic administration has been the least affected by the ferment of eastern European reform. The significant trends in the domestic policies of one member form a somewhat larger part of the early narrative than would ordinarily be justified in a history of an international agency. This, of course, is because, until 1956, the voice of the USSR was decisive in Comecon's councils.

The history is supplemented by the collection, as Appendices, of Comecon's three major documents and a tabulation, based on east European sources too numerous to list, of its agencies, conferences, and decisions.

Part II is addressed to the work of Comecon—in trade, in technical collaboration, in the evolution of a common price policy, and in attempting economic integration. It offers assessments of the present position and future development. The prospects for trade are perhaps the clearest. The average trade dependence of members is low, partly because their planning systems have been virtually incapable of evaluating the gains from trade: remedial principles of pricing and costing are, however, currently being introduced, and cannot fail to be fortified by the considerable devolution of trade-seeking authority

[1] G. Teich, *Der **Rat** für Gegenseitige Wirtschaftshilfe, 1949–63* (Kiel, 1966) provides a comprehensive bibliography of outside commentaries.

to producers, now also in debate. This would notably affect industrial imports, but it is also relevant that the industrialization achieved by Comecon members has not been accompanied by a commensurate development of agriculture. Although the present investment drives will redress some of the lag, it may prove cheaper—if self-sufficiency in foodstuffs were no longer needed for strategic reasons—to import sizeable quantities of farm produce, paid for by manufactures in which industrialization has yielded a cost advantage.

The commercial expansion that can confidently be expected will enlarge East–West turnover (comprising increased exchanges with the underdeveloped areas), certainly at a rate faster than that of trade within the group. While this conclusion is partly based on the mutual cost-advantages of trade with the West and the likelihood of their better exploration, it also has in view the restrictiveness of inter-member programming. In the first place, having abandoned moves towards supranational planning, Comecon members have virtually completed a network of bilateral relations between their plan commissions. Secondly, the 1963 clearing scheme requires the annual plans for inter-member trade to be built up bilaterally—with currency convertibility under very cautious discussion. Such bilateralism in Comecon planning will not demonstrate the options of trade as thoroughly as do the markets of the West.

The member states which already place more reliance on trade than their fellows are hence actively pursuing a commercial policy which they term 'the half-open door'. But access to the market economies is also intended as insurance against possible price imperfections within Comecon. Such pricing difficulties will only arise in trade with other members if Comecon establishes its own set of trade prices: opinions are divided and the 1966–70 goals for mutual exchanges were negotiated on the basis of world prices. World prices are more imminently needed to protect each national economy against domestic inefficiency—a hazard which increases as price-setting becomes decentralized.

As in a single economy, the Comecon group comprises producers at different costs for any one commodity. If the minimization of costs within the group as a whole were the sole aim, the least efficient sources would be closed or would remain unexploited. Comecon's principles, however, qualify the cost criterion by requiring that each member participates in the general development and maintains balance-of-payments equilibrium. Comecon attempted to reconcile all three objectives without ensuring either massive capital flows (even the wealthiest member is poor by west European standards) or major adjustment of its internal terms of trade (precluded by the alignment with world prices). Further, the Soviet Union—notably in the 1961 Programme of its Communist Party—saw its own, and the group's, rate of growth as the decisive indicator in 'peaceful competition' with the United States, and hence tended to favour maximum efficiency as the policy for Comecon. Its clash with Rumania—which sought the spread of development, even at higher cost—is still unresolved and leaves Comecon divided.

Comecon's Charter, in any case, limits common action to its advocates, and inevitably negotiation has returned to bilateral channels, although—as for most international bodies—a wide field for non-controversial and valuable collaboration remains. Such circumspection—and even that activity in isolation from the rest of the Continent—will scarcely satisfy a community of states dedicated to purposive planning throughout the fabric of their society. Renewed efforts to create a multilateral programme may not necessarily be kept within the bounds of their group. Soviet ideology has recently buried the hatchet which, at the time of Comecon's foundation, struck down Varga for discerning the feasibility of planning in the west European mixed economies, and a shared economic language is at least evolving as western Europe and the developing countries embody some of their policies in plans, nationally and internationally. One way for Comecon to enlarge this potential communication would be by the partial transposition of its multilateral programming to a wider arena, such as GATT or the United Nations Trade and Development Board, where the plans of developed and developing countries could best be confronted. Its members have long been on record as favouring an international trade organization, but have still to show what functions this should assume. The possibility is already being informally discussed within Comecon of inviting as observers those developing countries having substantial trade and aid links with members. Certainly Comecon remains the natural venue for the group to establish its commercial and lending policy *vis-à-vis* the rest of the world, and it is only surprising that it appears to have been hitherto little used for such co-ordination.

Faced in 1966 by a crisis in the military alliance which (with the exception of Mongolia) comprises the same membership as Comecon, the eastern European states are unlikely to abandon either of their major goals—national equality of development and rapid rates of growth. The disparity between members is, after all, about the same as it is within EEC, or EFTA; nor, at root, is it the crucial obstacle to integration. The difficulty seems rather to lie in the forms of central planning to be harmonized. The crisis through which Comecon passed in 1963–4 posed fundamental questions to members and may well have convinced them of the need for internal reforms. In a climate very different from that of 1949, the search for new techniques of collaboration between planned economies is again focused upon the need for modifying the domestic systems: happily there is no Stalin to inhibit invention.

Part I

THE HISTORY

II
CIRCUMSTANCES OF BIRTH

The foundation

A MARRIAGE on the rebound stands less chance of success than one between first loves. Comecon—the commonest English abbreviation of the Council for Mutual Economic Assistance[1]—began life after an alleged rebuff from the 'Marshall Plan' powers and as a riposte to the Organization for European Economic Co-operation (OEEC). The 1947 tripartite conference of the United Kingdom, France, and the USSR to discuss European acceptance of the American aid offered by General Marshall broke up on Soviet charges of intended violation of national sovereignty: the two eastern European countries which had decided to join such a programme (Czechoslovakia had formally accepted) withdrew, and the OEEC was set up in 1948 by sixteen nations of western Europe. As soon as Comecon had been formed, the eastern countries also withheld—from 1949 until 1953—practical co-operation within the only pan-European economic agency, the United Nations Economic Commission for Europe (ECE), created in 1947. The Soviet view was—and remains—that the Anglo-American bloc spurned East–West collaboration and persecuted its former allies. In the words of a Soviet standard work on Comecon, the reconstruction of the former all-European economy was opposed by the 'American monopolists . . . whose interests had nothing in common with those of the European peoples':

> A majority of the European people's democracies, subjected to discriminatory policies conducted by the Anglo-American bloc, were for long deprived of United Nations membership. In 1949 only Poland and Czechoslovakia were United Nations members, whereas the other European socialist countries were not accepted into the United Nations until 1955. The frequent proposals of the Soviet Union and other socialist countries on the development of international economic co-operation in the framework of the United Nations on conditions of equal mutual advantage were rejected

[1] Although formed from the English title (*Co*uncil for *M*utual *Econ*omic Assistance), it was apparently coined by analogy with the then extant Cominform and the previous Comintern. Eastern European publications normally employ the initials (and quotations here follow this by using CMEA) but those for foreign readers (e.g. *Soviet News* and *Soviet Weekly* of the Soviet Embassy in London) tend to use 'Comecon'.

by the United States and the other capitalist countries. The policy of a trade boycott by the imperialists was an attempt to provoke difficulties for the socialist countries.[2]

The economic division of Europe by political alliance—Finland, Spain, and Yugoslavia[3] were then unattached, and consequently in neither group—disrupted the restoration of prewar flows of trade and, in broad terms, grouped the richer with the richer and the poorer with the poorer. Only five out of sixteen members of OEEC (Austria, Greece, Italy, Portugal, and Turkey) had a per capita national income less than that of the richest member of Comecon (Czechoslovakia). The scission thus conformed to the postwar pattern of trade blocs—'horizontal integrations' at broadly the same level of development, in contrast to the prewar 'vertical integrations' whereby a developed country was associated with underdeveloped areas (exemplified by the British Commonwealth, and the French colonial empire).[4] Moreover, the affluent half of Europe, the OEEC, had come together to distribute among themselves gifts from outside, Marshall Aid, while Comecon members, the poorer area and the more war-devastated proportionally to their prewar wealth, were mostly paying reparations to the Soviet Union.

The decision to set up a new body was the more striking in the light of the evolution of the ECE. The virtually 'western' Emergency Economic Committee for Europe, established in May 1945, had been transformed into an all-European body early in 1947: the ECE was created by resolution of the United Nations Economic and Social Council dated 28 March and the organization was set up within two months. By the second Plenary of ECE that summer, even the non-members of the United Nations (other than Germany and Austria) were represented—and until the formation of Comecon the eastern European members played an active part in its work. At the 1947 conference on Marshall Aid, the Soviet Union—contrary to western expectations—had not proposed that ECE should distribute the United States funds, but had made a point of ECE's intended role in European co-operation. In these first postwar years the USSR (and

[2] Shurshalov, ed., *Mezhdunarodno-pravovye formy sotrudnichestva sotsialistichikh gosudarstv* (Moscow, 1962), pp. 271–2.

[3] The Yugoslav Foreign Minister, Kardelj, stated on 2 Feb. 1949 that his country was ready to enter Comecon if the Cominform expulsion were rescinded (A. Korbonski, *Int. Con.*, Sept. 1964, p. 55).

[4] See S. Dell, *Trade Blocs and Common Markets* (London, 1963).

the eastern European countries qualified for membership) joined those of the United Nations specialized agencies with which it had no ideological quarrel.[5]

The withdrawal of this collaboration began immediately after the creation of Comecon. The first sign was the Soviet withdrawal on 19 February from the World Health Organization, followed by the resignation of Albania, Bulgaria, Czechoslovakia, Poland, and Rumania; more significant was the departure of all these countries from the ECE technical committees. By January 1950, when the USSR absented itself from the Security Council, the eastern European boycott of every major United Nations body was complete—save only for continued participation at the International Court of Justice.

The separate European organization was founded at a Moscow conference in January 1949 (and, as described on p. 22, an unpublicized meeting in Hungary) by Bulgaria, Czechoslovakia, Hungary, Poland, Rumania, and the Soviet Union. Albania joined within a month and eastern Germany—the German Democratic Republic (GDR)—was accepted the following year, in turn seemingly as a political rejoinder, less than two weeks after the Anglo-American-French agreement to end the state of war with western Germany and to curtail the list of prohibited and limited industries. The Federal Republic had already been permitted (from October 1949) a delegation at OEEC and the Comecon move thus brought the two Germanies into symmetry *vis-à-vis* the rival group.

Comecon was the first formal assembly of the Soviet Union and its associates as states; the Cominform, convened in 1947, was a union of political parties, and the diplomatic and military alliance, the Warsaw Treaty, was not to be signed for another six years.

This circumstance combined with the allegations that the Marshall Plan subordinated its members to United States dominance to make national sovereignty the keynote of the first communiqué. Published on 22 January 1949—Comecon's only policy statement for eight years, and its substitute for a constitution for eleven years—the text must be quoted in full.

In January of this year an economic conference was held in Moscow attended by delegates from Bulgaria, Hungary, Poland, Rumania, the

[5] The ILO was 'evolutionary' and 'capitulationist', the World Bank and IMF were 'agents of finance capital', the FAO simply required regular farming statistics as a condition of membership.

USSR, and Czechoslovakia. The conference noted considerable successes in the development of the economic relations among the countries concerned and above all the great rise in the turnover of trade. As a result of the above-mentioned economic relations and the implementation of economic co-operation between the countries of people's democracy and the USSR, conditions have been created to accelerate the restoration and development of their national economies. The conference further observed that the Governments of the United States of America, of Great Britain, and of certain western European states had boycotted trade relations with the countries of people's democracy and the USSR because these countries did not consider it appropriate that they should submit themselves to the dictatorship of the Marshall Plan, which would have violated their sovereignty and the interests of their national economies. In the light of these circumstances, the meeting studied the question of the possibility of organizing wider economic co-operation between the countries of people's democracy and the USSR. To establish this wider economic co-operation between the countries of people's democracy and the USSR, the conference considered it necessary to create the Council for Mutual Economic Assistance between the countries represented—on the basis of equal representation and with the task of exchanging economic experience, extending technical aid to one another and rendering mutual assistance with respect to raw materials, foodstuffs, machines, equipment, etc. The meeting decided that the Council for Mutual Economic Assistance would be an organization open to other countries of Europe sharing the principles of the Council for Mutual Assistance and desirous of participating in the widening of economic co-operation with the above-mentioned countries. The Council for Mutual Economic Assistance would take a decision only with the agreement of the interested country. The Council shall meet periodically in the capital of each of the signatory countries in turn under the chairmanship of the representative of the country in whose capital the session takes place.

The principle of sovereignty

The emphasis upon national sovereignty in international co-operation was in deliberate contrast to the trend of thought in western Europe. The jibes about marshallization which then filled the Soviet press are beside the point: the United Europe and World Federalist movements in the West were public expressions of readiness to merge sovereignties, and the supranational bodies of 'Little Europe'—the Coal and Steel Community and later the Common Market—were to give them executive form.

It was, of course, also in blatant discord with the realities of eastern Europe, for at no time in their postwar history were their governments more subordinate to the Soviet will. Stalin was expert in verbal formulae which contradicted practice—the official *History of the CPSU* published in Moscow in 1959[6] complains that 'his words began to be more and more at variance with his deeds'—and not least in the sphere of sovereignty, mainly exposed in his pronouncements on the independence of the republics constituting the USSR.

Before the Revolution—in a speech of April 1917—he had admitted the right of Finland and of Transcaucasia to secede:

> If we . . . were to deny the Finnish people the right to declare its will on the subject of secession and the right to give effect to its will . . . , we would thereby put ourselves in the position of people who continue the policy of tsarism. . . A people has a right to secede, but it may or may not exercise that right according to circumstances.[7]

The latter proviso was written in obliquely to the clause of the 1919 Party Programme which recognized 'the right of colonies and non-sovereign nations to secede'. By 1930 Stalin had enlarged the circumstance of exception to the entire period of 'socialism in one country', and that of permission to 'the victory of socialism on the international scale', because the border nationalities might be taken over by their bourgeois compatriots. 'There is a Ukraine in the USSR but there is another Ukraine in other states.'[8] When his rule had ensured that no secession could in practice ensue, he felt able to lay down, in his report on the 1936 Constitution, that Union Republics must border a foreign state lest 'they have nowhere to go if they secede from the USSR'. 'Of course', he added, 'none of our republics would actually raise the question of seceding from the USSR.'[9] Since the establishment in 1944 of Union-Republican foreign ministries and the representation of the Ukraine and Byelorussia in the United Nations, Soviet commentators declare that 'Union Republics, as well as the Soviet Union as a whole, are truly sovereign states'.[10]

Meanwhile, with Vyshinsky as the spokesman, the proposition on international sovereignty was being developed. After the clearance of the opposition, led by Pashukanis, Vyshinsky's *Theses of Inter-*

[6] Trans. as *History of the Communist Party of the Soviet Union* (Moscow, 1960).

[7] J. Stalin, *Marxism and the National and Colonial Question* (London, 1936), p. 64.

[8] Ibid. p. 266.

[9] Stalin, *Problems of Leninism* (Moscow, 1947), p. 562. Thus in defiance of the natural boundary, the Baisun Tau mountains, Uzbekistan was given a 120-km.-wide corridor to the Afghan frontier.

[10] V. Evgenev, *Sov. gos. pravo*, no. 2, 1955.

national Law appeared in 1938.[11] The concept of 'the juridical equality of states' was put forward with Litvinov's definition as 'the possibility for each state to safeguard its own state form with its own social and economic system, in other words, the mutual non-interference in the domestic affairs of states'.[12] It was, however, by no means automatic that the sovereignties in postwar eastern Europe should be maintained. Kardelj, the Yugoslav Foreign Minister, told the Soviet ambassador in 1945 that 'our relations should be based on the prospect of Yugoslavia becoming in the future a constituent part of the USSR',[13] and later Stalin proposed that Yugoslavia absorb Albania. A Bulgaro-Yugoslav Union was seriously expected to follow the 1947 treaty between the two states. All this would have been in accord with the view of Marx and Engels in the Communist Manifesto that communists 'bring to the front the common interests of the entire proletariat, independently of all nationality'.

By making a virtue of sovereignty, the Soviet government feigned to justify its demolition of Dimitrov's project of Balkan federation, initiated in the Bulgaro-Yugoslav treaty of 1947, and of the economic union envisaged in the Polono-Czechoslovak treaty of the same year. Some of the co-operation schemes then destroyed were long afterwards reinstated. An agreement of 1947 for the dispatch of Hungarian alumina to Czechoslovakia, where its transformation into aluminium (a highly energy-intensive process) would benefit from much cheaper fuel costs, was revived in 1954 (see p. 58) and, on a larger scale, with the USSR in 1961 (see p. 127). Discussions during the same year between Hungary and Poland were broken off on Soviet orders: the project was for the former to invest in the Silesian mines (which yield double the calorific value by weight of the Hungarian deposits). This scheme, though with small sums involved, was eventually established in 1962 (see pp. 79 and 127). Hungary's moves towards economic co-operation with the other countries of east Europe had been effectively halted when Comecon was created (though not until after a sharp battle within the government), but there may have been significance in the Polish and Rumanian emphasis at the time on Comecon's avow-

[11] Ibid. no. 5, 1938. An editorial following Khrushchev's secret speech denouncing Stalin complained of 'the over-emphasis of the role of the scientific writings of A. Vyshinsky, the blind obeisance before the theses presented by him' (ibid. no. 2, 1956), and another called for the rehabilitation of Pashukanis (ibid. no. 6, 1956).

[12] M. Litvinov, *Vneshnyaya politika SSSR* (Moscow, 1937), p. 114.

[13] RIIA, *The Soviet-Yugoslav Dispute* (London, 1948), p. 38.

al on sovereignty. Both the main Warsaw newspapers, *Trybuna Ludu* and *Zycie Warszawy*, commented on 26 January 1949 that the new body 'would strengthen sovereignty', while the Bucharest *Universul* wrote of it 'protecting the rights and sovereignty of members of the Council'. The Bulgarian *Otechestven front* on the same day went no further than 'equality', and the theme of the Tirana press on Albania's admission (*Bashkimi* and *Zeri i popullit*, 23 February 1949) was solidarity with the Soviet Union.

It is, of course, Poland and Rumania which have most vigorously impressed their concept of autonomy on Comecon's history. In the late 1950s Gomulka sought to match a renascent political autonomy with enhanced economic power for Poland through the wider markets and the shared capital of a strengthened Comecon. He was behind Khrushchev's proposal—in 1962—to take this to the logical conclusion of joint planning and shared factories. The scheme was rejected by Rumania, which claimed in April 1964 that to transform Comecon into a supranational agency 'would be to turn sovereignty into a notion without any content' and that joint enterprises would restrict 'the fundamental, essential and inalienable attributes of the sovereignty of the socialist state'.[14] After fifteen years the Stalinist catchword which launched the marriage became the grounds for divorce.

Resources of the group

For the contemporary, however, the significance of the founding communiqué lay in the determination to divide the European economy. In the political schism, both halves of the continent contributed to the break. The western trade discrimination towards eastern Europe, of which the communiqué complained, had begun, though not to the degree that it was to assume the following year, when, with the creation of the Paris Consultative Group and its Co-ordinating Committee (Cocom), about 50 per cent of internationally-traded goods were under embargo to Comecon members and the People's Republic of China. This high rate of denial was to continue until 1954, when the strategic list was reduced to about 10 per cent of tradable items. From the divisive conference of 1947 until mid-1953 there were but eight months, October 1949 to June 1950, when East and West

[14] RWP Central Committee statement, *Sc.*, 26 Apr. 1964. This statement is referred to below as the Rumanian Declaration of April 1964.

were not at undeclared war—between the end of the Chinese civil war (and in Europe the quasi-belligerent Berlin airlift) and the outbreak of hostilities in Korea. The nationalization of foreign assets in eastern Europe, largely carried out in 1947 and 1948, with scant hope of compensation, did not, so far as western business was concerned, encourage the commercial evasion of politically-inspired embargoes.[15]

The disruption of traditional exchanges and the build-up of military supplies placed proportionately greater strain on Comecon members than on the OEEC group: they were poorer and East–West trade had bulked much larger in their commerce. Although the group's potential productive capacity was—in view notably of Soviet natural resources—vast, its pattern of prewar development had been non-complementary. Before the Second World War the Bohemian-Silesian triangle represented the one major industrial centre in a vast area of primary production which reached deep into the USSR, to the line of Leningrad, Moscow, and the Donbas. The Soviet Union had withdrawn into autarky during the First Five-Year Plan and the manufacturing nuclei outside the industrial triangle—virtually limited to each metropolis in Hungary, Poland, and Rumania—had been restricted by the predominance of German industrial exports. The occupation line in Germany had, however, left in the western zones the majority of the enterprises that had engaged in trade with eastern Europe, and the participation of the newly-created GDR did not add much more potential trade.

The crucial fact of Comecon's history from its foundation to the present is that the rapid growth of its aggregate production has not been accompanied, as in other world economic groups, by a relatively more extensive international division of labour, either among its members or with the rest of the world. As Chapter VII shows, it is the very disparity between growth and trade which is striking.

By the end of its first year of existence, each member had a long-term plan in operation. All but Bulgaria—which had a five-year plan to run to 1953—were operating five- or six-year programmes with

[15] Negotiations on compensation have been very protracted: Greece and Rumania, for example, reached agreement only in September 1966 and other western claims on Comecon members are still outstanding; see *The Times*, 15 Feb. 1967. The link of settlement with commercial prospects was evident from the rise of Rumanian trade with the West after the clearing up of most of its compensation in 1961.

1955 as a common target year; yet every plan was cast in precisely the same pattern and narrowed further the scope for exchange. A common plan methodology consolidated a preference for domestic sources over foreign supplies.

Soviet rules on industrialization

Why these countries did not from the start initiate an international division of labour is a political question: the obstacles to integration may be described in economic terms (see Ch. III), but the causation is to be found in the nature of the Soviet political system under Stalin.

Comecon included only states then in total political subordination to the USSR: the two important, professedly socialist, states—China and Yugoslavia—which were not in that dependent relationship remained outside. At first sight Soviet control of these economies may appear to be inconsistent with their autarkic industrialization: the interest of the USSR would seem to have required that eastern Europe become its economic complement (notably by the supply of raw materials) rather than its competitor. In fact, the autarky was not despite, but because of, the tutelage: the Soviet directives are attributable both to its standing ideology and to its contemporary practice.

The political theory engendered by Soviet postwar pre-eminence in eastern Europe called for the establishment of socialist regimes in countries detached from the 'imperialist camp', the adherence of which to the 'democratic camp' was to be assured by an administration conducted by communist parties in the image of the Soviet Party. How the USSR saw its new responsibilities and their discharge is enunciated in the *History of the CPSU* (pp. 637–8), already cited.

> The international character of the dictatorship of the proletariat gave rise to a fundamentally new, hitherto non-existent function of the Socialist State—the function of assisting other countries in the building of Socialism and of establishing international Socialist relations. . . . The Communist Party of the Soviet Union took an active part in creating and strengthening the community of Socialist countries. As the guiding force of the first country to have built Socialism, it shared, and continues to share, its experience of building a new life with the brother Parties, on a footing of equality. . . . The path travelled by the Soviet people is the highroad of Socialist development for the working people of all countries. The main features and laws of development of the Socialist revolution and of the building of

Socialism in the USSR are not of local, specifically national, significance: they are of international importance.

The USSR was exporting politico-economic management for the first time—its prewar experience in Mongolia was hardly relevant (implicit in the exclusion of that country from the Comecon of the day). It was simplest to transfer the Soviet structure in its totality to the new partners. So far as the economic system was concerned, Soviet planning decisions were made on rules rather than on judgements, and rationalized on the wider plane as demonstrating conformity to Marxist laws in lieu of the spontaneity held to be characteristic of capitalism. Industrialization on the Soviet pattern was embodied in the objectives of a socialist society, and because the Soviet authorities sought only to introduce their established pattern, any attempt at national adaptation was repressed. This was as much the case in planning as in any other sphere. In Poland, for example, the techniques used to draw up the Three-Year Plan, based upon a harmonious growth of consumption and investment, were replaced in 1949 by the much cruder Soviet procedure, which yielded a Six-Year Plan comprehending a concentration of industrial resources on capital goods on the one hand and on agricultural targets which were no more than fantasy on the other.

Lenin believed that 'the sole material basis possible for socialism is large-scale machine industry'; Stalin had been more specific. 'Not every development of industry constitutes industrialization', he said in 1926. 'The core of industrialization, its very basis, consists of the development of heavy industry (fuel, metal, etc.); in the expansion, in the last resort, of the output of the means of production of our own engineering.' His political rationale was that

> the country of the dictatorship of the proletariat, in conditions of capitalist encirclement, cannot remain economically independent if it does not produce at home the instruments and means of production. This means that industrialization should be understood above all as the development of heavy industry, and particularly of our own engineering, the very nerve of industry as a whole. Without this, no one can speak of the assurance of the economic independence of our country.[16]

Vast, untapped natural resources—'the exploitation of our domestic market and the extent of our resources, these are the bases of the

[16] *Sochineniya*, 4th ed., viii. 12–13.

expansion of our industry'—were an economic defence of Stalin's autarky, confirmed by the experience of the Plan's early years, when the violent fall of the terms of trade associated with the world depression greatly increased the cost of imported machinery in terms of Soviet primary exports.

None of these conditions of the 1930s obtained for the eastern European planners in 1949–50. Their flows of resources were obstructed by absolute deficits and immediate bottlenecks, which a switch of trade to their neighbours could only intensify: even where the East-West rupture did not eliminate imports altogether, it not only meant change in suppliers but often changes in supplies—Czech steel mills, for example, built for Swedish ore with a high iron and low silica content, had to be adapted for a furnace burden with low iron and high silica from Krivoi Rog. The economic hinterland of each was not the USSR of 'socialism in one country' which Stalin proclaimed, but over one-third of the world's population and a territory from Pilsen to Canton. Even primary terms of trade were on the upswing—though this trend might have been discounted, for it did not in the event outlast Comecon's first round of five-year plans.

But if Stalin's premises of his first five-year plan were absent in postwar eastern Europe, Stalin himself was notably present. His own predilection was for steel—though the '*stal*' of his *nom-de-guerre* antedated his economic ideology—and steel-using engineering. A decade later an American Iron and Steel Institute delegation to the USSR could still be assured that 'maximum production of iron and steel is the foremost goal of the Soviet Union'.[17] Throughout Comecon, therefore, the plans were centred upon metallurgy and machine-building, and upon their direct inputs of fuel, power, and ores. Even Albania put a steel smelter into its 1951–5 Plan (judiciously dropped as soon as Stalin died). The contemporary round of OEEC long-term plans—for plans for dollar viability in 1952–3 were a condition of Marshall Aid—were in revealing contrast: Norway and Greece were rebuked for wanting steel plants. The Comecon member's high priority for a section of 'heavy' (producer-good) industry went with a conversely low priority for agriculture and the 'light' (consumer-good) industries. Targets were set ambitiously, leaving little scope for domestic resource-shifts if they were not met, let alone for

[17] *Steel in the Soviet Union* (New York, 1959), p. 49.

manœuvrability in trade; this in turn made home production more desirable than imports. Strain was increased and the parallelism of objectives made more intense when, late in 1950, in face of the threat of extension of the Korean conflict—MacArthur was on the Yalu and Chinese intervention began—the munitions industries, and further earmarkings for heavy industry, were everywhere accentuated. In Poland, for example, 11 per cent of all industrial investment during 1951–5 went for military purposes.

The emphasis on the autarkic expansion of engineering during the period until Stalin's death virtually eliminated any hope for integration. Such investment priority limited the outlays available for other sectors, and, irrationally, even for the raw materials needed in the metal-using group. Eastern European economists have been unanimous in identifying the duplication of engineering capacity as the main obstacle to trade in Comecon's early years.

> Engineering was most affected. The various countries created enterprises and whole industries parallel to each other turning out products in excess supply and unsaleable at a time when other goods were everywhere unavailable. These factors hindered the development of the international socialist division of labour and made it hard significantly to increase foreign trade.[18]

> In 1951 all the European Popular Democracies raised substantially the targets in their production plans. The rates of growth of heavy industry and of capital construction were significantly accelerated. While it thus became all the more important to establish the right proportions within the socialist camp as a whole, the socialist nations continued to plan, to a large extent, in isolation. This led to uneven economic development—disproportions between industry and agriculture, between raw materials, fuel, and power on the one hand and manufacturing, especially engineering, on the other.[19]

The Soviet objective of more energy and more machinery seems to have been little more than the amassing of goods needed for reinvestment and defence. If there was further rationalization of duplicating this pattern, it was doubtless that eventual exports of these products to the USSR would contribute to its cycle of accumulation. Shipments of primary materials were less in demand, because the

[18] T. Kiss, *A szocialista orszagok gazdasagi egyuttmukodese* (Budapest, 1961), p. 110, quoted by I. Agoston, *Le marché commun communiste*, 2nd ed. (Geneva, 1965), p. 26.

[19] V. Kaigl, *Vopr. ekon.*, no. 10, 1957, p. 35, quoted by J. Montias, *Wld Pol.*, July 1966, p. 722. See also R. Nötel, *R. éc. et soc.*, spec. issue, Apr. 1963, pp. 77–106.

Soviet endowments of minerals (other than fuel), and of manpower for their extraction, were considered adequate, and because no food imports were required by the Soviet consumption plans.

Fundamentally, however, the Soviet policy favouring the creation of fuel and metal industries in the countries controlled was an autarky inherent in the planning system. At the time, this precept ran through both the manner in which the general lines—or 'proportions'—were drawn up, and the detail of planning. For sectoral ministries or producing enterprises, the overriding consideration was production: they were concerned with fulfilment of the production plan, with other criteria such as costs and wages effectively of minor account. As labour was consequently not strictly controlled, the level of output was chiefly determined by supplies of materials. Executants therefore tried to protect their inputs by furnishing as much as they could of their own supplies: a ministry would extract its own fuel, or an enterprise forge its own steel. This 'departmentalism' was not undermined until Khrushchev substituted regional authorities for the industrial ministries in 1957, and until the main plan indicator for an enterprise was shifted from output to costs in 1960. In the planning environment of 1949 the protection of supplies was a reflex easily carried over to the international scene. There were no Soviet calculations of comparative costs in trade, because in almost two decades a new generation of planners (those not purged in 1930 had mostly disappeared in 1936–8) had arisen with no idea of foreign-trade efficiency; indeed, even relative costs of domestic production were misleading until Voznesensky's price reform of 1949.

If Soviet officials on their home ground were stultified by following these conventions in composing and executing plans, there is no reason to suppose that those sent to advise east European governments were any more enterprising. The need for what they termed 're-insurance' was, if anything, stronger.

Abortive reforms

Within the Soviet government which convened Comecon in January 1949 there was one minister at least, Nikolai Voznesensky, chairman of the State Planning Commission (Gosplan), who was aware of some of the problems and was initiating reform. His dismissal in the following March was succeeded by a reversal of his measures, and

Comecon had no opportunity of operating within a new environment until Stalin died in 1953. No link is, of course, established between Comecon as such and Voznesensky (though Soviet writers are now beginning to reveal the history of the reforms and their author),[20] and, in any case, the chair at the initial meeting was taken by Mikhail Suslov, Secretary of the Central Committee since 1947, and then, as now, chiefly concerned with relations with foreign communist parties. The conference was not, however, at Party, but at economic-administrative, level, for the USSR had invited the senior planning ministers—e.g., Erno Gerö, the President of the Supreme Economic Council, and Imre Vajda, Chairman of the State Planning Office, from Hungary,[21] and Hilary Minc, Chairman of the Polish Central Planning Board. In this it may be distinguished from the other major economic conference of the East European states when Comecon had become quiescent, the 1950 Party meeting (see p. 49). The length of the founding discussions may indicate that, in January 1949 at least, the Soviet government was taking inter-member economic relations seriously. The session in Moscow was inadequate to reach agreement and discussions were resumed privately in Hungary—at a small resort, Matrahaza. Perhaps the failure of any official or eastern European source to cite a precise date for the founding meeting[22] implies unwillingness to reveal how protracted were the debates. But it must be observed that no agenda had been circulated and that the heads of plan offices reached Moscow unaware that a project for an organization was to be discussed. This situation was not unusual in the Byzantine environment of Stalin's rule, but patently it did not expedite the meeting. Such conditions could make it possible that a meeting of chairmen of planning agencies lacked the corresponding Soviet minister, but the circumstantial evidence on Voznesensky's policies seems enough to support the view that he was active in its convocation. Suslov's chairmanship of the actual meeting would imply that Voz-

[20] Voznesensky was formally rehabilitated, after Khrushchev's secret speech of 1956, as were others purged by Stalin, by an entry in the supplementary volume (vol. 51) of the *BSE*, 1958, but fuller appreciations have only recently appeared, notably by G. Sorokin, a former colleague in Gosplan, in *Vopr. ekon.*, no. 12, 1963, and by V. Kolotov and G. Petrovichev, *N. A. Vosnesensky; biografichesky ocherk* (Moscow, 1963). The Leningrad Institute for Finance and Economics has been renamed in honour of Voznesensky (*Vopr. ekon.*, no. 9, 1966, p. 156).

[21] The protagonists in the dispute, within the Hungarian government, on co-operation with east Europe other than the USSR (see p. 14).

[22] Including the Secretary's own official history of the agency, N. Faddeev, *Sovet Ekonomicheskoi Vzaimopomosh* (Moscow, 1964): see p. 26 for this period.

nesensky's authority was already weakening.[23] It was to be Suslov who led its public attack on Voznesensky in the wake of Stalin's last published work (see p. 34).

It was undoubtedly Voznesensky who, at the end of the war, had been instrumental in revising the decision of Malenkov's committee of the Council of People's Commissars on the dismantling of German industry for reparations deliveries to the USSR; the creation of Soviet-owned corporations (SAG) to manufacture for Soviet needs was Voznesensky's.[24] The issue was not the severity of the tribute from the ex-enemy states, but the strategy of relating, instead of devastating, the subordinate economies.

Voznesensky had been chairman of the Leningrad plan department and deputy president of the City Executive, when Andrei Zhdanov had been First Secretary of the City Party Committee; he was promoted at the early age of 34 to the chairmanship of the USSR Gosplan in December 1937. His ally in economic reform seems to have been Alexei Kosygin, the present Chairman of the Soviet Council of Ministers.[25] In September 1947 Zhdanov, by creating the Cominform as the planning staff for international political strategy, had explicitly given new significance to Stalin's doctrine of 'two camps', the socialist and the imperialist. But Zhdanov had scored the frontiers of socialism more deeply than Stalin's 'socialism in one country' two decades earlier, and under his lead the relative coexistence of the war period and its aftermath was abruptly terminated, both for the independent-minded within and for the former allies without. He died in August 1948, but Voznesensky remained Deputy President of the USSR Council of Ministers and chairman of Gosplan until March 1949. Kosygin, who had become Minister of Finance while Voznesensky's economic reform was being drafted, lost that post two months before the latter's dismissal. It was Kosygin, when he eventually became Chairman of Gosplan (1959–60), who signed the Charter of Comecon on behalf of the Soviet Government.

[23] For some evidence of this and a review of Voznesenky's place in domestic policy and marxist economics see the present writer, *Annuaire de l'URSS 1965* (Paris, 1965), pp. 555–69. G. Segal, *Problems of Communism*, Mar.–Apr. 1966, esp. pp. 4–7, adduces further evidence on economic reform in Leningrad by Voznesensky and Kosygin.

[24] See L. Schapiro, *The Communist Party of the Soviet Union* (London, 1960), p. 507. J. Nettl, *The Eastern Zone and Soviet Policy in Germany 1945–50* (London, 1951), dates the change as exhibited in actual dismantling as mid-1946 (p. 204).

[25] Kosygin had been Mayor of Leningrad before promotion as Minister of Textiles in 1939.

Comecon's founding communiqué proclaimed the importance attached by its authors to the need for a socialist contrast to the Marshall Plan. The significance of the Marshall Plan, and of the national planning which it subsumed (the four-year programmes to eliminate the dollar deficit by 1952), was in 1948 the subject of acute debate between Voznesensky's Gosplan and Academician Evgeni Varga, Director of the USSR Institute of World Economics. The public discussion crystallized around Varga's book, *Changes in the Economy of Capitalism as a Result of the Second World War*, and Voznesensky's *The War Economy of the USSR during the Patriotic War*.[26] Voznesensky's book had appeared after others had criticized Varga's standpoint—notably at an economists' conference in May 1947—but, although Varga's Institute and his house journal were liquidated, the debate proceeded, notably at a session of the Scientific Council of the USSR Institute of Economics in October 1948. For the relevance to Comecon's foundation, it is chiefly enough to examine the major denunciation from Voznesensky's side, an article by his protégé M. Myznikov[27] in the Gosplan organ, *Planovoe khozyaistvo*, no. 6 (Nov.–Dec.) 1948, entitled 'Perversions of Marxism–Leninism in the works of E. Varga', and frequently quoting Voznesensky's book as his authority against Varga.

> Comrade Varga especially revealingly exposed his point of view on the planned character of contemporary capitalism in his introductory remarks in the discussion [of May 1947]. He affirmed that the bourgeois state plans its economy not only in wartime but in peace, and that since the war in capitalist countries, for example, in England, there is even 'something of a Gosplan. . . . In the conditions of the given historical period', writes comrade Varga, 'only American and Canadian banks and firms can in fact provide credit to European countries. . . . Consequently the rates of recovery, of overcoming the underproduction crisis and of avoiding or limiting inflation in Europe depends in the first place on the export of American capital to Europe.' In this argument, comrade Varga flourishes the direct kinship of his views with the scribblings of bourgeois economists and politicians, preaching the 'Marshall Plan' as the means of curing capitalism of its irremediable infirmities. In this, comrade Varga does not even separate the people's democracies from the rest of 'continental Europe'.

[26] Respectively, E. Varga, *Izmeneniya v ekonomike kapitalizma v itoge vtoroi mirovoi voyny* (Moscow, 1946); and N. Voznesensky, *Voennaya ekonomika SSSR v period otechestvennoi voiny* (Moscow, 1948).

[27] He first appeared in the journal soon after Voznesensky took over Gosplan and left the Editorial Board shortly after his chief's dismissal.

It is possible to conclude that he denied so vehemently the parallels with western European planning because Gosplan was itself introducing an operational price mechanism into Soviet plan practice. This is perhaps supported by the recent acceptance in a Soviet historical journal of Varga's views on capitalist planning:[28] Voznesensky's reform is at last being consummated (by the wholesale-price revision scheduled for July 1967), but in conditions of coexistence with the West.

For Varga, as a Hungarian communist, the omission of the new socialist states of eastern Europe from an article dealing with capitalism was obviously not intended to exclude them from the scope of planning, but Myznikov's criticism of so trivial a point was significant. There was a Soviet choice between what Uschakow delineates as 'an autarkic national-egotistical economic policy', and 'global-area economic (*grossraumwirtschaftliche*) co-operation with the help of international trade'. Comecon was to be an expression of the latter.[29]

Stalin's reversal of Voznesensky's economic policies—described in the next chapter—cut away the criteria which could have been used for such collaboration. It was not until some of the eastern European members had begun seriously to examine the standards by which integration could be judged that Comecon took an operational form—by the establishment of standing technical commissions in 1956. The structure of consultative committees was given legal entity by the Charter of 1959, but member states were then adamant that a more closely-knit body could not emerge before they had defined the principles of integration. An east German writer in 1958 observed that the decisions of 1956 had been 'premature and not based on rational economic principles', and the Polish Deputy Prime Minister affirmed in 1959 that the Charter did not make Comecon a 'supranational body'.[30] Comecon's declaration of *Basic Principles* of 1962 collated, rather than composed, members' differences on the measure of rational integration, and the proposal which followed, to create a 'unified planning organ, empowered to compose common plans and to decide organizational matters', was lost. Once mere institutional reforms were

[28] *Vopr. ist.*, no. 1, 1964, pp. 124–5.

[29] A. Uschakow, *Der Rat für gegenseitige Wirtschaftshilfe, Dokumente zum Ostrecht II* (Cologne, 1962), p. 11.

[30] Respectively W. Mostertz, *Wirts.*, no. 5, 1958, and P. Jaroszewicz on Warsaw Radio, 17 Dec. 1959, both cited by Agoston, pp. 33 and 40.

shelved, the Soviet policy-makers began to examine an alternative, but within the USSR a solution is yet to be found. The absence of criteria whereby the Soviet economy can measure its own goals and its own performance has been the crucial issue on which Comecon integration has foundered.

III
ECONOMIC CO-OPERATION WITHIN THE INITIAL FRAMEWORK

The conditions for integration

A SCHEME of economic integration may be conceived either as the extension of a national system for the allocation of resources to the international plane, or as the addition of extranational goals to the national objectives for that allocation.

The transposal of the classical competitive system to international economic relations, with movements of labour and capital unrestricted by frontiers, would institute a market tending to equalize throughout the area the price of the same good, the wage for the same kind of labour, the rent for the same quality of land, and the return on a unit of capital under a comparable degree of risk. The operation of this mechanism under private ownership and profit-seeking enterprise has, of course, been modified in western Europe to include a substantial public sector and objectives of social welfare. This mechanism, too, can be extended throughout an integrated area, explicit derogations to market criteria and the movement of labour and capital then being made on the typical intranational pattern. In the case of the European Economic Community (EEC), for example, social-security systems are being standardized by international agreement, and prices of coal and steel are fixed by supranational authority. The formation of a common market for the products of the area (by the abolition of tariffs and quantitative restrictions on imports and of subsidies to exports) is an essential step, since such barriers to trade are not part of the national mechanism. It is naturally easier to eliminate elements alien to intranational allocation than to standardize deviations from market procedures: within the EEC negotiation has been particularly difficult on subsidies to farm produce, and the reconciliation of the French and Dutch plan procedures with the slighter controls of the others.

An alternative concept of integration is the achievement of purposes desirable for the group as a whole, but to which the national mechanisms do not conduce. It underlies all public programmes for foreign aid and, in an integration of the first type, is analogous to the development of depressed areas, and can be projected to the still wider aims of which Myrdal is the prime exponent.

> As between developed and underdeveloped countries, international trade . . . does not equalize factor prices but rather tends to set up a cumulative process away from equilibrium. . . . Economic development of the underdeveloped [countries] has become a recognized main goal of international economic integration. [But] international economic integration, like national integration, is at bottom a much broader problem than trade or even than economics. It involves problems of social cohesion and practical international solidarity, and the building up of machinery for accomplishing intergovernmental agreements and large-scale political settlements.[1]

An integration scheme can evidently combine collaboration along lines both of converting a national into an international economic system, and of widening the perspectives of national allocation. The European Development Bank, as an instance, is intended to serve the second purpose in the basic objectives of the EEC. For a decade Comecon embraced the first of these concepts, 'organizing wider economic co-operation between the countries of people's democracy and the USSR' and being 'open to other countries of Europe . . . desirous of participating in the widening of economic co-operation with the above-mentioned countries'. The 1960 Charter[2] added the second purpose, as 'the acceleration of economic and technical progress in [member] countries' and 'the raising of the level of industrialization in the less-developed countries'.

Centralism and collaboration

Trade and the many varieties of aid are means for the international allocation of the resources of contributory economies: they obviously do not constitute the mechanism of allocation, and the use that is made of them is a function of the economic system. In their relations with the capitalist world, Comecon members operate within the mechanism of the market; in dealing with each other the nexus is logically a central planning system transposed from their national practice. Comecon's founding rules, however, precluded integration based on

[1] G. Myrdal, *An International Economy* (London, 1956), pp. 339–40.
[2] See below, p. 236.

a centralist procedure. Furthermore, national decision-makers, employing no criteria independent of their own authority, lack a yardstick to measure national against extranational interest. Neither concept of integration could therefore be successfully implemented. The recognition of this impasse has brought both critical examination of the national mechanisms and a new appraisal of the role of trade with market economies therein.

Lenin's formula of 'democratic centralism' for the Soviet Communist Party and state had been adopted by all member states before their association in Comecon. It provided that elective bodies, and the administrations they authorized, 'form a single system built on the basis of the strictest subordination of lower units to the direction and control of superior agencies, the decisions of which are binding'.[3] Following from this, 'plans under socialism have a directive character; ... the planned management of the economy is based on the Leninist principle of democratic centralism'.[4] Comecon could not be administered in this fashion because from the start it had declared that 'on the basis of equal representation' it would 'take a decision only with the agreement of the interested country'. Its later Charter permitted it to make decisions only 'on organizational and procedural matters'; substantive affairs are the subject of 'recommendations'. Its International Bank requires unanimity for any decision except on liquidation.[5]

The basic incompatibility has by no means prevented the adaptation of certain planning techniques to Comecon collaboration, notably the establishment of supplies and requirements for goods in physical terms on the lines of the Soviet 'material balances' (the accountancy of inputs with outputs by product in physical units as opposed to money values). But the reconciliation in such balances of the aim of production efficiency for the group with that of the acceleration of growth in the least developed has been inhibited by the lack of adequate criteria for choice among national uses; this lacuna is inherent in the Soviet system of values.

[3] Definition of 'democratic centralism' in *BSE*, vol. xiii; on the people's democracies see ibid. vol. xlvi under 'centralism'; in this connexion Lenin's most frequently-cited statement is that 'Our task now is exactly to introduce democratic centralism into the economy, to ensure absolute order and unity in the functioning of... economic enterprises' (*Sochineniya*, 4th ed., xxvii. 181).

[4] *Politicheskaya ekonomiya*, 4th ed. (Moscow, 1962), pp. 462–6 (the standard Soviet textbook on economics).

[5] A two-thirds majority is sufficient for liquidation.

The incubus of sovereignty

Reference to sovereignty in Comecon's founding declaration was consistent with Soviet claims that 'marshallization' of the OEEC members subjected them to United States domination. The Soviet government did not then see this formula as a potential obstacle to group action. In its relations with Comecon governments it was *de facto* as much at the head of a centralist administration as *de jure* within its own frontiers. Inside the USSR, the exercise of Union-Republican sovereignty in any restrictive or pre-emptive sense was held to be impossible. Litvinov (p. 113) contended that 'it is because rights are equal that in the Soviet Union there is neither national majority nor minority, because no nationality has, theoretically or practically, more right or access than another to cultural or economic development'. In Lenin's political theory, the merging of economic interest within multinational Russia even under capitalism was the precursor of an international socialist community. While demanding minority protection, he opposed declarations of minority nationalism in his *Theses on the National Question* (1913): 'The slogan is incorrect because already under capitalism, all economic, political and spiritual life is becoming more and more international. Socialism will make it completely international.'[6] This remains the long-run view held by the Soviet government, as Khrushchev stated in a speech at Leipzig in 1959:

> with the victory of Communism on a world scale, state frontiers will disappear, as Marxism–Leninism teaches. Only ethnic borders will be likely to survive for a time and even these will probably subsist merely as a convention. . . . The common economic base of world socialism will grow stronger, making the question of borders a pointless one.[7]

The latest Programme of the CPSU, adopted in 1961, conceives of communist intra-state relations as 'self-administration', though in forms still to be determined. But even at the present stage of Soviet political structure, the national decision-maker is not compelled to weigh the equity of the development of one region against another, nor to assess the balance of payments of one in relation to the other. It is of course precisely these considerations which are crucial to negotiations in Comecon, and on which Soviet procedures are no

[6] Lenin, *Works*, 4th ed. (Moscow trans.), ix. 246. [7] *Pr.*, 27 Mar. 1959.

guide. Moreover, if the national authority resolves upon the acceleration of growth in a given region, the capital flows or the setting of favourable terms of trade can be effected by instruments at hand: in developing Central Asia, for example, the Soviet government has both financed regional investment and shifted the prices of steel and cotton to the advantage of the latter.[8] Internationally, such capital aid or price changes have to be explicit and negotiated.

The Soviet planning authorities had occasion to appreciate the niceties of such dealing when faced with intra-Soviet sovereignty by the reforms of 1957. In the devolution of industrial management to regional bodies, and of segments of other controls to the Union Republics, they found both the advantages of initiative on the spot and the frustrations of 'localism'. This *mestnichestvo* within the USSR was evidently the parallel of national interest in Comecon, resurgent after the revolutions of 1956. It seems significant that when, in 1962, the Soviet government retrenched on the 'territorial principle of management' at home, it also called for central economic planning in Comecon. The USSR did not revert to the full rigour of the earlier centralism, but, in deferring to proposals then being advanced by Liberman—a professor at Kharkov University[9]—to enlarge the authority of a producing enterprise within rules of profit maximization, it provided no alternative to the directive in home planning. The opposition of Rumania to such centralism is well known. Its Declaration of April 1964 claimed that

> the idea of a single planning body for all CMEA countries has the most serious economic and political implications. The planned management of the national economy is one of the fundamental, essential, and inalienable attributes of the sovereignty of the socialist state—the state plan being the chief means through which the socialist state achieves its political and socio-economic objectives.

The coincidence of Soviet policies towards Comecon and on domestic planning should not be overstressed, but after supranational planning had been abandoned in the one, the Liberman scheme for the other was (in August 1964) returned to public discussion.[10]

[8] See the special study of Soviet Central Asia in *Econ. B. Eur.*, ix/3.

[9] For a convenient summary see, among a number of studies, *Econ. Survey Eur. 1962*, pt 1, pp. 45–47; A. Nove, *Survey*, Apr. 1963, pp. 112–18.

[10] See V. A. Trapeznikov, *Pr.*, 17 Aug. 1964.

Material balances and international planning

In the year Comecon was formed, the eastern European states were consummating their transitions to Soviet-type practice, but they took over not the macro-economic value planning which Voznesensky was beginning to introduce, but the principle of instruction to enterprise managers in terms of physical goals of production. The consistency of these goals was effected, as it had been since 1930, by a complex of 'material balances', but because the units of each were physical (tons, metres, boxes, bales), there was no aggregation, and hence no procedure to reach an optimum, that is, a set of plans which would maximize output and minimize input. More importantly—for the effect on Comecon—the prices of the goods balanced in physical terms were all but irrelevant for the producing enterprise.

Voznesensky's domestic reforms are concentrated in the period December 1947 to January 1949. At the first of those dates he cut out the inflationary pressure of accumulated war and postwar purchasing power by a drastic monetary reform and by a sharp retail price rise to revalue consumer-good supplies at the level of money wages. In the same December the planning institutions were radically reorganized. The programme of 'material balances' was passed over to a new agency and Gosplan was left with plan composition in money terms. Such programming was based essentially on the so-called 'national-economic proportions' (the distribution of national product between consumption and investment and the sector allocation of the latter) and on purchasing-power projection. As a Soviet rehabilitation puts it,

> Voznesensky affirmed that socialist planning requires a knowledge of the economic laws of production and distribution and their skilful use to obtain proportionality in economic development. . . . Of great interest are Voznesensky's propositions on the function of the law of value in the socialist economy and on material incentives for the expansion of production. Scientific socialism, he wrote, cannot deny a role to the law of value, to retail pricing, or to profit-and-loss accounting in a socialist economy.[11]

Gosplan's concentration on value programming was made complete the following August, when the statistical administration was hived off. Throughout 1948 the wartime proliferation of economic ministries was overhauled.

[11] G. Sorokin, in *Vopr. ekon.*, no. 12, 1963.

But the most important feature of the year was the elaboration of the first major set of wholesale-price changes since 1936 and their first thoroughgoing reform since value planning was renounced in 1930. On 1 January 1949 the new planning prices replaced the 'constant 1926/7 prices'.[12] When Voznesensky was arrested in March 1949 he was composing a theoretical exposition of his economics: his *Political Economy of Communism*, 'which he called his credo as a communist and as a scholar; doubtless this work was seized in the house-search and it has disappeared'.[13] Two days after the announcement of Voznesensky's dismissal, Varga wrote in *Pravda* (15 March):

> I wish to protest most strongly against the dark inferences of the war instigators that I am a man of 'western orientation', a defender of the Marshall Plan. Today, in the present historical circumstances, that would mean being a counter-revolutionary, an anti-Soviet traitor to the working class.

This may rather be seen as Stalin's clearance of an ideological path to his theory of 'two world markets'. In his *Economic Problems of Socialism in the USSR* (1952), Stalin claimed that 'the disintegration of the single, all-embracing world market must be regarded as the most important economic sequel of the Second World War and of its economic consequences' caused by an economic blockade of 'the USSR, China, and the European people's democracies, which did not join the "Marshall plan" system . . . [and by] the fact that since the war these countries have joined together economically and established economic cooperation and mutual assistance'.[14] But Stalin's method of implementing that 'economic cooperation' rejected Voznesensky's crucial principles.

Rejection of the money mechanism

Voznesensky's three lines of economic policy were discarded with their author. On 1 March 1949—as every year afterwards under the Stalin and Malenkov administrations—retail prices were substantially cut: this marked a shift from a wages policy which was sensitive to individual or sector incentives towards a manipulation of the aggre-

[12] For a detailed contemporary analysis of this reform see the present author's 'Soviet planning and the price mechanism', *Econ. J.*, Mar. 1950.

[13] Sorokin, *Vopr. ekon.*, no. 12, 1963. In the October 1948 debate Paltsev, an economist who also advocated a price mechanism and value balancing, obliquely referred to this work.

[14] Moscow trans., pp. 34–36.

gate price-level, which could only reflect overall changes in productivity. On 1 January 1950, and again on 1 July, wholesale prices were sharply reduced, nullifying much of the careful balance with cost patterns and retarding the repeal of subsidies to producers' goods. Both these price deflations reflected Stalin's earliest contentions in the debates preceding the First Five-Year Plan, against which Preobrazhensky had given warning as 'an utterly mutilated and distorted operation of the law of value'.[15] Voznesensky's economic-administrative pattern was not formally disturbed until 1953 (by Malenkov), but during 1950 a plethora of medium-term sector programmes made nonsense of global quinquennial or longer-run planning. Although Molotov announced in March 1950 that a new national five-year plan was being drafted, no text appeared until August 1952.

The fulcrum of Stalin's dispute with Voznesensky on economic management is phrased in Soviet writing as 'the law of value'. In *Economic Problems of Socialism in the USSR* Stalin denied that producers' goods could be defined as 'commodities': they 'are not "sold" to any purchaser, they are not "sold" even to collective farms; they are only allocated by the state to its enterprises', which 'are deemed to be agents of the state in the utilization of the means of production in accordance with the plans established by the state'. Such goods, Stalin went on, were priced within the USSR only in formal accountancy, for enterprise control, and 'to conduct sales of means of production to foreign countries'. While consumer's goods had to be sold 'as commodities coming under the operation of the law of value', the level of those prices in no way determined the macro-economic 'proportions'[16] between investment and consumption. Stalin made no explicit reference to Voznesensky, but in *Pravda* of 24 December 1952 Suslov linked Stalin's work with a condemnation of Voznesensky's 'hotch-potch of voluntarist views on the part to be played by plans and the state in Soviet society and of fetishism of the law of value—which was allegedly the governor of the distribution of labour between the sectors of the USSR economy'. It is not unrealistic to infer that value-guided choice in international planning became equally impolitic.

[15] E. Preobrazhensky, *Novaya ekonomika* (Moscow, 1926), p. 197. For the context see trans. by B. Pearce, *The New Economics* (Oxford, 1965) p. 177, and for an analysis of the dispute see A. Erlich, *The Soviet Industrialization Debate 1924–8* (Cambridge, Mass., 1960), p. 103.

[16] Moscow trans., pp. 23, 58–59.

The implications for Comecon of the Voznesensky approach were, it may be suggested, trade arrangements based on the analysis of comparative costs and permitting the evaluation of multilateral exchanges. Two rumours current just after Comecon was established illustrate what might have become the trend. One—described more fully in Chapter IV—was that a Comecon currency-clearing was under discussion; another suggested that the USSR was proposing to sell its shares in the eastern European 'mixed companies'. Those companies, which exported directly to the USSR, were in effect instruments of physical planning outside national pricing, and were not in the event to be sold back until 1954. A 'law of value' operating between Comecon members would have furnished criteria for the rational specializations undertaken in the context of co-ordinated long-term planning. An annual trade agreement was, in the conditions of the time, no more than an exchange of those goods surplus to domestic needs against those which could open home bottlenecks. If—then, as now, among Comecon members—industrial capacity is not to be left idle, decisions on output and trade specialization are fundamental to investment planning, and vice versa. To co-ordinate plans on physical balances alone may ensure mutual consistency, but makes no contribution to optimality.

To emphasize, it would seem, the divorce of 'commodity' pricing from intra-Comecon trade planning, the exchange value of the rouble was substantially raised in March 1950. Ostensibly to free the rouble from the peg to the dollar (fixed in July 1937 at 5·30 to the \$) and to define it uniquely in terms of gold, the act of further overvaluation (to 4 roubles to the \$ and *pro rata* with respect to other currencies, including those of Comecon members) removed intra-Comecon exchange rates still farther from a reflexion of domestic cost-levels, and from their consequential use in measuring the efficiency of foreign trade. Contemporary observers could only attribute the move to the prestige of a higher—but nevertheless nominal—gold content, and the exaction of higher costs for maintaining embassies or sending trade delegations to Moscow.[17] For the student of the Soviet economy, the revaluation was the contrary of what would have been expected, given the trends in Soviet and world prices: the 1936 wholesale-price

[17] The Commercial Secretariat at H.M. Embassy, Moscow, was in fact closed, not to open again until Macmillan undertook its reinstatement during his visit to the USSR in 1959.

reform (which, like that of 1949, had raised the prices of, and eliminated subsidies to, producers' goods) had been accompanied by devaluation of the rouble. The 1950 appreciation was not annulled until 1961, when, following Comecon discussions on foreign-trade pricing and efficiency (described in Ch. IX), devaluation was explicitly undertaken to facilitate policy-making in external commerce.

Integration by mandate

For Comecon planning, the Soviet measures of 1950 implied reliance on mandatory, and the renunciation of the permissive, instruments. Once a policy of integration is adopted by a pair or group of market economies—by the lowering, say, of the internal tariffs of the European Common Market—the flow of goods across the frontiers is correspondingly altered, simply because the incentives—in this case lower customs duties—have only to be exhibited for trade to be diverted. The governments agreeing upon the integration do not have to adjudicate upon international cost comparisons, because this function is fulfilled by the market. Where, of course, the market-price mechanism has been distorted, e.g. by subsidies, such adjudication must be made: the Franco-German dispute over integration for agricultural produce in the Common Market is a case in point, and represents the sort of decision which must be made within Comecon.

Planning by 'material balances' became and (according to A. Sokolov in *Voprosy ekonomiki* for January 1967) remains the standard technique for Comecon. The balances, interlocked from product to product (viz. after 1956, from one commission or secretariat department to another within Comecon), can assure consistency among production goals: in the Comecon context, the system can demonstrate the trade flows in, say, iron ore and coking coal needed for members' steel outputs, and the corresponding flows of steel underwriting the mining investment to provide the ore and coal. As has been pointed out above, balances do not in themselves gravitate towards an optimal solution as would an international market mechanism. The two inhibitions to the attainment of rationality are, put technically, the fact that transformation coefficients are hard to use as a planner's variable and that the iteration starts from the output side.

In the Soviet practice of material balancing, the output of an industry—say, coal—is allocated to other users; these other users calculate the output of their product which is feasible with that coal (and other inputs similarly passed to them—in the case of steel, say, iron ore and limestone). By applying 'transformation coefficients' (the tons of coal, ore, and limestone needed per ton of steel), a planned output is calculated and this output, in turn, is allocated to other users. The users would include the coal industry, which then applies its own transformation coefficients to verify that it could produce the draft plan of coal. If an imbalance is shown (e.g. not enough steel to support the mine-sinking programme to extract the planned coal output), the procedure must be repeated ('iterated') with variant figures.

In the international arena, the transformation coefficient comprises not only the technical (physical) relationship of input to output, but also the gain from trade arising from the national differences of production cost. Ricardo in 1817 formulated the generation of foreign trade by the comparison of costs in terms wholly appropriate to Comecon's material balancing and manhour costing. The argument may therefore be recalled in his original words:

> England may be so circumstanced, that to produce the cloth [sold to Portugal] may require the labour of 100 men for one year; and if she attempted to make the wine [bought from Portugal], it might require the labour of 120 men for the same time.... To produce the wine in Portugal, might require only the labour of 80 men for one year and to produce the cloth in the same country, might require the labour of 90 men for the same time.... Though she could make the cloth with the labour of 90 men, she would import it from a country where it required the labour of 100 men to produce it, because it would be advantageous to her rather to employ her capital in the production of wine, for which she could obtain more cloth from England, than she could produce by diverting a portion of her capital from the cultivation of vines to the manufacture of cloth.[18]

For any member of the trading group, the input needed to derive a given output becomes the export proceeds to cover a given import from another member. It is shown in Chapter IX that Comecon members have computed ingenious physical coefficients, as well as labour costs, to measure the rate of international transformation, but two problems remain. In the first place, there are difficulties in aggregating the apparent gains from trade—there may be a comparative cost advantage for one partner in terms of raw-material inputs, but

[18] D. Ricardo, *The Principles of Political Economy and Taxation*, ed. P. Sraffa (Cambridge, 1951), p. 135. In Marx's terms, 'capital' may here be regarded as 'embodied labour'.

for the other in terms of manpower. In the second place, it is the planner who has to assess the alternatives to the existing coefficients. There is hence a built-in adherence to actual flows of trade. National agencies operating on the material-balance principle are slow to make radical changes in their planned coefficients—as witness the recent Soviet problems in introducing new materials (e.g. plastics) or techniques (e.g. railway dieselization); the invention of new flows of trade poses the same question for Comecon commissions.

Moreover, a complication arises which is not found in national planning: any country deprived of one export possibility by a decision on international specialization—i.e. a change in trade flow based upon an evaluation of comparative costs—needs to replace that export to maintain its balance of payments. Cases of refusals to adhere to Comecon specialization agreements because of balance-of-payments difficulty have rarely been discussed publicly in eastern Europe (see p. 164), but Pryor has collected from dissertations at the GDR Hochschule für Ökonomie evidence that they have occurred.[19]

Aggravating the difficulty of assessing the comparative costs in physical units is the parallel operation of price measurements. Enterprises and countries calculate their transactions in money: the one uses the domestic-price relationships, the other prices in the capitalist world market. Neither set of prices reflects the physical-input coefficients used by the planners—national or international—and the concerns of the monetary planners (the enterprise accountants, the Ministry of Finance, or the foreign-settlement department of the national bank) will differ from those running the physical programmes.

Material balances and the demand for trade

The second broad problem generated by the 'material-balance' approach is the start from the production side. In market economies the allocation of resources theoretically originates in consumption—the patterns of consumer demand and the efficiency of use of investment goods (or 'derived' demand). For a national 'material balance', the fact that production is the starting-line tends to induce a certain automatism in allocation: users are put down for the same shares year after year because assessment of the relative utility of each use is not

[19] F. Pryor, *The Communist Foreign Trade System* (London, 1963), pp. 212–13.

the responsibility of the producer. Obviously demand influences are exerted upon domestic planners: consumers' preferences are revealed by market surveys or by empty or over-full shelves in shops, investment efficiency by technical projection; but the complaints throughout eastern Europe of the rigidity of production patterns of retail and capital goods testify to the difficulties.

In planning the allocation to, and within, foreign trade, something of the same fossilization is apparent. The national 'material balances' exhibit a surplus of one product and a deficit of another, and these become respectively the export availability and the import requirement. A Comecon commission, or a bilateral negotiation, thus becomes a bartering place for these residuals and trade flows without rational justification. Where export residuals entered—or import substitutes stopped—intra-Comecon exchanges in the early, autarkic, period, continuance of the trade is almost certainly less than optimal. Yet no country is prepared to scrap plants constructed in those days (until 1956 obsolescence was held to be theoretically indefensible); it seeks instead markets, but for goods produced at a cost level higher than those available from other sources. The potential partners may be in Comecon or in the West, and in the latter case there may be technical difficulties in cost comparisons (examined in Chapter IX). The present Czechoslovak policy of the 'half-open door' is partly inspired by the need for cost measurement, and the Rumanian Declaration of April 1964 similarly emphasized the role of East–West trade in Comecon. Moreover, all the members are now more careful of their outlays (they have consumers whose share in national income cannot be compressed as in the 1950s), and are unwilling to sacrifice rational purchasing to amortize a neighbour's white elephant. Flows of labour and capital which in an integration of free markets would tend to equilibrate cost differentials have been inhibited by the exclusive concept of sovereignty. As Chapter X shows, there has been little inter-member investment and virtually no movement of labour.

Under a market mechanism, moreover, foreign trade arises more from the seeking of sales than from the disposal of output; yet 'material balances' are an instrument of the latter rather than the former. Similarly, because Comecon members—until very recently—traded bilaterally (or, at most, trilaterally), with inconvertible currencies, the adherence to existing flows has been still more closely stratified by country: new sources of an import requirement, or new outlets for an export, are less actively sought than by a market trader.

Objectives of production

Naturally neither production nor trade is an end in itself, and a broad objective, 'to accelerate the restoration and development of their national economies', was set out in the founding communiqué of Comecon. In 1952 Stalin wrote of

> the fact that during the postwar period these countries joined forces economically and organized economic co-operation and mutual aid. . . . As a result, we have high rates of industrial growth in these countries. . . . The basic economic law of socialism might be formulated roughly as follows: to assure maximum satisfaction of the constantly-growing material and cultural requirements of the entire society through the constant growth and improvement of socialist production on the basis of highest technology.[20]

But his decisive rule of production, which he then reiterated, was that of 'the preferential growth of means of production'. A decade later the Third Programme of the CPSU echoed these concepts, which were in their turn reflected in Comecon's *Basic Principles*:[21] '. . . above all maximum development of each country's socialist industry as the leading branch of the national economy, with priority given to the output of the means of production'. Yet in twenty months—in February 1964—this was being questioned in *Pravda*:

> In the interpretation of a number of economists, the law of preferential growth of the output of producers' goods is transformed into an end in itself. . . . Marx and Lenin never divorced production from consumption . . . Lenin sought the roots of the preferential growth of the first category not in [Marx's] formula of expanded reproduction but in technical progress.[22]

But Comecon still has no criteria for running economies on other lines. A young Soviet economist, discussing the dilemma, recently commented,

> If the answer to what are the main criteria for the economic efficacity of the international socialist division of labour has already been given in the *Basic Principles*, the other, more important question—how practically to apply these criteria—is for the present still unelucidated. Of course, this is

[20] *Economic Problems of Socialism*, pp. 35–36. [21] See below, p. 253.
[22] A. Arzumanyan, *Pr.*, 25 Feb. 1964.

far from being accidental. The economists of socialist countries have failed to solve many major problems of determining the economic efficiency of production even at the national level, let alone at the scale of the world socialist economic system.[23]

[23] O. Bogomolov, *Vopr. ekon.*, no. 11, 1963, pp. 5–6.

IV

AD HOC MEETINGS, 1950–5

The slow start

FROM the foundation until 1956 Comecon's relatively few conferences were convened strictly *ad hoc*. As it had no Charter until 1960, its statement of 1949 served as the 'organizational arrangements',[1] expanded by an unpublished resolution of the Fourth Session (1954) 'defining the further tasks of the CMEA and the legal basis for its activity'.[2]

The period before Comecon attained definite form falls into three parts. An initial round of consultation brought long-term agreements on mutual trade, the introduction of triangular deals which began to break the restrictiveness of bilateralism, and permanent arrangements for technical assistance. From 1951 until after Stalin's death, national planning was sacrificed to Soviet insistence, regardless of cost, upon the priority of the metal-using industries, including the munitions programme associated with the Korean War. Inter-member relations deteriorated under 'extraordinary tensions in economic relationships ... the result of serious errors of ... Party and economic leaders'[3] and exchange with the rest of the world was curtailed and envenomed by NATO controls. Such an environment soon left Comecon with no substantive role to play, and a miniscule staff then busied itself with the standardization of trade statistics and of contract practices. A third phase was initiated by a change in Soviet policy: nearly all mixed companies in Bulgaria, Germany, Hungary, and Rumania were dismantled; Soviet exactions of Polish coal ceased; the pre-eminence accorded to heavy industry was relaxed; and everywhere a 'New Course' emerged with more emphasis on consumers' goods. Comecon was able to take up the threads of its earlier activity: for long-run trade planning, 1960 was selected as a common horizon; for the short term, triangular commercial links were extended to virtually all

[1] *Uchreditelnye polozheniya* (Shurshalov, pp. 373–4; Faddeev, p. 20), a peculiar term otherwise unused in the terminology of Soviet international law.

[2] Ibid. The same wording is used in both sources.

[3] *Imre Nagy on Communism: in Defence of the New Course* (London, 1957), p. 238: writing in early 1956, he was specifically referring to Hungarian relations with Czechoslovakia, the GDR, and Rumania before June 1953.

members; and technical-assistance liaison was established through the good offices of the permanent delegations in Moscow. But new scope for collaboration was not provided until twelve standing commissions were established in 1956.

Comecon published two communiqués on meetings in 1949; until March 1954 it was silent. As the official history shows, one Session was held during the quiescence (in November 1950), but by then Soviet references had long ceased. In eastern Europe Comecon seems to have been officially mentioned only once during 1950: there had been talk of it at a Czechoslovak historians' conference in November 1949 and in the Rumanian Grand National Assembly on 28 December 1949, but in 1950 it was mentioned only in the Hungarian Parliament on 6 December. In the summer of 1950 the Soviet delegate at the annual session of the ECE contrasted the Marshall Plan exploitation of western Europe with the 'mutual assistance' within eastern Europe, but made no mention of Comecon by name.[4] In the years 1950–3 not one word appeared in the Soviet press about Comecon; it was neither spoken of nor represented at the 1952 International Economic Conference in Moscow. In a memorandum addressed to his Party Central Committee in early 1956, Imre Nagy, appointed Secretary of the Hungarian Workers' Party in 1951 and Prime Minister from July 1953 to April 1955, concluded that 'although the economic cooperation and mutual assistance between the socialist countries brought significant results, the activity of CMEA from the point of view of industrial production and development was exceptionally limited during the period of the First Five-Year Plan (1950–1954)'.[5]

The First Session convened by the signatories of the January declaration met in Moscow in April 1949. It created the nucleus of an organization, but it can be nicely debated whether an organization was set up *stricto sensu*. Comecon did not have its juridical entity defined until 1959—the Charter was ratified in 1960—and for ten years its formal standing derived solely from the founding communiqué. A Bulgarian lawyer has asserted that 'the act of international law whereby CMEA was founded is the published communiqué',[6] and there are authorities

[4] Reproduced in the *Vnesh. pol. SS 1950*. This annual collection of foreign-policy documents contained nothing about Comecon, although the 1949 issue reproduced both Comecon statements. The *Current Digest of the Soviet Press* records no reference to Comecon during 1950–3.

[5] Nagy, p. 189.

[6] M. Genovsky, *Politicheska i pravna kharakteristika na saveta za ikonomicheska vzaimopomoshch* (Sofia, 1959), p. 43.

in both eastern and western Europe who maintain that a communiqué may be tantamount to a treaty.[7] Relying on these, Uschakow concludes that it is enough that the communiqué fulfilled the essential criterion, 'namely, an international agreement among states to create an institution', but goes on to cite the requirement that a central agency (*Hauptorgan*) be created.[8] Until 1954 the conference of member states (entitled the 'Session of the Council') was Comecon's only formal body. The First Session did, however, deal with organization and an interim 'Bureau' was created. The size and composition of the Bureau in the first year is unknown, but there is reason to believe that at the nadir of Comecon's activity it comprised not more than two or three people.

The national composition of the first Bureau has never been stated, but by 1955, when the author first met members of the Secretariat in Moscow, Aleksandr Pavlov, a former Soviet Deputy-Minister of Foreign Trade, was Executive Secretary and his senior deputy was a Czechoslovak, Frantisek Hamouz (at the time of writing his country's Minister for Foreign Trade);[9] in the following year, a visit to the Comecon office showed that a multinational staff of perhaps forty was installed. As a staff, the majority of whom were national delegates and the minority an international secretariat, it was not unique in international economic organization—there is a close parallel in the European Danube Commission of 1856 to 1939, and a still closer one in its exclusively eastern European successor, the Danube Commission, created no more than six months before Comecon.

The founding conference of January 1949 had not publicly expressed any view on the location of the Secretariat. Two agencies of the 'socialist camp' were already based on Rumania. The Cominform was then operating from Bucharest (originally in Belgrade, but hastily removed after the Tito–Stalin break in 1948), and the Danube Commission was in Galatz,[10] but the quartering of other international organizations in different eastern European capitals had begun. In any case, with centripetal policy-making, the Soviet city was the obvious

[7] Uschakow; the Soviet lawyers whom he cites are N. Minasyan and V. Shurshalov, the western authorities G. Dahm and E. Meyers.

[8] Referring to K. Zamenek, *Das Vertragsrecht der internationalen Organisationen* (Vienna, 1957).

[9] W. von Knorre, *Zehn Jahre Rat für gegenseitige Wirtschaftshilfe* (Würzburg, 1961), p. 15, says another Deputy was then H. Rozanski (in 1967 dep. Polish delegate).

[10] Rumania was in fact to lose both; the Cominform was liquidated in 1956 and the Danube Commission was transferred to Budapest in 1954.

choice; had Comecon been envisaged as an outward-looking trade group, Prague would doubtless have been more indicated.

Besides creating the organizational nucleus, the First Session, also held in Moscow, reviewed objectives in the field of mutual trade and technical assistance. No communiqué was issued—among succeeding sessions only that of 1950 was similarly unpublicized—and it is unlikely, in view of the shortness of the meeting and the need for constitutional decisions, that this was any more than a general *tour d'horizon*. A study by a Soviet international lawyer on 'Legal Aspects of the Activity of Organs of the CMEA' lists recommendations as beginning to be made only at the Second Session.[11] Agoston believes that Comecon was used to co-ordinate the economic blockade of Yugoslavia.[12] The absence of documentary evidence for this view does not, of course, controvert it while so little of the early history has been published. On the other hand, the western powers preferred to create a body independent of OEEC, Cocom, in January 1950 to administer the embargo on exports to the Sino-Soviet group, and the presumption could be that if any corresponding body had been established in eastern Europe it would also have been separate. Nevertheless, the trade problems with which Comecon was to deal would have involved the reallocation of supplies and deliveries which, until mid-1948, had been exchanged with Yugoslavia.

First recommendations

Sofia was chosen for the Second Session (in August of the same year) because Bulgaria headed the Russian alphabetical order of founder members;[13] this session began one of the most fruitful aspects of the organization's work by drawing up procedures for scientific and technical co-operation, among them the establishment of bilateral agencies for such exchanges. The network of such joint commissions was largely created within a year. Thus Hungary created commissions with the USSR and Czechoslovakia in 1949 and with Bulgaria, the

[11] V. Morozov, *Sov. gos. pravo*, no. 10, 1961, p. 150. The brief description of the work of the First Session comes from the summary—presumably furnished by Comecon—of its history in V. Solodovnikov, ed., *Mezhdunarodnye ekonomicheskie organizatsii* (Moscow, 1962).

[12] Agoston, p. 26.

[13] Albania had been accepted a month after the constituent conference, but, as an isolated Cominformist beset by the violence of quarrels with its neighbours, Greece and Yugoslavia, it was no suitable venue for an international meeting. In fact, Tirana was not used by Comecon until a working group of its Agricultural Commission met there in January 1958; a Council Session was held in May 1959, when a second alphabetical round began.

GDR, and Rumania in 1950; similar commissions with non-member planned economies did not come for a long time—with North Korea and Yugoslavia in 1956, with Mongolia in 1958, with North Vietnam in 1960, and with China in 1963. Soviet technical-assistance treaties with Czechoslovakia and Poland had been signed in 1947, but all the others were in the Comecon period: after that with Hungary, those with Bulgaria and Rumania were agreed in 1950, with the GDR in 1951, and finally with Albania in 1952. The exchange of technical documentation—free, except for the mere cost of reproduction—was especially opportune at this time, because the round of long-run plans set off a burst of investment projects in 1950–2 which severely strained resources of qualified designers.[14]

The Second Session also made the important recommendation that members change their mutual trade agreements from an annual to a long-term basis. The framework for inter-member trade had already been largely—though not completely—settled by bilateral agreements and, so far as concerned the USSR and the other founder members of Comecon, was complete by February 1950. The Soviet Union had concluded trade and payments treaties with Poland in 1945, with Czechoslovakia, Hungary, and Rumania in 1947, and with Bulgaria in 1948. The GDR and Albania—neither founder members of Comecon—were omitted from these arrangements, and the USSR did not sign trade and navigation treaties with them until 1957 and 1958 respectively. In a similar network Czechoslovakia signed its agreement with Poland on economic co-operation in July 1947 (its provisions other than on technical interchange were suspended in 1949),[15] a trade and payments agreement with Rumania in the same year, with Bulgaria and Hungary in 1948, with Albania in 1949, and with the GDR in January 1950. When this was complete, each member negotiated trade and payments treaties with China—the USSR first in April 1950, Czechoslovakia and the GDR the same year, Poland and Hungary in 1951, Bulgaria and Rumania in 1952, and Albania in 1954. China's own network with the Asian socialist countries was being simultaneously created—by treaties with North Korea in 1951, with Mongolia in 1953, and with North Vietnam in 1954. The standard agreement was for a strict bilateral balance of trade each year tem-

[14] See S. Jedrychowski, *Inwest. bud.*, Jan. 1954, p. 32.

[15] J. Marczewski, *Planification et croissance économique des démocracies populaires* (Paris, 1956), pp. 236–7.

pered by credit (at 2 per cent interest) for a maximum of three months. Within the frame of these enabling treaties, Comecon members concluded long-term trade agreements with each other, and—with the highly significant exception of the USSR itself—with China.[16]

The practical precondition for the move to long-term trade planning was self-evidently the start of long-term planning itself (see Chart 1, p. 66). The five-year plans of Bulgaria and Czechoslovakia had already begun in 1949, that of Hungary and the Polish Six-Year Plan were to start in 1950. The current Soviet Plan was running from 1946 to 1950, and in March of 1950 Molotov had stated that the follow-on draft (1951–5) was being prepared. Albania, Rumania, and the GDR were operating on annual plans and envisaging five-year plans 1951–5 in line with the USSR. The link implied by the choice of period by these countries was, of course, intimate because their export commitments effectively were made in Moscow. Albanian dependence, after the split with Yugoslavia, was complete: it traded only with Comecon members and the USSR took two-thirds of its exports. In Rumania the Sovrom mixed companies, and in the GDR the SAG, were run on Soviet orders, and the share of reparations in exports was much higher in these countries than in the other ex-enemy territories.

It is clear from both contemporary and retrospective statements that intra-Comecon planning was on the agenda of the Second Session. On his return from Sofia, Hilary Minc, a Polish Deputy Premier and Minister for Trade and Industry, wrote in the Cominform Journal that Comecon 'strengthens planning in the people's democracies and makes it possible to extend the coordination in planning between several countries'.[17] His use of the word 'extend' doubtless referred to the joint planning already undertaken between Poland and Czechoslovakia under the 1947 treaty just mentioned. A brief history of Comecon in a Soviet compendium of international economic agencies states that the Session 'was concerned with the organization of planning the co-ordinated development of basic, interrelated branches of members' national economies'.[18] There was even a rumour at the time that the discussions centred on a twenty-year perspective and a

[16] A. Eckstein, *Communist China's Economic Growth and Foreign Trade* (New York, 1966), p. 140; on the Soviet failure to make long-run arrangements with China, see below, p. 72.

[17] *For a Lasting Peace, for a People's Democracy*, 18 Nov. 1949.

[18] Solodovnikov, p. 301; it is to be considered at least semi-official.

100-m.-rouble clearing fund;[19] this would have been of the order of 4 per cent of their mutual exports and hence a reasonable lubricant for multilateralism.

Planning for longer than a five-year period had been dropped by the USSR with many other programming techniques in 1930, and had been taken up again at the start of 1941 as a 'Genplan' for fifteen years; Stalin's proposition of fifteen-year goals in 1946 had indicated a resumption—now attributed to Voznesensky.[20] From 1950 until 1957 nothing was heard of either very long-run programming or of multilateral clearing. Both ideas were then taken up by Comecon, and it is relevant that the clearing arrangement set up by it in that year and in 1963 fixed the credit limits at 3 per cent of mutual exports—close to the original scheme. The very vagueness of the communiqué of this Second Session—'the Council discussed the current questions of its work and took corresponding decisions'—may imply that no substantive agreement was reached on what were in effect major policy matters. It may well imply also that a Charter was discussed, but not finalized: every other postwar agency in which the USSR played a leading part (see App. IX) produced its formal Statute or Constitution within a year of its creation.

Measures on trade and payments

If no consensus was then found on a general move from bilateral barter towards price-costed multilateralism (for the latter by definition cannot be on a barter basis), three members soon afterwards, and for the first time, made trilateral deals. Trade agreements were signed in Moscow in June 1949 between Finland, Poland, and the Soviet Union, and between Finland, Czechoslovakia, and the Soviet Union. The pattern of exports in millions of roubles was as follows:

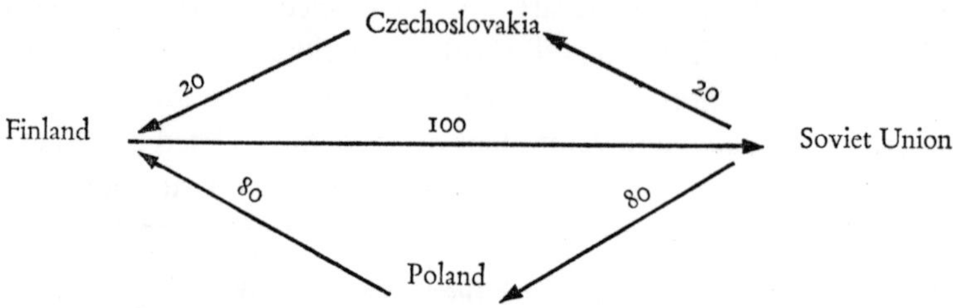

[19] Reported by M. Dewar, *Soviet Trade with Eastern Europe, 1945–9* (London, 1951), p. 5.
[20] Sorokin, *Vopr. ekon.*, no. 12, 1963, p. 152.

The three parties from the Comecon side were the obvious participants among the members, for they were the only wholly free agents: the other Comecon members, as already observed, had much of their exports determined by the USSR.

From that meeting until a year after Stalin's death, there was only one other Session of the Council, in November 1950, to which no reference was made either in a contemporary communiqué or in any eastern European narrative, and whose very date is an enigma.[21] It is possible that no such session took place, or—if it occurred in Moscow as stated—that it was to accept or elaborate on decisions taken at a highly secret meeting in Hungary. The production and trade plans of Comecon countries were radically changed at a meeting of Party leaders at Hollohaza, a village of 1,000 inhabitants on the frontier with Czechoslovakia, and far from large towns (Miskolc is 65 km. away). The Party officials, accompanied by economic advisers, were told by the representative of the Soviet Communist Party that the five-year plan targets for heavy industry of each country would have to be revised upward, partly to meet the armament requirements of the Korean War and partly to satisfy Stalin's urge for ever-greater accumulation.[22] Five members had already published their long-term plans: three, Czechoslovakia, the GDR, and Hungary, promulgated revisions in early 1951,[23] Bulgaria announced that a revision had been made but never divulged details,[24] while for Poland 'it is doubtful whether (the balances) were completely recast, as they should have been, after the radical revision of output targets pressed on the Poles by the Soviet Politburo in 1950'.[25] The key sectoral plan in Poland, however, was promulgated only in 1951, and incorporated the higher targets. The Albanian and Rumanian overall plans similarly did not appear until after Hollohaza and clearly took account of the new priorities.

[21] The exact date was not, it seems, made available until a list appeared in V. Polozhaev and G. Yakobson, *Mezhdunarodnye ekonomicheskie organizatsii i soglasheniya* (Moscow, 1961), p. 188; they gave, however, 25–27 November, whereas later documentation published by the Comecon Secretariat shows 24–25 November, as does L. Ciamaga, *Od wspolpracy do integracji—zarys organizacji i dzialalnosci RWPG w latach 1949–1964* (Warsaw, 1965), p. 200. Faddeev, p. 26, gives 24–25 October.

[22] Khrushchev, in his closed-session speech at the Twentieth Party Congress in 1956, described some of the fiscal burdens Stalin proposed to support the Soviet increase in forced saving.

[23] *RP*, 25 Feb. 1951; *Schriftenreiche der DDR*, no. 8, 1951; *Sz. Nep*, 16 May 1951.

[24] See *Econ. B. Eur.*, iii/1, p. 20, and *Econ. Survey Eur. since the War* (Geneva, 1963), pp. 29–31.

[25] J. Montias, *Central Planning in Poland* (New Haven, Conn., 1962), p. 150.

Hungary was in line for a Comecon meeting since it was the next in Russian alphabetical order after Bulgaria, the place of the Second Session. Certainly more substantial business was transacted at Hollohaza than in any formal Session in Moscow. The most that published sources have revealed[26] on the Third Session—no earlier than ten years after the event—is that it dealt with the same question as the Second, namely, the network of long-term trade agreements. This was in any case under construction. Thus the USSR had established its 1951–2 and 1953–8 trade with Poland in July 1950 and its 1951–5 arrangements with Czechoslovakia in November 1950, the turnover for 1951–5 having been settled with Finland in June by virtue of the trilateral scheme just described. Czechoslovakia as early as 1948 had exchanged provisional lists of mutual deliveries in the period to 1953 with Poland and with Hungary, but both were superseded in 1951 by new arrangements running to 1955. The round of long-term agreements with the USSR went on to completion, in the course of the next year, all with 1955 as the horizon: Albania in February, Rumania in August, and the GDR in September 1951. In 1951 also the network between Comecon members other than with the USSR was similarly advanced. This may be seen from the situation by the end of the year set out in Chart 2 (p. 67): the GDR had been brought into long-term relations with all the others save Bulgaria (which in turn remained at the stage of annual agreements with Hungary) and the only country not properly interlocked was Rumania.[27] The Hungarian Deputy Minister for Foreign Trade, Laszlo Gay, writing in the Cominform Journal, was able to state:

The mutually-concluded long-term trade agreements are of vital significance for the establishment of planned trade between the people's democracies. At first the situation was such that, while a country with a planned economy could calculate for years ahead its vital import requirements and its export possibilities, it could not be sure that it would definitely get everything it needed in future years from the other planned economies, or that it would definitely supply them with certain goods. Today, however, the long-term trade agreements serve as a solid basis for planning foreign trade for years in advance and in this way create prerequisites which will enable the countries marching along the pathway to Socialism to co-

[26] Solodovnikov, p. 302, and Morozov, *Sov. gos. pravo*, no. 10, 1961.

[27] Korbonski (*Int. Con.*, Sept. 1964, p. 38), records that in 1950–1 Rumania used its surplus with Bulgaria to buy Bulgarian tobacco with which it settled for imports from Czechoslovakia, the GDR, and Hungary. This trilateral barter seems to have been the only form of Rumanian multilateral trade at the time.

ordinate plans for production and capital investments in individual branches of the economy by means of trade agreements. . . . The year 1952 is the first year when the bulk of the foreign trade between the Soviet Union and countries of people's democracy is being conducted on the basis of long-term trade agreements.[28]

Taking this as an expression of full satisfaction with the completion of the long-term trade net, it could be argued that there was nothing more for Comecon to do until a new round had to be started in 1955 (the terminal year of most plans, as Chart 1 shows). A Soviet record of the agency does in fact take this view: 'In the initial years the activity of CMEA chiefly consisted of the strengthening and extension of trade links between member countries, because at that time the predominant form of economic co-operation was trade relations'.[29] It could in any case be maintained that while the Korean War lasted, the advance planning of trade flows had to be subordinated to military logistics; moreover, when rigorous strategic controls were imposed by the United States in October 1951 (with similar restrictions by other NATO powers), long-term projections of trade with the West were out of the question.

Writing in this period, and while Stalin was still living, Oskar Lange, later chairman of the Polish Economic Council but then without any governmental position, nevertheless pointed the steps Comecon should have taken, namely 'not only bilateral agreements, but the co-ordination of trade and co-ordination of plans of production between all countries of the socialist camp'.[30] Quoting this, an American economist considers that the bilateral agreements even conflicted with Comecon's professed aim of co-ordination.[31] The facts of Comecon's history appear to be that after 1950 there was some work by its 'Bureau' on the standardization of foreign-trade contracts and statistics; the Fourth Session of the Council was not convened until mid-1954.

So unimportant do two Soviet writers on Comecon seem to consider the post-1950 years that their narrative leaps straight from the accession of the GDR in September 1950 to the Session authorizing

[28] *For a Lasting Peace*, 14 Nov. 1952 (the English of the original has been slightly clarified).
[29] Solodovnikov, p. 302.
[30] O. Lange, 'The Disintegration of the Single World Market and the Formation of two Parallel Markets in the World Economy', *Ek.*, no. 1, 1953.
[31] N. Spulber, *The Economics of Communist Eastern Europe* (New York, 1957), p. 428.

the Charter in December 1959. The chief Polish and Rumanian delegates to Comecon in recent articles date the co-ordination of plans within Comecon only from 1955.[32]

Trade statistics and contract uniformity

The carrying out of the recommendations of the first round of Comecon meetings on the conclusion of long-term trade agreements was not impeded by the quiescence of the formal Session. They were concerned with bilateral deals, not with co-ordinated planning. Bilateral balancing, which was carried down to six-month periods not only for trade but for all payments,[33] was even defended as 'creating favourable conditions for the conduct of foreign trade, since neither side can run up against any serious difficulties in settling its accounts'.[34] At the time, the Secretariat of the ECE observed that this 'strong bilateral character' explained 'the lack of attention to international differences in costs', and that 'there would be little point in creating a more complicated system unless it were desired to take advantage of different relative-cost conditions'.[35]

One of its two known acts after the 1950 Session was the 'acceptance by members of CMEA in 1952 of "Basic Indicators for the Application of Operational Reports on Foreign Trade", permitting the creation of uniform primary reporting in international trade'.[36] The body, or meeting, which took this decision has not been indicated, but the following year it was the Bureau which drafted a 'Uniform Foreign Trade Classification'. The classification proposed was a very broad one, comprising only five main commodity groups and sixty product groups; the corresponding list adopted by the United Nations in 1950, the Standard International Trade Classification (SITC), had ten sections in 150 commodity groups comprising 570 items. After discussion among member countries, a much finer classification was adopted in 1954, comprising nine main commodity groups. The Soviet Union adopted it forthwith,[37] but its general use was not formally recommended for all member countries until a 'meeting of foreign-trade

[32] P. Jaroszewicz, *N. Drogi*, no. 11, 1962, p. 16; A. Birladeanu in *Pr.*, 25 Oct. 1963.
[33] This situation was 'uniform for all countries in the democratic camp' in 1953 (*Sov. gos. pravo*, no. 6, 1953, p. 96).
[34] A. Chistyakov, 'The Development of Economic Co-operation between the Countries in the Socialist Camp', *Komm.*, no. 15, 1954, p. 58. Shortly afterwards, he was appointed head of the USSR permanent delegation to ECE.
[35] *Econ. Survey Eur. 1954*, pp. 127 and 128 respectively.
[36] *Vest. stat.*, no. 5, 1959, p. 77.
[37] *Edinaya tovarnaya nomenklatura vneshnei torgovli* (Moscow, 1954).

statisticians from CMEA countries' on 5–9 March 1959 in Moscow, when 1960 was proposed as the first year for uniform classification. The same 1959 meeting recommended a unification of foreign-trade volume indices arising out of the 1952 proposal.

It is reasonable to ask why a uniform nomenclature was needed so soon after the elaboration of SITC by the United Nations Statistical Commission and on which the USSR, Poland, and Czechoslovakia had the opportunity of commenting. The draft SITC had been submitted to all United Nations members and consequently amended between June 1948 and April 1950. The Soviet delegation to the Statistical Commission, however, did not support the classification and declared it unsuitable for Soviet trade. In approving SITC, the Economic and Social Council recommended (in July 1950) that

> the attention of all United Nations organs, regional commissions and specialized agencies, and of other inter-governmental bodies, be drawn to the establishment of this classification and that they be requested to formulate their requests for international trade data [i.e. from their members] in terms of the new classification.

Comecon was theoretically among these 'other intergovernmental bodies' but in practice there was no contact with the United Nations at the time: when its own classification appeared, it proved to be conceptually the same as SITC, and, like it, an improvement on previous usage.[38] But whereas the SITC was coded to the United Nations *International Standard Industrial Classification* (1949), Comecon was not to start work on its *Uniform Classification of Industrial Groups* until May 1958 (completing it in January 1965); nor was Soviet revision of its prewar classification to start for some years.[39] As the Comecon grouping did not follow the extant Soviet industrial list, it could hardly have been imperative for domestic planning convenience. Yet the facts that it took years for its use to be extended to other Comecon members,[40] and that its one major divergence from the SITC pro-

[38] The Comecon list, like SITC, was decimal but used one more digit to identify goods. The League of Nations *Minimum List of Commodities* had had cardinal numbers (unusable for finer breakdowns) and the *Tariff Nomenclature* of the European Customs Union Study Group employed a combination of figures and letters.

[39] See F. Fedorov, 'Questions of the Classification of Production', *Vest. stat.*, no. 2, 1955.

[40] Bulgaria and Poland did not change their published trade statistics to the Comecon classification until 1960. Both Czechoslovakia and Hungary used it when they first published a commodity breakdown in 1957, but the former regrouped the Comecon classes. Albania showed the Comecon list when it published a commodity table in 1962, as did Rumania in 1964. The GDR has not yet published commodity tables.

cedure to suit Soviet practice was long a subject of contention,[41] imply that the initiative was wholly Soviet, a step towards group autarky or, as Stalin put it at the time, 'the formation and consolidation of the new, parallel world market'.

The other act of Comecon between the Sessions of 1950 and 1954, the Uniform Foreign-Trade Contract agreed in 1951, was part of the same policy, but to the practical advantage of all signatories. It covered conditions of delivery, quality of goods, packing, guarantees, payments, compensation, and arbitration. It seems to have been immediately applied, and has since been supplemented by twenty-eight further standard contracts.[42] The general use of new settlement arrangements also dates from this period, viz. the 'rapid settlement system' first tried out between the GDR and Czechoslovakia in 1951.[43]

The first conflict of interests

The first round of long-term plans had already been twice revised before the Fourth Session was convened in Moscow in March 1954. As already described, the first revision had been made under the impact of the armament needs of the Korean War and by Stalin's decision further to mobilize resources for the development of heavy industry. In 1953 this pressure was relaxed by the Panmunjon armistice and by the death of Stalin. The plans of every member were rewritten to accord higher priority to consumption—the 'Malenkov policy' in the USSR, the 'New Course' in eastern Europe. Major investment projects in producer-goods sectors were everywhere slowed down or abandoned. Some—the Main Turkmen Canal in the USSR or the Danube–Black Sea Canal in Rumania, the steel smelter in Albania—were never to be resumed, others—the steel works in Hungary at Sztalinvaros or in Poland at Nowa Huta—lost their urgent priority. Import programmes, once geared to heavy industrial equipment, were reoriented to the purchase of consumers' goods or to machinery for light industry, until the end of 1954 when priority was again given to heavy industry. Although each member later produced a report on the fulfilment of its long-term plans, each economy

[41] Viz. Comecon item 16, 'Equipment and material for complete plants', entered under the separate components in SITC.

[42] B. Dutoit, *L'Union soviétique face à l'intégration européenne* (Lausanne, 1964), pp. 102–3.

[43] I. Aizenberg, *Vnesh. torg.*, no. 1, 1962, p. 43.

was in fact run on annual programmes until the end of 1955 (see Chart 1, p. 66).[44] The network of long-term trade agreements fell into similar desuetude.

The revisions, however, were of a different nature to those of 1951. Under the decisions of Hollohaza the seller's market in Comecon was accentuated, but trade fell behind the growth of production because all were competing for the same inputs and producing roughly similar outputs. The plan changes of 1953–4 diversified the demand for primary products and reduced that for manufactures. Orders placed in Czechoslovakia and the GDR for capital equipment were cancelled as investment plans were drastically scaled down, thus adding to the excess of engineering capacity in relation to the flow of raw materials. The 'New Course' involved a general raising of food supplies: Czechoslovakia and the GDR depended on the other members for the additional grain, but at the same time had their export earnings reduced by the cancellation of orders. The primary producers, too, had their commitments to improve consumption: Hungary, Poland, and Rumania reduced the sales of farm produce to other members, in at least one case—Rumania to Czechoslovakia—breaking in 1953 and 1954 the foodstuff contracts which it had undertaken in the long-term trade agreement. While, however, reducing their traditional exports, the three agrarian economies, Bulgaria, Hungary, and Rumania, were faced with balance-of-payments difficulties with the USSR: the USSR had been taking its share of the output of 'mixed companies' outside commercial channels: in 1954 the sale of these companies to the national authorities required annual repayments under trade agreements, in goods which were by no means necessarily the same as those produced by the companies. This was a severe problem in Rumania where the two main products of such companies, timber and petroleum,[45] had been over-exploited: the government's response—as it had been before the war—was to try to persuade its partners to take more refined petroleum (a proposition Czechoslovakia declined, turning to the USSR for crude supplies) and more of its own machinery. The decline in Czechoslovak-Rumanian trade epitomized

[44] In the USSR a two-year programme 1954–5 enlarging the outputs laid down for consumers' goods superseded the 1951–5 Plan, but it was operative only in 1954. A Bulgarian Five-Year Plan 1949–53 was wound up in 1952 and one for 1953–7 introduced; it was revised almost as soon as published and the original investment rate planned was not regained until 1956–7.

[45] Sovromles was sold back in 1954, Sovrompetrol in 1955.

the clash that Comecon was to face between international efficiency—as represented by Czech engineering—and national development—Rumanian industrialization.[46]

Trade with western Europe if anything exacerbated the conflict. The sharp reduction in the Cocom embargo already mentioned had ironically been initiated by an informal démarche by the Czechoslovak UK delegation at the Plenary Session of the ECE. Western equipment was thus made available embodying advances in technology that had been unavailable or stultified by autarkic growth: in the short run, it had been cheapest to continue to make machines already in production and to set up factories at home or in the less-developed members on established techniques. It could moreover be purchased rapidly, in contrast to the delays which a seller's market had engendered in Comecon states. In 1953 imports from western Europe had just regained the 1949 peak (see Ch. VII), but by 1954 they were 24 per cent and in 1955 32 per cent above it; exports to western Europe were in 1953 and 1954 below 1949 but rose 23 per cent in the later year and 24 per cent in 1955. The further revision of plans and the emergence of idle engineering capacity led to some disruptive cancellations of orders during 1955, such as those for textile machinery placed by Soviet corporations with British firms the year before.

Finally, in 1953, reparations deliveries from the GDR, Hungary, and Rumania were terminated, and trade agreements had consequently to be revised: the GDR, for example, set its 1954 foreign-trade plan at 30 per cent over the 1953 volume.

There was little point, when Comecon was reactivated, in using the organization for negotiations on the trade needs of the plan period to 1955. There was no question of co-ordinating plans for new capacity, and exchanges from current output had to be effected by bilateral contract. With the 'New Course' posing radically-changed policy principles for the next long-run horizon, it was obvious that Comecon should direct its attention to 1956–60. This period, that of the Soviet Sixth Five-Year Plan, was available for the next round by all Comecon members save Bulgaria, which envisaged a Three-Year Plan to follow

[46] The genesis of this confrontation, amply documented from Czech sources, was first analysed by Montias, in *Wld Pol.*, July 1966, pp. 722–5, in *Sov. Stud.*, Oct. 1964, esp. pp. 127–31, and in *J. Int. Aff.*, no. 1, 1966, esp. pp. 55–61; his principal references are D. Machova, *CSSR v sotsialisticke mezinarodni delbe prace* (Prague, 1962), J. Novozamsky, *Vyrovnavani ekonomicke urovne zemi RVHP* (Prague, 1964), and J. Vanek, *Ekonomicky a politicky vyznam vyvozu vyrobku z CSSR* (Prague, 1960).

its 1953–7 programme, and thus could also use 1960 as a target date. The Fourth Session hence tried to look beyond immediate difficulties and recommended members to conclude long-term trade agreements for the period to 1960.

Talks on international specialization

Two meetings were held in quick succession, both in Moscow. The Fifth, three months after the Fourth, Session must have taken up the problems of investment distribution in each national plan when long-term trade began to be discussed. The communiqué of that conference (July 1954) briefly stated that

> the Council discussed questions of the further development of the different branches of industry and agriculture on the basis of economic co-operation between member states. The Council also concerned itself with questions concerning the trade of members of the Council with other countries.

The problem of the 'different branches of industry and agriculture' was, presumably, the confrontation of enlarged import demands for foodstuffs and consumers' goods with reduced export availabilities. This was an immediate prospect as the share in national product devoted to consumption rose, and a long-run problem as investment cuts decelerated the rate of growth. It left open the decision as to who was to carry the burden of investment in producers' goods. A Hungarian newspaper, the following year, stated this question succinctly:

> Is it possible to suggest to a people's democracy, which has more favourable conditions of raw material production, that it should develop only its heavy industry, while we develop only light industry, and agriculture? It is known that the development of heavy industry is much more costly than that of light industry. Can we demand of a friendly country that it should have a substantial part of its national income invested in coal mining, metal production and other branches of heavy industry, and leave us to develop only the cheap branches of the national economy?[47]

The 'trade with other countries' which the Fifth Session discussed must chiefly have concerned balances with western Europe. Since the Fourth Session the USSR had suspended its sales of gold (approximately $150 m. between late 1953 and the spring of 1954), and Fin-

[47] *Sz. Nep*, 31 July 1955.

land had received $10 m. from the USSR in gold and convertible currencies to settle its export surplus with eastern Europe (under the triangular agreements described above). The USSR, moreover, was shortly to grant (in October 1954) a loan to China of $130 m.

Not surprisingly in these circumstances, the July 1954 Session reached no recommendations on trade,[48] but it was one of the three consecutive sessions (Fourth to Sixth) which advocated inter-product specialization.

The Fifth Session, discussing the question of reaching agreement between member countries on plans for capital investment, recommended the conclusion of bilateral and multilateral agreements between members on mutual aid and collaboration in the development of specific sectors of the economy.

The 1954–5 meetings examined the situation in fuels and raw materials and recommended such concentrations of primary industry as a very broad review of natural endowments could have revealed. This appraisal was certainly based on no detailed cost comparisons, which were to begin at a much later phase of Comecon activity and which are not yet complete, but in effect it ratified the halt to autarkic investment in this sector, upon which members had severally resolved in their national policies.

The first moves in joint planning were bilateral, although they must have been discussed at the Comecon meetings of the time: the creation of an international grid and co-operation in 'production-line' (i.e. series-produced) engineering are recorded as having been on the agenda of the Fourth to Sixth Sessions, and joint projects were first recommended at the latter. The electric grid scheme then propounded —but not operative until 1962—linked in bilateral negotiations Bulgaria and Rumania, Rumania and Hungary, Hungary and Czechoslovakia and the GDR. Hungary in 1954 signed agreements with Czechoslovakia and with Rumania on joint projects in aluminium and in chemicals respectively. Specialization among products (inter-product) made little progress until the 1956 Session, but the first steps were taken on specialization within products (intra-product), under bilateral, rather than Comecon, arrangements.[49] Hungary agreed in

[48] Shown by the absence of the Fifth Session from the lists of trade recommendations given by Morozov (*Sov. gos. pravo*, 1961, p. 150) and Shurshalov, p. 293.

[49] The main contemporary Soviet study describing these (Chistyakov, *Komm.*, no. 15, 1954) makes no mention of Comecon.

1954 with Czechoslovakia and with Poland on the production of types of rolled steel, and with Rumania on ball-bearings: the latter agreed on tractor specialization with Poland. At the beginning of the year, the GDR signed a protocol allocating types of manufactured consumers' goods between its industry and that of Poland, a year later with Czechoslovakia and Hungary in the same sphere, and with Poland and with Rumania on chemicals; at the same time Czechoslovakia drew up agreements with Hungary and with Bulgaria on consumers' goods.

The reappraisals of 1954

It was doubtless difficult at that stage to take further either co-ordination among themselves or policies towards the rest of the world: between July 1954 and December 1955 there was no Session. Perhaps it would even have been unrealistic to convene a Session while fundamental changes were being elaborated. In the sphere of economic relations between members, the striking reform was the dismantling of the network of Soviet-owned companies during 1954: in March the SAG were made over to the GDR government (save for one, converted to a 'mixed company'); a Soviet-Rumanian treaty liquidated all but two of the 'mixed companies' in September; similar terms were accorded Bulgaria, excepting only one company, in October, and Hungary in November 1954.[50]

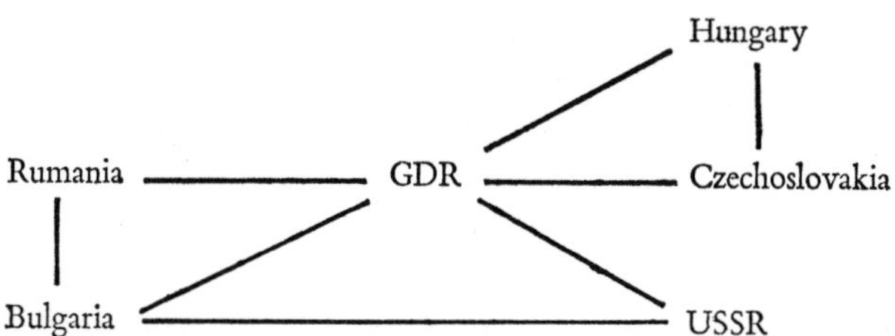

A modest break was made with strict bilateralism in a return to the trilateral dealings of 1949, in the new instance centred upon the GDR (instead of, as before, the USSR). As the diagram of agreed links shows, it was the only country which effectively had multilateral

[50] For the details see Spulber, pp. 202–6, and Montias, *Slav. R.*, Sept. 1966, pp. 427–9. Soviet concessions toward Mongolia—admitted to Comecon in 1962—lagged behind that towards eastern Europe. The Sovmongolmetall mixed company was not abolished until 1957—the Soviet share to be repaid without interest over 1962–92; see S. Sergeev, *Ekonomicheskoe sotrudnichestvo i vzaimopomoshch sotsialisticheskikh stran* (Moscow, 1964), p. 178.

dealings with the rest of Comecon (save Poland, which did not enter the scheme).[51]

The substantial easing of western strategic controls on exports to Comecon, already described, presented members with a real choice between barter among themselves and sales and purchases on a multilateral basis—at least within the framework of EPU convertibility and trade agreements with western governments. The annual trade confrontations arranged by the ECE brought together eastern and western European partners even where diplomatic relations did not exist. With the signature of the Austrian State Treaty in May 1955 and the reduction of the armed forces in all but one Comecon member (the GDR) which followed, the political environment for East–West trade was further improved. The Soviet state visit to Belgrade in May 1955 revoked the Soviet restrictions on trade with Yugoslavia.

These must have been the factors inducing, in the hiatus between Comecon's Fifth and Sixth Sessions, a reappraisal of the measure of the efficiency of foreign trade. The first issue—October 1954—of a new journal of the Hungarian Academy of Sciences carried a paper by T. Liska and A. Marias on 'Optimum Returns and the International Division of Labour'.[52] The authors observed that although it was government policy to

> turn to account the advantages arising from an international division of labour . . . we have not yet succeeded in switching over. . . . The theory of autarky still survives in our Party teaching, our periodicals, our planning methods and in the minds of certain of our economic leaders. . . . While the production plan, it is true, is supposed to take into account the international division of labour, no calculations have been made for this purpose.

Since these authors were concerned 'exclusively with formulae reflecting value relationships', they were inevitably despairing of the usefulness of the existing domestic-price system. The GDR, Poland, Rumania, and the USSR did in fact introduce a measure of wholesale-price reform in 1953–4, and, to the extent that a closer concordance was effected with costs, one obstacle to international comparison was partly lowered.

[51] From the report in *Auss.*, 7 Sept. 1954, it seems clear that the initiative came from the GDR. In the light of Pryor's account of these deals (pp. 194–5), one may surmise that Poland was holding out for a fully multilateral arrangement.

[52] *Koz. Sz.*, no. 1, 1954, pp. 75–94: the significance of the paper was such that an abridged trans. was published by the ECE in the *Econ. Survey Eur. 1954*.

A significant factor inhibiting a renewal of negotiations on long-term trade planning was the end of the 'New Course' and the return to priority of heavy industrial development, albeit with a higher ranking for farm investment and incentives than under Stalin. In 1955, the year of the creation of the Warsaw Treaty Organization,[53] it is not surprising that defence requirements were cited as another factor underlying the new policy, as in an article in *Pravda* by its editor, Shepilov.

> Some propose to supplant the Party line of accelerated development of heavy industry, as the only solid basis for the flourishing of all branches of the socialist economy and as a mighty source of growth in the people's prosperity and the country's military invulnerability, with another line of economic development, . . . that we should give the privilege of accelerated development of heavy industry, engineering, power, chemicals, electronics, jet technology, automation, etc. to the imperialist world.[54]

There was doubtless significance in the resignation of the Minister of Trade, announced the day after the publication of this article; it took place two weeks before Malenkov resigned as Chairman of the Council of Ministers, as—so far as the public were concerned—the culmination of a debate in which *Pravda* had followed its editor's line and *Izvestia* had supported Malenkov's policy. Mikoyan, as minister in charge of both foreign and domestic commerce, had frequently gone on record as supporting the expansion of consumer-goods output.

A similar resumption of the priority of heavy industry was declared by the other eastern European governments.

> It would be incorrect to think that the creation of the material basis for socialism is proceeding without difficulties. Reorganizing the entire technical base of a national economy requires large capital investments, new trained personnel, and great experience. The difficulties undergone by the economies of the people's democracies were manifested first of all by a number of economic disproportions. The decisions of the administrative bodies of the Communist and Workers' Parties of the people's democracies point out the fact that the rate of growth of agriculture is insufficient to meet the working people's growing demands. The development of the raw-materials and energy base is lagging behind the needs of industry. In certain of the people's democracies the regrouping of investment effected

[53] For a parallel between the creation of Comecon and of the Warsaw Treaty Organization see ch. VI (pp. 122–3).
[54] *Pr.*, 24 Jan. 1955.

to liquidate such disproportions was interpreted by some as a renunciation of the preponderant development of heavy industry. The Party press of these countries writes that these views, basically incorrect and injurious to the cause of socialism, are being severely criticized.[55]

Collaboration outside trade

Plan co-ordination through Comecon was halted while the broad policies for the new programmes were being reshaped, but co-operation outside the formal structure accelerated. The exchange of technical documentation and expertise, recommended by the Second Session (in 1949), seems to have been taken up on a particularly broad scale. In the first half of 1955 alone technical-collaboration agreements and exchanges were announced, linking not only each member with the USSR but every member with the others.[56] Between 1955 and 1956 the requests of the GDR for technical documentation which were filled by other Comecon members rose from 470 to 600 and the requests of other members filled by the GDR rose from 480 to 850.[57] Impetus was given to this sort of exchange by a conference convened by the Central Committee of the Soviet Communist Party, on technical progress, and attended by delegates of all Comecon countries (save Albania) and of China and North Korea. National delegations at Comecon headquarters played a significant part in helping to ensure that requests for assistance reached the right technical department in their country.

A further element in technological co-operation was a resolution of the 1955 Session of the ECE recommending that its technical committees should 'devote more attention to the exchange, on a reciprocal basis, of production experience and scientific-technical and statistical information'. All Comecon members had by then resumed participation in the ECE committees. Albanian attendance was, however, rare, for the non-political reason that the few multilingual officials could not easily be spared for international conferences: when Albania was admitted to the United Nations late in 1955 the permanent mission to ECE was closed, as the delegate moved to New York and could not be replaced. At that time also GDR participation—on an equal basis with ECE members in technical committees—was regular, but

[55] I. Dudinsky, ibid. 21 Mar. 1955.
[56] The 1955 network was exhibited by the ECE in *Econ. B. Eur.*, vii/2, p. 31.
[57] Pryor, p. 207.

it was later suspended as a protest against the status accorded the German Federal Republic. One of the immediate outcomes of technical co-operation within ECE was a study tour in Poland by its Housing Committee—the first of many in eastern and western Europe by the various committees—in May 1955.

Two other major steps were taken in specialized collaboration, which were to lead to the creation of new agencies (unconnected with Comecon) the next year. In July 1955 a conference in Berlin discussed the co-ordination of railway traffic and was attended by all eastern European countries and China, Mongolia, North Korea, and North Vietnam. This led, in June 1956, to the Sofia meeting of Ministers of Rail Transport of these states, to establish the Organization for Railway Co-operation. In the field of nuclear research, the USSR early in 1955 signed agreements with Bulgaria, Czechoslovakia, the GDR, Hungary, Poland, and Rumania to furnish each with an experimental reactor. In March 1956 a conference of these countries, together with Albania, China, North Korea, and Mongolia, set up the United Institute for Nuclear Research at Dubna (USSR). Comecon's restriction to European nations was probably responsible for the separate identity of these conferences and agencies.

Preparation for new plans

When the Sixth Session convened in Budapest in December 1955, it resumed the constitutional rotation which was completed in 1958. Albania started a second round in 1959 but, after reaching Rumania, the rota was again interrupted. Moscow did not take its alphabetical turn in 1958 but—as in 1950–4—seems to be chosen when the sessions are in some manner exceptional, viz. in mid-1962,[58] when the Executive Committee was created.

The Soviet delegation to the Session must have had with it the final draft of the Soviet Sixth Five-Year Plan (which was made public the next month). To set their targets for 1960 (and preliminary views were also exchanged at the Session on prospects for 1965 and 1970), the other members of Comecon had to know Soviet export availabilities of raw materials. A GDR commentator was to say of this period:

[58] Doubtless termed an 'Extraordinary Session' because of the location: under the Charter (then unamended) it was otherwise a regular biannual meeting.

> In spite of intense foreign trade and, on the whole, steadily expanding markets, there are important parts of our industrial capacities less than fully utilized, while expansion rates have been too low during recent years. The main reason for this is the lack of basic and raw materials, as is well known, not only in our country but in the whole socialist camp.[59]

Of Comecon members other than the USSR, only Bulgaria had a long-term plan in operation—the revised Five-Year Plan 1953–7—but it too, as already observed, was intending to use 1960 as a horizon (by means of a transitional three-year programme for which no targets had then—or were, in the event, ever to be—published). Rumania was the only country to have put out 1960 targets, quoting them as ranges of output. Czechoslovak and Polish sources had given goals for the expansion of farm output (both remarkably modest in comparison with earlier targets, but maintained in the final version). Apart from the Rumanian Five-Year Plan, which was published—one might assume deliberately—at the same time as the Soviet one, the European plans appeared four to eight months after the consultations at the Comecon Session. The Five-Year Plan for the GDR was published in April 1956, for Czechoslovakia and Albania (which made a point of stating that it was 'in full harmony with other socialist countries') in June, for Hungary in July, and for Poland in August.

The consultations on long-term specialization by type of product were rather successful, to judge by the number of products covered by agreements reached either then or at the Seventh Session five months later, viz. 27 types of metal products, 90 types of farm machinery, 23 chemical products, and 16 groups of farm produce.[60] Product specialization proved less susceptible to agreement, although by the May 1956 Session discussions had touched on virtually the whole field of production. A Soviet record states: 'At the Seventh Session questions were reviewed of the co-ordination of the development of ferrous and non-ferrous metallurgy, engineering, the coal, chemicals, and light industries, and the agriculture of these countries for 1956–60'.[61] Just over a year later—apparently referring to this period—Khrushchev remarked to a party of Hungarian journalists:

> We said long ago that a better co-operation should be established between our countries. It is impossible to develop everything everywhere simultaneously. Unfortunately we have often spoken in vain. Hungarians, Poles,

[59] *Auss.*, 5 Dec. 1957. [60] *Tars. Sz.*, no. 11, 1958, p. 84. [61] Solodovnikov, p. 306.

Rumanians, and the others have tried to build up everything by themselves. Perhaps it is only little Albania which has not attempted this. . . . In the Soviet Union this naturally is not the same problem as elsewhere, since Soviet industry produces for a vast demand. The same applies to China with its immense population. But for small countries this creates very great problems, for which solutions cannot be found within national boundaries.

As regards tractor or motor vehicle production, for example, the situation today is that tractors and motor vehicles are produced not only in the Soviet Union but by Poland, Czechoslovakia, Hungary, and Rumania. Thus production is not always profitable. The sooner and the better we develop the division of labour between our countries, the stronger will our economies be.[62]

The Soviet position at the 1955–6 Sessions on co-ordination to 1960 was that inter-product specialization should be effected between members other than the USSR. The Soviet Union would commit its exports under planned trade, but reserved to itself the production of a full profile of outputs. The attitude that Comecon was something essentially for the other parties was tacitly reflected in the press. During 1954 and 1955 the Soviet press restricted mention of Comecon to the bare communiqués of Sessions. Even when the *Large Soviet Encyclopedia* (published in its second edition from 1949 to 1958) reached the entry for CMEA in March 1956 (vol. xxxix), it accorded it a mere third of a column, and simply paraphrased the founding communiqué,[63] an entry shorter than those for Soviet treaties with individual countries in the same volume. It was not until May 1956 that the USSR showed its readiness for real commitment in Comecon.

[62] *Nep.*, 21 July 1957.

[63] Still briefer paraphrases were included in other articles in volumes published in 1951 and 1954, but the absence of a 'q.v.' from the former implies that the editors were not then planning even a separate entry for Comecon.

CHART 1: *The Long-term Plans of Comecon States*

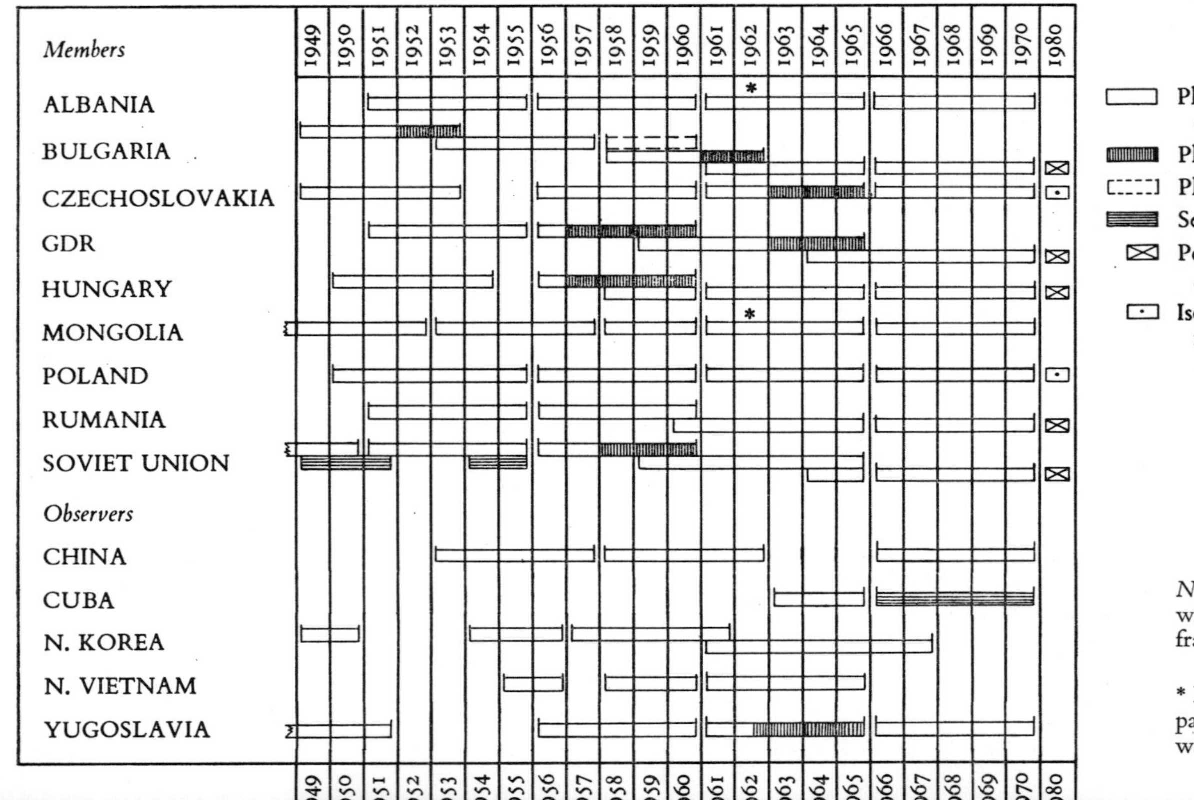

Note: Revisions to targets within the formal plan framework are not recorded.

* In 1962 Albania ceased to participate in, and Mongolia was admitted to, Comecon.

CHART 2

Network of Long-term Trade Agreements concluded between Comecon Members in 1950–1

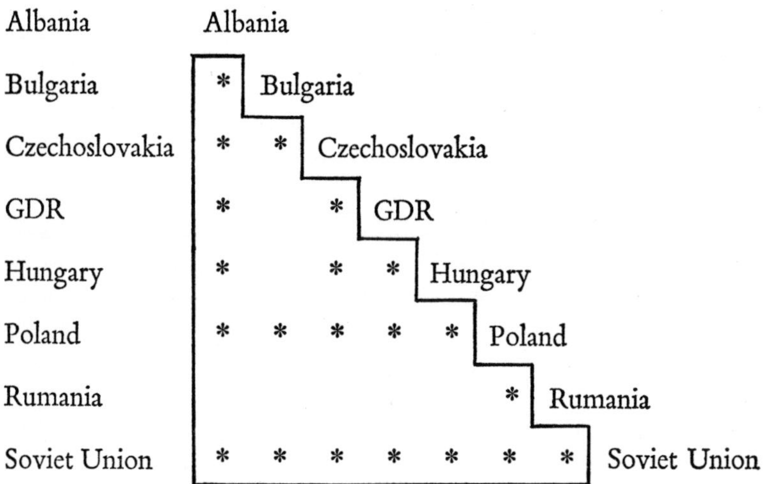

	Albania	Bulgaria	Czechoslovakia	GDR	Hungary	Poland	Rumania	Soviet Union
Albania								
Bulgaria	*							
Czechoslovakia	*	*						
GDR	*		*					
Hungary	*		*	*				
Poland	*	*	*	*	*			
Rumania						*		
Soviet Union	*	*	*	*	*	*	*	

CHART 3
Membership of Comecon and Related Agencies

Country	*Danube Commission**	*Comecon*	*Warsaw Treaty Org.*	*Org. for Railway Co-operation*	*United Inst. Nuclear Research*	*Org. for Co-op. Soc. Countries Telecom. & Posts*	*Mixed Comm. for Danube Fisheries*
Founded:	1948	1949	1955	1956	1956	1957	1958
Europe							
Albania	—	†(1949)	†	†	†	†	—
Bulgaria	†	†	†	†	†	†	†
Czechoslovakia	†	†	†	†	†	†	—
GDR	—	†(1950)	†	†	†	†	—
Hungary	†	†	†	†	†	†	—
Poland	—	†	†	†	†	†	—
Rumania	†	†	†	†	†	†	†
Soviet Union	†	†	†	†	†	†	†
Yugoslavia	†	‡(1956, 1965)	—	—	—	—	†
Asia							
China	—	‡(1956)	—	†	§(1966)	†	—
Mongolia	—	‡(1958) †(1962)	—	†	†	†	—
N. Korea	—	‡(1957)	—	†	†	†	—
N. Vietnam	—	‡(1958)	—	†	†(1956)	†	—
America							
Cuba	—	‡(1963)	‡(1965)	—	‡(1965)	†(1965)	—

* Austria admitted 1955 as observer, 1959 as full member. Federal Republic of Germany admitted 1959 as observer, 1965 as full member.
† Founder member, unless date (of admission) quoted.
‡ Observer status (with date of first attendance).
§ Founder member (with date of withdrawal).

V
INSTITUTIONAL REINFORCEMENT, 1956–60

Consolidation without China

FROM mid-1956 to mid-1962 the history of Comecon is one of gradual strengthening. The Seventh Session—an eight-day meeting in Berlin and the longest to date—was a turning-point: twelve standing commissions were set up and observer status was recognized. In 1957 the first multilateral treaty embracing all Comecon members—on the clearing of payments balances—was signed, but in the event scarcely used. Further commissions were set up, and provision for more regular multilateral action (the joint construction of a major pipeline and of an international electricity grid) was made in 1958. In 1959 the organization obtained a formal Charter; and in 1962 an Executive Committee, composed of vice-premiers of member-countries, sought to endow it with decision-making power at the highest level. But at that point the pressure to pursue this consolidation overreached itself, and in the face of the Rumanian obduracy more reliance had to be placed on forms of bilateral co-operation evolved during 1956–60.

In retrospect, the strengthening of Comecon can be seen as isolating China. The Session of May 1956 admitted China and Yugoslavia only as observers, and thereby maintained the restriction of membership to the industrially-advanced group of the 'socialist world market'. The share of Comecon at that time in the production of all socialist states was 94 per cent in electric power, 99 per cent in crude oil, 95 per cent in steel, 91 per cent in pig iron, and 88 per cent in cement.[1] It has been suggested by Schlesinger that

> such a unit, mainly composed of industrialized countries, may ally, but not identify, itself with underdeveloped countries making their first steps in industrialization. . . . The very state that planning is in at present, in particular in the Far Eastern Socialist countries, excludes world-wide integration of the grade of precision aimed at by Khrushchev for Comecon. In the economic field, too, there would be a broader, and one or more narrower,

[1] V. Zolotarev, *Vneshnyaya torgovlya sotsialisticheskikh stran* (Moscow, 1964), p. 164.

circles; of course the Chinese might establish a similar grouping in the Far East, once their own planning has reached the state of precision and reliability that is required for its international coordination.[2]

The Asian plans at that time coincided neither with their neighbours' nor with the common period that Comecon was introducing. The Chinese First Five-Year Plan (1953–7) had the same term as the Mongolian Second Five-Year Plan. North Korea had a Three-Year Plan in operation, but to end in 1956, with a First Five-Year Plan to start in 1957. North Vietnam was still at the annual planning stage (although its programme for 1955–6 is described in some sources as a Two-Year Plan) and did not start on a lengthier horizon until 1958 (see Chart 1, p. 66).

There was a certain irony in the choice of Berlin as the venue—by the chance of alphabetic order—for the half-hearted attempt to bring China into Comecon. Like the Chinese communist government, the government of the GDR had not been in existence when Comecon was created, but had been set up, in October 1949, a mere eleven days after the Chinese People's Republic. Yet the GDR had been admitted to full membership in less than a year, while China was let in after a lapse of nearly seven years to the same observer status accorded to Yugoslavia. That country still had a 'revisionist' communist party, had been originally rejected for membership, and was being accepted less than a year after the 1955 Belgrade declaration which ended the 1948 split.

The contrast was still harsher in terms of Soviet economic aid. Yugoslavia was that year offered a credit of $160 m. to develop its metals industry (although because political relations deteriorated, the USSR did not ratify payment until ten years later—in September 1966). China, on the other hand, had been granted Soviet loans of only $300 m. in 1950 and $130 m. in 1954; in each case the bargaining had been hard and protracted (the first required the personal intervention of Mao Tse-tung with Stalin and the second had not been gained until Stalin died); Mao's reported request for a third loan, when he visited Moscow in 1957, was rejected.[3] Not only were Chinese development needs vastly greater than the Yugoslav, but the USSR had taken Manchurian plant in 1945 to a value estimated

[2] R. Schlesinger, 'The Sino-Soviet Dispute', *Science & Society*, Summer 1963, p. 281.
[3] Eckstein, pp. 143–4.

at as much as $2 billion. As Eckstein observes, 'the Soviets were in effect returning new equipment for the old they had taken away earlier, but the Chinese had to pay for it out of credits and current exports'.[4]

Some slight precedence was recognized for China, for it attended, after the 1956 Session, a number of the standing commissions, whereas Yugoslavia was invited only to the annual Session (until its observer status lapsed at the June 1958 Session) and to the one subcommittee (on the Danube) in which its co-operation was essential, and which in any case overlapped with a body of which it was a full member (the Danube Commission). As Chart 3 shows, Yugoslavia has not been invited into the socialist-group agencies of which China is a full member.

The other Asian members of the socialist group entered Comecon as observers gradually—North Korea in 1957 and Mongolia and North Vietnam in 1958. Only Mongolia eventually reached membership, and this after the alignments of the Sino-Soviet dispute had been made clear. Their immediate participation in the agencies other than Comecon (the Vietnamese delay in entering the United Institute for Nuclear Research was a matter of six months) lends some support to the suggestion that China intended to form its own economic union of the Asian states.

In the decade since 1956 the Chinese antipathy towards the USSR has deepened into enmity. With hindsight over those ten years, it may be asserted with some confidence that the offer of full membership to China—a proposal not apparently made until 1963 and then in conditions which ensured Chinese rejection—would not have made a real contribution to preserving the alliance. When the Session which was to allow only observer status convened in May 1956, the first Chinese démarche to the USSR was a month old: in April Mao Tse-tung had expressed his reserves to Mikoyan on Khrushchev's closed-session speech at the Twentieth Party Congress two months previously. He stated his view that Stalin's 'merits outweighed his faults' and that 'an all-round evaluation' was needed. On 23 October, when telling the Soviet Ambassador to Peking, 'Stalin deserves to be criticized, but we do not agree with the method of criticism', he added

[4] Ibid. p. 142; and see F. Mah, in C. Remer, ed., *Three Essays on the International Economics of Communist China* (Ann Arbor, Mich., 1959), and C. Li, *Economic Development of Communist China* (Berkeley, Calif., 1959), esp. chs. 5 and 6.

that there were 'other matters at issue between China and the USSR'.[5]

If the 'other matters' included economic issues, May 1956 may well have been too late for an offer of economic co-operation. It is unlikely that at that, or any, time the Chinese leadership was defending Stalin as anything but a symbol of its own objectives: it was later to record that 'in handling relations with fraternal parties, he made some mistakes'.[6] It declared:

> We have always had a proper appreciation of the friendly Soviet aid which began under Stalin's leadership. . . But we must point out that, so far from being free, Soviet aid to China was rendered mainly in the form of trade and that it was certainly not a one-way affair. . . Even the war *matériel* supplied to China in the war to resist US aggression in Korea has not been given gratis.[7]

The aid which 'began' under Stalin was at its most generous after his death. As mentioned above, a second loan had been furnished in 1954, the naval bases at Port Arthur and the Sino-Soviet mixed companies had been liquidated with the respective stores and equipment handed over on credit, rail communications were developed, and numerous agreements were concluded on technical aid.[8]

Soviet credits were exhausted by the end of 1956, and China not only paid for all subsequent exchanges, but began repayment of the earlier debts. Eckstein concludes that

> The Chinese resisted measures towards economic integration because they perceived these as designed to maintain more or less of a status quo, to perpetuate the economic gap between themselves and the Russians. They were apparently reluctant to enter into long-term trade agreements with their leading economic partner because flexible quantities and mixes of imports could provide a cushion for poor harvests, planning errors and other unanticipated short-term changes.[9]

Soviet efforts to reach a long-term trade agreement were rebuffed.[10] Paradoxically the Soviet economy was not developed highly enough for integration with China. With a broader gamut of production, less strain on stocks, and a better-distributed burden of investment—all

[5] *Peking R.*, 13 Sept. 1963, pp. 8–9, citing an editorial in *Renmin Ribao*, 6 Sept. 1963.
[6] Ibid. 20 Sept. 1963, p. 10. [7] Ibid. 8 May 1963, pp. 13–14. [8] Eckstein, pp. 143–4.
[9] Ibid. p. 141.
[10] See O. Hoeffding, in K. London, ed., *Unity and Contradiction: Major Aspects of Sino-Soviet Relations* (New York, 1962), pp. 295–312.

problems particularly acute in 1956, as the resolutions of the CPSU Central Committee revealed in December—the USSR could have more readily accommodated the fluctuations of Chinese needs. With the lower costs to be associated with a higher degree of industrialization, the USSR could have offered China at least as good terms of trade as those prevailing with developed capitalist countries. 'It is necessary to add', the Chinese government complained, 'that the prices of many of the goods we imported from the Soviet Union were much higher than those on the world market.'[11] Although formally defending Stalin, the Chinese Communist Party can find more to blame in him than in his successors. The belief embodied in the slogan painted by the Red Guards on the Soviet Embassy in Peking in August 1966 that 'all the old and new hatred is graven on our hearts'[12] must be seen with its roots in 1949, but the aversion to participate in an international economic community must be measured by the millennium: as FitzGerald concludes, 'The Chinese view of the world has not fundamentally changed: it has been adjusted to take account of the modern world, but only so far as to permit China to occupy, still, the central place in the picture.'[13] Chinese desire for hegemony in one group would have reinforced unwillingness to submit to the then evident Soviet dominance in Comecon.[14]

The new shape for Comecon

If China had desired integration in the Socialist world market, a new agency would have been needed to erase the record of Soviet dominance in Comecon. For the European members, on the other hand, 'any attempt to create another international body would probably have met serious opposition . . . particularly from countries most strongly affected by past Soviet policies conducted in the name of proletarian internationalism'.[15] Comecon had not been used for Stalin's exploitation, and can be seen (as in Ch. II) as an attempt—probably unsure and certainly abortive—at a common market. For socialist states west of Russia, its framework was hence open for use.

The major organizational change made at the May 1956 Session

[11] *Peking R.*, 8 May 1964, p. 13. [12] *Komsomolskaya pravda*, 22 Sept. 1966.
[13] C. FitzGerald, *The Chinese View of their Place in the World* (London, 1964), p. 71.
[14] M. Dewar, 'Economic Cooperation in the Soviet Orbit', *Yb. Wld Aff. 1959*, p. 66. The same point was made by E. Klinkmüller and M. Ruban, *Der wirtschaftliche Zusammenarbeit zwischen den Ostblockstaaten* (Berlin, 1960), p. 254.
[15] Korbonski, *Int. Con.*, Sept. 1964, p. 11.

F

provided permanent bodies for technical consultation. Since 1954 the permanent delegations to Comecon had formed a standing body, the 'Delegates' Meeting', of which *ad hoc* working parties were formed from time to time. As the delegates and their staff were not Foreign Service officials, but experts from technical ministries, the consideration of specific problems could be competently dealt with at this level. It was these working parties of experts in Moscow which, during 1954–5, made the recommendations on bilateral specialization described above. Although the decisions of the Delegates' Meeting were not binding, a certain national commitment was thereby made, because decisions could only be taken at Delegates' Meetings if the chief delegates were present in person. 'This strict juridical formula was called into being by the need to ensure the functioning of the Delegates' Meeting not only as formal representation, but with the necessary competence and continuity.'[16]

During 1955 these *ad hoc* committees of the Delegates' Meeting proliferated, some even to the extent of forming subcommittees. The main fields covered were engineering, timber, coal, electric power, agriculture, and foreign trade. They met during the 1955 and 1956 Sessions, often far into the night, and it is clear that they had become genuine *fora* of negotiation. The bargaining at the 1956 Session, both in the committees and in the plenary meetings, was such that the delegations of the GDR and of Hungary proposed that the proceedings be published. They complained that if, as in the past, all that the outside world was to know of Comecon was a brief and vague communiqué, public opinion in their countries would hold that the governments were 'selling out' to the Soviet Union and that the latter was unilaterally imposing its economic demands upon the others. Such speculation, the proposal is said to have concluded, would be effectively checked by publication of the debates, showing the results as a matter of fair give and take. Neither this suggestion, nor that of the Yugoslav observer which would also have abated secrecy, was adopted, but they were referred back for further study. The Yugoslavs had proposed that the United Nations Secretariat be invited to all those Comecon commissions which overlapped with ECE tech-

[16] Morozov, *Sov. gos. pravo*, no. 10, 1961, p. 154. Uschakow (p. 51) remarks that, until a deputy could be made a plenipotentiary under the 1960 Charter, unavoidable absence from Moscow must have 'seriously damaged its functional efficiency'.

nical committees.[17] This was not mainly to make a more open organization, for ECE technical committees meet in private, and only their annual reports must be published. Rather, Yugoslavia was chiefly seeking to strengthen its position in international sectoral collaboration, for among the many European economic bodies it was a full member only of ECE. It had gained observer status with OEEC, which had similar technical committees to Comecon and ECE, in February 1955, but was then using the ECE as its main European negotiating instrument. Its treaty with Austria on the operation of power stations on the Drava river had been agreed under the auspices of the ECE Electric Power Committee and it was promoting Yougelexport under the same aegis with Austria, the Federal Republic of Germany, and Italy. The Executive Secretary of ECE had in fact proposed reciprocal Secretariat representation at technical committees to the Secretary of Comecon two months earlier, and even the year before representatives of each of the two Secretariats had met in Geneva and in Moscow.

The twelve standing commissions created by Comecon in 1956 were each allocated to a member country, although the staff was to be carried on the general Comecon budget.[18] The Agricultural Commission was set up in Sofia, Chemicals in Berlin, Coal in Warsaw, Electric Power, Ferrous Metals, and Foreign Trade in Moscow, Engineering in Prague, Non-Ferrous Metals in Budapest, and Oil and Gas in Bucharest. The choice allowed every capital—save only Tirana—at least one commission and reflected a major industry of the country concerned. A senior official, usually the Minister, of the national department administering the sector was appointed chairman (see App. VII). Three other commissions were created (Timber and Cellulose, Forestry, and Geology) but were abolished in 1958, when a further four were added (Construction, Economic Questions, Transport, and Light and Food Industries). All met usually twice a year and in the city where their secretariat was located. Their subcommittees (termed 'sections') and working parties (some *ad hoc*, others permanent) proliferated and with other seminars and conferences under the same auspices contrasted sharply with the limited opportunities for contact

[17] Viz. the ECE Committees on the Development of Trade, on Timber, on Coal, and on Agricultural Problems.

[18] See Shurshalov, p. 291.

between experts and professionals afforded before 1956. Klinkmüller and Ruban[19] list fifty-five eastern European conferences, mostly under Comecon auspices, taking place in 1958 alone.

The Iron Gates project

The immediate consequence—and no doubt the occasion—of Yugoslavia's participation was the creation of a 'standing commission for the exchange of electric power among members of the CMEA and for the use of the hydro-resources of the Danube'[20] and an agreement to regularize its flow at the Iron Gates. Hungary and Yugoslavia would benefit from soil melioration, Rumania was to gain irrigation water, and all members within grid access would have cheap hydro-electric power. The scheme could have been arranged at any time through the Danube Commission, which had undertaken the existing regularization and of which the three states immediately concerned were members. It was argued that the Commission should remain confined to navigational affairs and that Comecon would be the best agency to promote the supplementary investment. A discussion of finance from members other than the three interested states was deferred until technical details were ready. These technical meetings ran for a year, and at least one of them (in Moscow, September 1957) had observers not only from Yugoslavia but also from China.

The Chinese interest is presumably explicable by the start, in 1956, of a joint Sino-Soviet survey of the hydro-electric resources of the Amur river. The Danube subcommittee, so described, met in Bucharest in April 1958 with observers from Yugoslavia and the Danube Commission (which thus gained belated entry). This was apparently the last meeting, for the talks fell victim to a deterioration in Soviet-Yugoslav relations: by June 1958 Yugoslav observer status in Comecon had lapsed, and the *ad hoc* committee on the Danube had ceased to function, but a mixed Romano-Yugoslav technical commission seems to have continued to meet whenever the political relations between their countries were favourable. This bilateral commission drew up a technical-economic memorandum on the project, which

[19] pp. 156–8. 39 may be identified as of Comecon bodies, 4 of the Railway Organization, 1 of the Warsaw Treaty Organization, 1 of the Postal Organization, and 1 of the Danube Commission (see App. IX). They list 59 conferences in all but four appear to be continuations of others on the list.

[20] *Ezhegodnik BSE, 1958* (Moscow, 1958), p. 374.

was signed by the two authorities in 1960; Rumania established a similar technical agreement with Bulgaria, as did Czechoslovakia and Hungary, for other Danubian power stations in 1959. The Comecon Session of May 1959 also studied a possible grid link between Rumania and Bulgaria which the Danube station would feed. Yugoslavia was also a party to the Sofia agreement of 1959 establishing direct rail connexions for Danube shipping.

Multilateral clearing

The 1956 meeting recommended that some form of multilateral clearing arrangements be set up for members; details were worked out during the year—doubtless with interruptions under the strain of political upheavals, in October in Poland, in November in Hungary, and early 1957 in the USSR. A draft agreement was put before the Eighth Session (convened in Warsaw in June 1957) and signed in the course of the meeting. It was of very limited operation and involved neither subscriptions (as did its successor of 1963) nor any special institution beyond an earmarked account at the State Bank of the USSR, and corresponding balances in members' national banks. Its provisions, more fully described on pp. 169–70, were the first automatic—that is supranational—commitments made by Comecon members *in corpore*: a swing-credit was required to be granted by the clearing bank in Moscow to any member, albeit within only one year and very small limits. The principle of sovereignty, with this miniscule breach, was protected by the requirement that the settlement of clearing disequilibria was to be effected by bilateral negotiation.

The decisions of the 1956 and 1957 Sessions other than on these organizational novelties embraced the recognition of the need for planning beyond five years, before, in fact, it had become official policy in the USSR, and an extension of specialization arrangements.

The disruption of plans in 1956

These latter, however, were overshadowed, at the 1957 meeting, by measures to support the 'rescue operation' in the form of supplies of food, clothing, and raw materials and of convertible currency to Hungary. From a November 1956 trough of 21 per cent of the September level, output of Hungarian large-scale industry had by March 1957 reached 80 per cent of that level. The chairman of the

Hungarian Price Board observed: 'By consuming government stocks, by contracting foreign credits and by retaining exports, the appearance can temporarily be created of an economic "miracle", but no economic consolidation can be established on such a basis.'[21]

All Comecon members save Albania and Rumania granted credits to Hungary in the first quarter of 1957, although the initiative was made through diplomatic and Party channels, not, it would seem, as an effort of Comecon, although its technical bodies continued to meet unaffected by political events. In January Bulgaria offered \$1¾ m., the GDR \$25 m., and China \$50 m. (of which half in convertible currency); in February Poland gave \$10 m. and in March Czechoslovakia provided \$19 m. and the USSR \$190 m. (of which \$50 m. in free exchange); in addition, the USSR (which since October 1956 had made two other convertible-currency loans to Hungary aggregating \$10 m.), cancelled the remainder of the Hungarian debt incurred in buying back the mixed companies, and moratoria on debt service were granted by the USSR and Czechoslovakia.

The Comecon Session of June 1957 thus faced distortion of such 1956–60 production plans as it had been able to co-ordinate at its 1955 and 1956 meetings, with more imports by, and less exports from, Hungary and—in the case of the Soviet Union (and China), which gave convertible currency—the need for higher exports (or gold sales) to western countries. The main outcome was, reasonably enough, a short-term revised trade plan, covering the remainder of the period to 1960.

With Gomulka's accession, Poland had had its foreign obligations reduced, by the Soviet agreement to cancel debts of \$525 m. in consideration of the Polish deliveries of 65 m. tons of coal from Silesia during 1946–53 at a price covering only the cost of transport (a Soviet gain, at world coal prices of around \$14 per ton, of some \$900 m.).[22] This coincided with a revision of the plan to 1960, which decelerated the rate of growth but raised the share of investment so as to open bottlenecks and to absorb the inflow of labour from agriculture and from demographic expansion. The Polish balance-of-payments imbalance which this policy would induce was eased by agreements with two Comecon members, viz. GDR and Czechoslovak investments of \$25 m. and \$63 m. respectively in Polish coal-mining and a further

[21] *Nep.*, 17 Mar. 1957.

[22] A. Zauberman, *Industrial Progress in Poland, Czechoslovakia, and East Germany, 1937–62* (London, 1964), p. 292 n. 27.

$25 m. from the latter for sulphur extraction: all three loans were to be repaid in kind.

The first joint-investment project

The arrangement between the GDR and Poland was the first joint-investment project within Comecon, whereby foreign capital is directed towards a specific scheme, and repayment and interest made from the eventual output. Previous intra-Comecon credit had been extended on a government-to-government basis without attachment of the loan to a project. In 1959 Poland and Hungary developed the concept of joint investment into that of the joint enterprise, whose plant was held in common: for five years the Haldex corporation—to process coal slack—was the only example of its kind (see p. 127).

The Eighth Session 'noted with approval the agreement between Poland and the GDR on the building of new mines in Poland and the fact that other countries had expressed their readiness to undertake similar negotiations with Poland', but only Czechoslovakia made such offers. Immediately after the Session it granted its credit to exploit sulphur deposits in the Tarnobrzeg area (repayment in products started in 1961, as agreed). Both it and the USSR, however, declined participation in Polish coal-mining at the Session. The latter is reported to have done so on the grounds that it was already developing the Volyn coalfields (the prewar Polish Volhynia), which would supply the regions within the Polish delivery radius, and that in any case it was committed to a preferential development of oil. Czechoslovakia was concerned that Polish production costs were above its own (outside evidence on the cost relationship is conflicting),[23] but it accepted the scheme in October 1957, mainly for mines around Turoszow, near the Czech frontier. The GDR joint investment was also in a frontier area, the Bogatynia 'peninsula' of the Polish western territories, and its readiness to participate might conceivably be associated with an expectation that it would revert to Germany if a Peace Treaty tidied up that part of the Oder–Neisse Line.

The Czechoslovak-Polish agreement of 1957 also made another innovation. Echoing the provisions of their treaty of 1947, it authorized contacts between the corresponding technical and administrative agencies of the two countries—the first such 'decentralized' arrange-

[23] See ibid. pp. 163–9.

ment among Comecon members—and created the precursor of the many Intergovernmental Commissions on Economic, Scientific, and Technical Collaboration (see Chart 4, p. 120). Both types of collaboration were to be the main means of bypassing the crisis of 1963.

With the important exception of the USSR, the joint-investment project and the mixed planning commissions were soon taken up by the other members. Rumania was the leading beneficiary: it received capital from the GDR and Hungary for chemical projects, while an immense paper-making mill at Braila on the Danube Delta, the reeds of which were the raw material, was financed by Czechoslovakia, the GDR, and Poland. Later Czechoslovakia participated in sinking copper-mines in Bulgaria and Poland, and equipping a fertilizer plant at Pulawy in Poland. As in the prototype, each foreign share was eventually to be bought out by repayments in products at the prices ruling in intra-Comecon trade at the time of delivery. The bilateral planning commissions also found favour: as Chart 4 shows, more were set up in 1958 than in any subsequent year.

The USSR was to take part in neither of these forms of collaboration until 1963. The balances of availability and requirements of basic materials drawn up in this period covered only the 'European people's democracies', with the USSR statement of its trade balance added.[24] In the many inter-product specialization agreements of the period, the USSR refused to accept any suspension of its own production-lines and the consequent reliance for supplies on another member. This position seems to have been maintained until 1962, when Khrushchev declared: 'International specialization is advantageous not only to small countries, but also to such large states as the Soviet Union. . . . The Soviet Union is even prepared to reduce its output of some kinds of manufactures if it proves more expedient to produce them in other CMEA countries'.[25] Until that year, the Soviet attitude to the practical activity of Comecon was benevolent detachment: it regarded such matters as the affair of other members.

Multilateral projects

A form of investment which did not involve international capital flows and in which the USSR fully joined was nevertheless also

[24] Cf. notably the communiqué of the Eleventh Session.
[25] N. Khrushchev, *Komm.*, no. 12, 1962.

evolving. This was the construction of projects under common technical control, but with the national segments being financed by the country concerned. The erection of a Comecon electricity grid was first mooted at the Fifth Session (1954), developed at the Seventh (1956), and approved at the Eleventh (1959). Its major connexion was to be through the GDR, Poland, Czechoslovakia, and Hungary; others were to link Rumania and Czechoslovakia, and Hungary and Poland with the Soviet grid—respectively the Western Ukraine and former East Prussia (Kaliningrad *oblast*). When the main stage came into operation in mid-1962, a central control office was set up in Prague; the connexion with the Soviet grid was made in 1963 and Bulgaria was joined to it via Rumania in 1967 when a transmission line was set up spanning the Danube.[26]

At the Tenth Session (1958) another transmission project was agreed —named the 'Friendship Pipeline'—to transport crude oil from the Soviet oilfields in the Urals to Poland and the GDR (where refineries were to be built at Plotsk and Schwedt-on-Oder respectively). The scheme was accomplished and the first oil reached Schwedt in 1964. A branch pipeline, completed in 1963, was to supply Hungary and Czechoslovakia with a major new refinery at Bratislava. The project involved no long-term international finance—each country was responsible for its own section—but, by exporting crude instead of refined products, the USSR made a real contribution to the importers' balances of payments. In the case of the GDR the capacity at Schwedt appears to allow for substantial export, and the USSR forgoes the earnings on refined products it might have earned by domestic processing. At the previous Session Bulgaria had persuaded the rest to afford it preferential prices for its primary exports. This lends some credence to the rumour that Rumania opposed the oil pipeline project on the grounds that it would restrict its own export prospects—either in price, for Urals oil was cheaper, or in quantity. Though the causal connexion cannot be affirmed, it did shift its long-term oil policy shortly after the Session, towards home use of crude oil in petrochemicals. Nevertheless Rumanian deliveries of oil pipe for the project furnished substantial earnings in the short run.

[26] *Rab. delo*, 25 Jan. 1967. The link had been envisaged in the 1962 plans: see *Information on Economic Cooperation* (Comecon), p. 8.

Agencies parallel to Comecon

The same distinction between technical collaboration—the Soviet provision of expertise, for example, seems to have been unstinted—and the commitment of substantial resources did not apply to the other agencies of the socialist group set up in the mid-1950s. Soviet engagement in the military alliance of 1955 was of course fundamental to its foreign policy; the other new bodies involved the work of only a few technicians. The counterpoise to NATO, the Warsaw Treaty Organization, was established in 1955, with the immediate purpose of associating the GDR in a military alliance, as a reply to the participation of the Federal Republic of Germany in Western European Union. The first economic conference of the Treaty Organization was reported in 1957, and it is rumoured that there is a more formal link between the Economic Commission of the Organization and a 'Defence Industry' Commission of Comecon: for evident reasons this sort of arrangement is not in the public domain. Whatever institutions there may be at the intergovernmental level to integrate defence production with aggregate planning, the two problems were to become intimately related during 1965–6 (see pp. 122–6). Of the three specialized agencies set up in 1956–7—for nuclear research, railways, and posts and telecommunications—the first two are congruent with organs of Comecon. The Dubna Institute is devoted to pure research in nuclear physics, and, as an intergovernmental undertaking, exactly parallels CERN in Geneva (indeed, the interchange between Dubna and Geneva is about the least political and most fruitful of any East–West relationship). The application of nuclear energy for peaceful purposes is run by a Comecon Commission, established in 1960 and which has much the same functions (though far from the same powers) as the western Euratom.

The Organization for International Railway Co-operation (ORC), decided upon at a conference in June 1956, though not formally founded until September 1957, was similarly followed by the establishment of a Comecon agency. An 'operational group' on transport had met frequently in the year before a Comecon Transport Commission was set up (June 1958), at the demand of Poland and Czechoslovakia, two of the countries which are members both of the ORC and of the long-standing International Union of Railways (UIC).[27] Ar-

[27] The members of Comecon not participating in either agency are Albania, Mongolia, and

rangements for close collaboration between the ORC and Comecon (chiefly through its Transport Commission) were made in 1961.[28] Since then Comecon has elaborated recommendations jointly with the ORC on railway electrification, road feeders to international rail connexions, etc.[29]

The Organization for the Co-operation of Socialist Countries in Telecommunication and Posts, founded in December 1957, does not overlap any Comecon work, and should be seen as a counterpart to the five other regional postal unions of the world within the Universal Postal Union. As Chart 3 has shown, it was to become the only agency of the socialist countries to embrace all qualified states as full members. A Mixed Commission for the regulation of Danube fisheries was established in January 1958.

In 1958 also were held the first meetings of *ad hoc* conferences which have developed a momentum of reconvocation without a formal secretariat—of central banks, of tourist offices, and of ministers of social affairs. The bankers' conference, which—at the outset at least—included the Asian socialist countries, is not primarily an operational organ.[30] Central bankers are an eminently 'clubbable' group, as much in eastern as in western Europe, at least as demonstrated by the success of the Bankers' International Summer School (held in Moscow for the first time in 1962). They have mainly conferred on domestic banking techniques, although the relaxation of banknote transactions may have arisen from their second meeting, which it closely followed. On 12 December a statement by the USSR State Bank announced an agreement with the central banks of all Comecon members and the four Asian countries that their nationals could import and export limited amounts in cash. Only Poland and Hungary had permitted even the carrying of their currency abroad. It was a welcome concession, which did away with an anxious (and often hungry) wait on arrival until travellers' cheques could be encashed; but was not—as reports of the time had it—a move towards convertibility.

---

the USSR. Both the former have built railways only since the war (the UIC was set up in 1922); the USSR was a member until the outbreak of war and has recently renewed its relationship.

[28] Faddeev, p. 51. The ORC, the Waggon Pool, and the Ship Charter Bureau (see p. 262) were, for example, all represented at the Transport Commission in January, 1967, as were Cuba, Korea, Vietnam, and Yugoslavia (*Sc.*, 18 Jan. 1967).

[29] See V. Savarin and Yu. Syurin, *Vnesh. torg.*, no. 5, 1963, pp. 17–24.

[30] See reports of the meetings, e.g. in *Fin. SSSR.*, no. 8, 1958; *Prob. econ.*, no. 12, 1959.

Consolidation in reply to the Common Market

On 24 March 1957 the Treaty of Rome established the EEC, and the European Atomic Community (Euratom) was set up. A week previously on the 16th, the Soviet Foreign Ministry had delivered to the missions of all European countries with which it had diplomatic relations, to the American Embassy and to the Executive Secretary of ECE (who happened to be in Moscow after a tour of Central Asia) a 'Declaration on the Plans for Creating Euratom and the "Common Market"'. Its political premises apart, it marked Soviet concern with the loss of markets which the common tariff of the eventual EEC might imply, despite most-favoured-nation clauses with individual member countries. The communiqué of the Eighth Session of Comecon (June 1957) echoed this anxiety, for the same fears were beginning to inspire the Polish government. Gomulka is reported to have personally proposed to Khrushchev that Comecon be developed as the answer to the Common Market. The reaction of the Czechoslovak and Hungarian governments at the time seems also to have been to face integration with integration. This, however, as the debates at the May 1956 Session had shown, could not begin from positions of sensed inequality, and the Polish and Hungarian crises of the autumn evoked the Soviet Declaration of 30 October 1956 'on the bases for the development and the further strengthening of friendship and co-operation between the Soviet Union and other Socialist states'. The political concessions to the east European states which followed included the settlement of claims concerning property in the Baltic states and other areas incorporated into the USSR between 1939 and 1945, the establishment of the rights (including that to repatriation) of their citizens on the territory of the USSR, the improvement of consular dispositions, the delineation of the competence of national judiciaries, the reduction of Soviet garrisons—save evidently in Hungary—and the regularization of the status under which the remaining forces were to stay.[31] These measures were a prelude to the convocation in November 1957 of a Conference of Representatives of Communist and Workers' Parties of Socialist Countries, coinciding with the celebration of the Fortieth Anniversary of the October Revolution. The Soviet delegation sought to establish a new

[31] A list of the various agreements and declarations of 1957 and 1958 is in *Ezhegodnik BSE, 1958* (pp. 34–45) and *1959* (pp. 38–51).

relationship not only with the eastern European countries, but with the dissentient Chinese, and the final declaration affirmed that

> the basis of the mutual relations of the countries of the world socialist system and of all communist and workers' parties is the putting into practice of the principles of Marxism-Leninism, of the principles of proletarian internationalism.

Intercourse within the socialist group had soon after the war been termed in the USSR 'a new type of international relations'.[32] The leading Soviet international lawyer, G. Tunkin, representing his country at the International Law Commission, wrote in 1959:

> Although the new type of international relations has been established for only a relatively short period of time, the communist and workers' parties . . . have elaborated durable and stable principles for such relationships. . . . The principles of proletarian internationalism include full parity of rights, the respect for territorial integrity, for state sovereignty and for non-interference in the domestic affairs of another state. . . . A principle of proletarian internationalism also penetrates the economic . . . relations between socialist states. . . . Economic co-operation between socialist countries is directed towards the elimination of existing inequalities in the level of economic development.[33]

To determine these economic applications a conference of party leaders of Comecon countries was convened in Moscow in May 1958—the first of a series of 'summit meetings' on Comecon affairs (see App. III). Its communiqué listed for the first time 'the aim of raising the level of industrialization of the countries with less-developed industry', which became Comecon's formal policy in its 1960 Charter. It is of course significant that, although the general conference of the Parties in November 1957 had included China and the three other socialist nations of Asia, the membership of the economic meeting was restricted to Comecon states, with the Chinese, Korean, Mongolian, and Vietnamese parties present as observers. China had already begun to come to Comecon in 1956 (see p. 69), and it had been joined by North Korea for the June 1957 meeting; the two others entered at the Bucharest Session of June 1958 which followed the Party leaders' conference.

[32] F. I. Kozhevnikov, *Sovetskoe gosudarstvo i mezhdunarodnoe pravo 1917–47* (Moscow, 1948).
[33] G. Tunkin, *Sov. gos. pravo*, no. 1, 1959, pp. 82 and 87.

Trade and specialization

The meeting of Party representatives in Moscow, and the Ninth Session in Bucharest, were faced by the need to revise the production and trade plans. In the year since the previous Session a new Soviet government had been installed and a Seven-Year Plan was in draft to supersede the Sixth Five-Year Plan. The Albanian, Bulgarian, and Rumanian plans nominally pursued their course (see Chart 1, p. 66), but in early 1958 each came under the influence of the Chinese 'Great Leap Forward'. The ideology of the immediate transition to communism and the belief in the practicability of an unprecedented mobilization of resources appealed to the three largely agrarian members of Comecon: the communes and 'backyard' steel of China became the talking-point of their press. Only Bulgaria explicitly elaborated a plan for the economic 'leap forward', but during the year—in February in Albania and in April in Rumania—a far-reaching intensification of the industrial drive was resolved upon.[34] In the Albanian case, the Second Five-Year Plan, which had stated its aim as development 'in full harmony with other socialist countries' and the elimination of the balance-of-trade deficit by 1960, was revised in favour of a much heavier investment programme and the expansion, well beyond the original targets, of producer goods. The Soviet cancellation of Albania's debts and the strike of a new oilfield contributed to this change of programme, but the theme of expansion and the launching of a collectivization drive were doubtless motivated by ideology. The Rumanian campaign to transform the loose working associations of peasants into full-scale collective farms was announced by Gheorghiu-Dej in a speech at Constantza on 3 April 1958, but the decisions on industry appear to have been formulated towards the end of the year.

The GDR, Hungary, and the USSR abandoned their long-term plans: the two former were able to count on more imports from the latter (both received credits, while the GDR benefited from the scaling-down in 1957 and 1958 of occupation costs and the receipt, from 1959 onwards, of Soviet support costs as an invisible export).[35]

With these changes in trade plans went a fundamental revision in trade planning. The bilateral deals for the next round of long-term

[34] For studies of these countries at the time see *Econ. Survey Eur. 1960*, ch. VI (Albania and Bulgaria), and *Econ. B. Eur.*, xiii/2 (Rumania).

[35] H. Rau, Minister of Foreign Trade, *Auss.*, 13 Jan. 1959.

plans were drawn up before, instead of after, the production programmes. Thus the Soviet government announced the start of work on the Seven-Year Plan (1959–65) in September 1957 and the draft plan itself in November 1958. It made its 1961–5 trade agreements about half-way through this drafting period—with Czechoslovakia in April, with Bulgaria and North Korea in May, with Hungary in June, with the GDR and Rumania in July, and with Mongolia in August. Since the Albanian transactions would be largely underwritten by the Soviet loan agreement, only trade with Poland was not covered. The other members of Comecon had initiated their negotiations on intra-trade in the spring, and the June session recommended that quantitative agreements should be concluded by the end of October for at least 70 per cent of the projected trade.[36]

The longer economic perspective and the brighter political prospects combined to make this period particularly effective for inter-product specialization within the Comecon framework. In November 1957 alone agreement was reached between Poland and the GDR on heavy engineering, electrical equipment, and locomotives, between Poland, Czechoslovakia, and the USSR on shipbuilding, and between the GDR and the USSR on motor vehicles, agricultural engineering, and steam turbines.[37]

As early as June 1957, a Rumanian economist had voiced his country's dissatisfaction with the trend of specialization, and at a conference at Liblice (Czechoslovakia) soon afterwards Rumanian views, as an underdeveloped member of Comecon, were contrasted with the Czech, as the most developed.[38] By April 1958 the Rumanian position was still more explicit. A paper by Horowitz made three major points —that world prices do not reflect the dynamic positions of developing countries, that the criterion of efficiency in current costs would 'perpetuate the backwardness of the underdeveloped countries', and that a developing country may protect high-cost industries on the traditional arguments about balance-of-payments disequilibrium.[39] The

[36] Pryor (p. 89) understands that this deadline was essentially met.

[37] Shurshalov, pp. 295–6.

[38] The retrospective analysis of this source is due to J. P. Saltiel, *Cahiers de l'ISEA*, Dec. 1965, p. 70: the references are to T. Pavel, *Prob. econ.*, no. 6, 1957 and, on the opponents at the conference, I. Anghel and V. Kaigl, ibid. no. 1, 1958.

[39] M. Horovitz, *Prob. econ.*, no. 4, 1958, pp. 10–20. Its significance was generally unnoticed until Montias (*Sov. Stud.*, Apr. 1964, pp. 131–2) deciphered its careful phrasing. As he pointed out (p. 149), an author in western Europe had at the time cited the article 'as evidence of the

Czechoslovak 'answer' came in March 1959, namely that efficiency required supply by traditional producers, with the less developed building upon their raw-material endowment: he cited as examples Rumanian chemicals based on oil and gas and Bulgarian engineering founded on non-ferrous metals.[40]

With this background, the two Sessions of 1958 confined themselves to the rather easier task of intra-product specialization: multilateral agreement was reached on 13 groups of engineering goods and on 117 types of bearings. At the Eleventh Session (May 1959) a division of rolling-mill components was made between Czechoslovakia, the GDR, Poland, and the USSR; for machine-tools in the ball-bearing industry 55 types were allocated to the USSR, 40 to the GDR, 12 to Poland, and 10 to Czechoslovakia. Specialization on chemicals took longer, but as much as 80–85 per cent of chemicals production had been distributed under such agreements by the Fourteenth Session (February 1961).

To take intra-product and product specialization a logical step nearer integration, the GDR proposed discussions on sectoral planning. This involved the establishment of 'material balances' for all the products of a given sector and for the inputs subsumed by those targets. The Sessions of December 1958 and May 1959 pursued this for fuel and energy and for the rolling-mill and pipe sectors of the steel industry and made recommendations for national outputs to 1965.[41]

The Sofia Session took the sector-balance approach, earlier used for fuel and power and rolled products, on to agriculture, and approved the Agricultural Commission's projections for wool, fruit, grapes, and vegetables. So far as the last three were concerned, the chief trade flows were from Albania, Bulgaria, Hungary, and Rumania, but the absence of a price clause threw the shortcomings of the balance method into relief. For fuels and rolled steel the general understanding on world market prices was acceptable enough to producers and consumers, but it was inadequate for the dates and composition of deliveries of fruit and vegetables.

---

complete subordination of Rumanian views on integration and foreign trade to the Soviet Union'.

[40] V. Kaigl, *Voprosy filosofii* (Moscow), no. 3, 1959, pp. 37–8, also illuminatingly interpreted by Montias, *Sov. Stud.*, Apr. 1964, p. 133.

[41] Shurshalov, p. 297. For a discussion of the targets themselves, see *Vopr. ekon.*, no. 9, 1959, esp. p. 101.

Agricultural problems were the subject of a Party conference in February 1960, unlike its general predecessor of 1958 confined to 'European socialist countries', and hence to Comecon without, it would seem from the communiqué, any Asian observers. Its main task was to review the state of collectivization—the drive to virtual completion, everywhere save in Poland, was soon undertaken—but it discussed matters normally within the competence of Comecon. It called for more intensive study by Comecon of specialization in agricultural production itself and in the production of farm machinery and chemicals. It reflected the current general preoccupations in demanding expansion of fodder crops, and Khrushchev's particular predilection for maize. The policies enunciated at the Party leaders' conference were implemented as Comecon recommendations at the Thirteenth Session, in Budapest in July 1960.

Growth of the organization

The appointment of Nikolai Faddeev as Secretary by the June 1958 Session was in itself a strengthening of the organization, for his predecessor and compatriot, Pavlov, had been in poor health for some time, and on one occasion had been too ill to attend the Session. The new head of the secretariat evidently saw some need to improve working efficiency, because the following Session, in December 1958, 'exchanged views on the work of the organs of CMEA in executing the decisions of the Council Session'. The staff had been enlarged around 1956 to about 100 (including ancillary services, typists, and the permanent missions) and seems to have remained more or less at this level. This was possible because most of the new work was shouldered by the various committees and working parties set up to deal with specific problems, or by the standing commissions themselves. Since such expert groups, and not the Secretariat, were responsible for the substantive research and consultation, and because problems sometimes crossed the lines of their terms of reference, working methods included joint sessions (e.g. of the Commissions for Ferrous Metals and for Coal in April 1959) and combined studies, such as that of the Commissions for Agriculture, for the Light and Food Industries, and for Foreign Trade, to draw up the agricultural long-run balance-sheet presented to the Sofia Session. This procedure also explains the mobility of Comecon meetings, in contrast to the almost invariable convocation of OEEC meetings in Paris and ECE meetings in Geneva, for more experts could thereby be brought in to the discussions. Thus the Commission for Ferrous Metals had the first of its two 1958 sessions in Dnepropetrovsk, planned the second for Leipzig and eventually held it in Moscow; the Chemicals Commission, normally convened in Berlin, met in Warsaw in November 1958. Subcommittees and working parties were still more peripatetic, and there were meetings not only in capital cities, e.g. Tirana (wool, January 1959), Bucharest (maize, February 1957), Budapest (railway electrification, March 1958) but in other towns, such as Leningrad (synthetic rubber, May 1958) and Gdansk (shipbuilding, March 1957).

Comecon also began a modest programme of international publications. As early as 1957 the Agricultural Commission began its *Mezhdunarodny selskokhozyaistvenny zhurnal* (which appears in six languages with a combined circulation of 25,000), and the Timber and Cellulose Commission founded an information bulletin (which appears not to have survived the demise of the Commission). The Secretariat itself circulated Russian translations of significant articles from members' technical journals quarterly from 1956 (*Sbornik perevodov*) and has issued its own quarterly journal (*Byulleten ekonomicheskoi informatsii*) since 1959. In the same year the Building Commission launched a journal (*Informatsionnye soobsheheniya Postoyannoi Komissii po stroitelstvu*), chiefly devoted to the standardization of construction design and modular co-ordination.[42] Comecon's publications programme has, however, never matched the output of similar European agencies.

A multilateral initiative of considerable practical significance was the conclusion on 13 December 1957 by the Foreign Trade Commission of 'General Conditions for Deliveries of Goods among Foreign Trade Corporations of CMEA members'.[43] It replaced—from 1 January 1958—the separate agreements annexed to annual trade protocols.

The need for further consolidation was nevertheless felt to be increasing with the rapid development of EEC and EFTA. The Treaty of Rome had come into force in January 1958, the first 10 per cent

[42] Faddeev, p. 50. Comecon's only other publication is a stud-book (see p. 158).
[43] *Hand. zag.*, no. 8, 1959; the German text is in Uschakow, pp. 119–39. For a legal commentary see A. Kanda, *Vliv zmeny pomeru na trvani zavazku* (Prague, 1966).

cut in internal tariffs had been made, on schedule, on 1 January 1959, and the GATT had acquiesced in the procedure establishing the Common Tariff; in the one year 1959 the intra-trade of the Common Market had risen by 18 per cent and imports from the European Free Trade Area (EFTA) had risen by 8 per cent, while trade with the rest of the world had fallen. The agreement on EFTA was initialed in Stockholm on 20 November 1959, and a 20 per cent tariff cut on intra-trade was scheduled for 1 July 1960, to catch up with the Common Market. The loose directives of 1949 were valid neither as an expression of the complexity of Comecon, nor as an answer to its west European rivals. Drafting of a Charter began and Statutes were agreed at the Twelfth Session, at Sofia, at the end of 1959.

The Charter, reproduced in Appendix IV, entered into force on 13 April 1960, as did the Convention on Immunities (App. V) establishing an international civil service; with two revisions (never ratified), they are still operative. The amendments replaced the Conference of Representatives, which formalized the earlier 'delegates' meeting', by an Executive Committee (Art. VII) and excised 'European' from Article II (2). But the only non-European state which asked to join was Mongolia; by 1962 the rift between China and the Soviet Union was too deep for any realistic hope that Comecon might embrace the entire socialist world.

VI

DIVERGING INTERESTS, 1961–6

The new role of Bucharest

OVER the past seven years Bucharest has been the epicentre whose tremors have shaken the east European alliance. In June 1960 the Third Congress of the Rumanian Workers' Party brought to Bucharest representatives of forty-nine fraternal Parties: Khrushchev, personally leading the Soviet delegation, took the occasion—unexpectedly, according to the Chinese, although they had launched their polemic in April[1]—of presenting those from socialist countries (Comecon and the four Asian states) with a bill of protest against China. At a larger meeting in Moscow the following November, the Soviet and Chinese viewpoints (the latter supported by the Albanian Workers' Party) were more acrimoniously argued. A Declaration was drafted and signed by 81 Parties—all the participants save the Yugoslav League of Communists, who thus renewed their dissidence. The Declaration did not choose between the Chinese or Soviet ideological contentions, but rather set out both in a form which, superficially, was mutually acceptable.

The usual biannual Session of Comecon met (in Budapest) soon after the Bucharest Party consultation and discussed very long-term planning. So distant a horizon as 1980 demanded fundamental decisions on the pattern of development and the Rumanian view of its own industrialization came to be the nub of dissent. Preoccupation with the Moscow meeting—which ran on into December—postponed the Comecon Session, normally held in that month, to February–March 1961 in Berlin. There the co-ordination of plans to 1980 was further reviewed and the need became evident for commonly-agreed guidelines on the international division of labour. Doubtless to allow time to draft such a text, no mid-year meeting was held in 1961, but the *Basic Principles* (see App. VI) were laid before the subsequent Warsaw Session in December. Albania did not attend the meeting, but a new dichotomy of views became evident, for the Principles, like the Declaration of the 81 Parties, listed rather than

[1] *Peking R.*, 26 Apr. 1960.

resolved the points of conflict. In June 1962 a 'meeting of representatives of the Communist and Workers' Parties of member-states of Comecon' ratified the *Basic Principles*, and the concurrent Sixteenth Session created an Executive Committee composed of deputy premiers of member governments. The Executive virtually supplanted the Session of the Council. The Seventeenth and Eighteenth Sessions met normally in December 1962 and July 1963 at the alphabetical turns of Rumania and the USSR (the out-of-rota Sixteenth having been termed 'extraordinary'). In 1962 the number of statutory meetings of the Session had been reduced to one,[2] by an amendment which remains unratified (for the reasons set out on pp. 245–6). It was intended that the Session be held in June,[3] but that for 1964 was delayed until January 1965, and that for 1966 until December of that year. The meeting which constitutionally should have been convened in June 1965 never took place.

In the three years to mid-1963 the seventeen meetings of the Council or its Executive were significantly confined to three capitals: Moscow, Bucharest, and Warsaw. On the Executive each member occupied the chair as the initial letter of his nationality dictated, but the Rumanian, Soviet, and Polish delegates held it for two meetings apiece. Even without an analysis of national statements, these pointers might suffice to indicate the predominance, in the disputes of these years, of the USSR, Rumania, and Poland.[4]

Repercussions of the Sino-Soviet dispute

The triangular debates of Rumania, the USSR, and Poland during 1961–4 were intertwined with a series of membership problems which formed part of the Sino-Soviet dispute. The fundamental issues of the political schism need hardly be examined in the present study: the domestic politics of both sides, the differences in foreign policy, and the extent of the Soviet military commitment to China have all been involved. In the narrower context of economic collaboration, the turning-point seems to have been November 1957. In broad sum-

[2] Art. VI of the 1960 text laid down that the Ordinary Session meet twice a year in each capital in turn; the Extraordinary Session is convened at the request of not less than one-third of members.

[3] The original Rules of Procedure specified June and December (Shurshalov, p. 286).

[4] When the alphabetical rota began again (at the December 1964 Executive), with the Bulgarian representative presiding, each began to hold the Chair for two consecutive sessions; Mongolia, however, did not make use of its turn and Jaroszewicz (Poland) presided out of order at the September 1965 meeting, as well as in his country's turn in April and June 1966.

mary, the Eighth Congress of the Chinese Communist Party had in September 1956 ratified a policy of comprehensive economic development for China, explicitly with the help of Soviet experts and supplies, but its resumed session of 1958 transformed this into one of independent and self-sufficient development. China and North Korea had accepted observer status in Comecon in 1956 and 1957, and the other two Asian states had done so in 1958; from then until December 1961 all appeared regularly at Sessions. In 1960 and 1961 the Soviet Union concluded substantial aid agreements with the three smaller states. In October 1960 Korea was excused $190 m. debts to the USSR, and repayment of $35 m. was postponed; in December an aid agreement was signed covering deliveries in 1961–7. Vietnam obtained credits for 1961–5 in the same month, and Mongolia concluded an aid agreement for the same period in April 1961, implementing the offer of $154 m. made the year before. Of the three, Mongolia had received by far the greatest attention: Mongolian delegations were in Moscow almost continuously during 1960–1, resulting in no less than fifteen economic agreements other than on trade.

China did not make use of its observer status at the December 1961 Session of Comecon, but Korea, Mongolia, and Vietnam were represented. At the following meeting Mongolia was the only Asian state present, and became a full member. From then until October 1963 Korea and Vietnam continued to boycott the Executive Committee, a period coinciding with the ascendancy of Chinese influence in Pyong-yang and Hanoi. Joan Robinson finds that the Korean Seven-Year Plan changed from the Chinese to the Soviet type in 1964[5] and by mid-1966 its foreign policy was of neutrality with preference towards the USSR.[6] In Vietnam the sharpening of the war has increased the dependence of Hanoi on Soviet assistance, while requiring a relationship with Peking which would preclude full membership of Comecon. The absence of these states from Comecon during 1962 and most of 1963 was not only a reaction to Chinese desires, but may well also have been attributable to the probable Soviet view that the transformation of Comecon into a supranational body would have left no place for observers, and hence that those who would not accept the full responsibility of membership should withdraw. This ex-

[5] J. Robinson, *Collected Economic Papers*, iii (London, 1965), p. 209.

[6] See editorials in *Rodong Shinmoon*, 12 and 15 Aug. 1966.

planation is further pursued in connexion with the Yugoslav application for observer status (see p. 100). The session of the Executive Committee (October 1963) to which Korea and Vietnam returned was almost certainly concerned with their membership for, just afterwards, the Rumanian Premier, Ion Maurer—who himself led the Rumanian mediation mission to Peking, Pyong-yang, and Moscow—wrote that only membership of 'all socialist countries' could be 'a lasting material basis for the unity and cohesion of the socialist system'.[7] According to the Moscow correspondent of a leading Yugoslav newspaper, full membership had in fact been offered to China, North Korea, and North Vietnam at the June 1962 Session and this had been immediately declined.[8] In the light of Maurer's article, a direct refusal seems unlikely, but the offer may have been conditional on terms unacceptable to China.

None of the Asian observers reappeared at sessions of the Executive after October 1963, but until then they had made eclectic appearances at certain commissions. In December 1961 China did not participate in the Non-Ferrous Metals Commission although its exports to Comecon members of lead, tin, tungsten, and zinc gave it a major interest. Korea, Mongolia, and Vietnam, on the other hand, were present, and in the same month, at the Council Session. China returned to the commissions which directly concerned it in 1962. China and Korea were at the April meeting of the Oil Commission—Soviet oil is their main source of supply, whereas Vietnam takes very little (at least, directly). During 1963 China, Korea, and Vietnam appeared at the Trade Commission in April, at the Engineering Commission in November, and at the Economic Commission in September, but China failed to attend the Currency and Finance Commission of the same month, although Korea and Vietnam did so. They were both at the Agricultural Commission at the end of November 1963, when —in a gesture which, it seems, was not repeated—Rumania abstained in company with China. China was absent, too, from the 1965 Session held in Prague, and the Czechoslovak representative, who presided, made a pointed reference in his opening address to the provision that Comecon was open to 'all Socialist countries'. North Korea and North Vietnam attended as observers in 1965 but not in 1966.

Asian participation in the non-Comecon agencies (Chart 3, p. 68)

[7] *Sc.*, 4 Nov. 1963; also published in *Wld Marx. R.*, no. 11, 1963. [8] *Politika*, 18 June 1962.

was not limited until 1966, when China withdrew its nationals from the United Institute for Nuclear Research; two years before Chinese scientists at Dubna had been reported in the Soviet press as more numerous than 'any other group from the Popular Democracies'.[9]

The Soviet-Chinese rupture also changed the European composition of Comecon: Albania, siding with China, was barred from using its membership, and Yugoslavia (Soviet policy towards which was always the inverse of its attitude to China) was readmitted as an observer.

Albanian support for the Chinese case had been first publicly voiced at the Third Congress of the Rumanian Workers' Party in Bucharest in June 1960, and in September one of the most senior members of the Central Committee of the Albanian Workers' Party, Madame Liri Belishova, was dismissed from the Committee for 'grave political errors', revealed, three years later, to have been an alleged pro-Soviet plot. The following May, a political trial—ostensibly for treason with Yugoslavia and Greece, but patently directed against Soviet sympathizers—resulted in the death penalty for, among others, a former Albanian representative to Comecon. During the rest of 1961 Albanian-Soviet relations rapidly deteriorated, and on 12 December the USSR announced the withdrawal of its diplomatic mission to Tirana. On that day a meeting of the Comecon Executive Committee opened in Warsaw, without a delegate from Albania. The Polish Vice-Premier, who presided, gave an assurance at the press conference that Albania was still a member, and a Soviet source later stated that 'the Albanian representatives refused to participate in the Fifteenth Session of CMEA'.[10] The Albanian subscription to Comecon, which fell due in September 1961, was not paid, and the Secretary stated at the December 1962 Session that he had ceased to issue invitations on that ground. Article XII of the Statute requires that members bear the cost of the Secretariat and it must presumably have been argued that failure on this score amounts to loss of membership. By analogy, the six-months' notice of withdrawal (Art. II (3)) could be applied to the non-payment of dues, and Albanian membership could thus have lapsed in March 1962. The 1960 Charter is remarkable for its lack of provision for the suspension or expulsion of members, or even for the termination of the organization. The Albanian protest, published in *Zeri i popullit*, 6 June

[9] *Pr.*, 22 Jan. 1964. [10] *Ezhegodnik BSE, 1962*, p. 196.

1962, stated that Albania had not been invited to 'certain' meetings of 1962—bearing out the supposition of a March deadline—and claimed that Comecon decisions taken in the absence of its representatives were invalid.

In April 1962 the Chinese Communist Party declared its willingness to renew discussions with the Soviet Communist Party if the latter took 'positive steps to restore normal relations' with Albania. Before the meeting opened on 5 July, such a gesture was made by the arrival in Moscow of an Albanian trade union delegation. After the breakdown of the Sino-Soviet talks, relations deteriorated further. If Comecon expulsion had in fact been ostensibly on a financial ruling, Albania later took a neat retaliation when it sequestered the Soviet embassy building in Tirana because the Soviet government had not paid a debt of 1·5 m. 'clearing roubles' for its construction.[11]

The Albanian departure is exclusively a political question. There have been general statements on the Soviet side about disruptive activities by Albania within Comecon, but the specific accusations have been reserved for the Party conflict. In 1962 a semi-official Soviet record of Comecon had it:

> The shameful course adopted by the Albanian leaders and their attempts to weaken the unity of the socialist camp evoke among countries of the socialist community a feeling of deep anxiety concerning the future development of Albania. The schismatic policy of the Albanian leaders, who forget the significant help given their country by the Soviet Union and other socialist countries, could lead to their alienation from the socialist camp and cause immense harm to their nation. Violating the standards of mutual relationship between socialist states, the Albanian leaders are attempting to undermine the concerted activity of the socialist countries in the international arena and in particular in the CMEA.[12]

But the more usual Soviet attitude is to ignore Albania's absence. In another brief Soviet history of Comecon published also in 1962, the only members noted as entering since the foundation were the GDR and Mongolia; Albania did not gain a mention, either in its coming or in its going.[13]

At least one attempt, however, was made to attract Albania back to

[1] *Zer. pop.*, 28 Feb. 1964. *Iz.* (24 Feb.) claimed that 'Albania had put all kinds of obstacles in the way of the Soviet [caretakers, who] were shadowed, whose electricity and water were
[12] cut off, and so on.'
[13] Solodovnikov, p. 316.
V. Sergeev in A. Stupov, ed., *Ekonomicheskoe sotrudnichestvo i vzaimopomoshch sotsialisticheskikh stran* (Moscow, 1962), p. 14.

membership. When Sino-Soviet tensions had been slightly relaxed by Khrushchev's departure, Poland sought to mediate to gain Albanian attendance at the Nineteenth Session, convened for December 1964 but held in January 1965 in Prague. In the latter month the Political Consultative Committee of the Warsaw Treaty Organization met—on east German initiative—in Warsaw:[14] to emphasize that Albania had been invited, but had declined to attend, four empty seats were left at its place around the conference table. In a note of protest after the meeting, the Albanian government complained to Poland that it should have been consulted on the agenda in advance, thus implying that it considered itself, as in Comecon, a full member deprived of its constitutional rights. The note renewed the complaint that the Soviet Union was seeking to disrupt the Albanian economy by a trade embargo. It could hardly have criticized Poland itself in that respect: with Rumania, Poland had increased trade with Albania since 1961, while the other eastern European states had diminished—and the USSR eliminated—exchanges. In 1964 Polish exports to Albania ($6·85 m.) had been just on double their 1961 level ($3·75 m.). Moreover, Albania's trade surplus of 1961 and 1962, of $0·25 m. and $1·45 m. respectively, had reverted to its earlier debtor position: with Polish shipping to pay for, the Polish credits must have exceeded the value of the trade balance allowed ($1·65 m. in 1963 and $0·83 m. in 1964).

The Albanian rebuff to Polish mediation in the two agencies brought the credits to a sharp halt. In 1965 the trade balance was reversed, and Polish exports to Albania fell short of its imports by $1·35 m.; trade returns for early 1966 showed a still larger gap, but the balance was reversed in the course of the year. Even so, the Polish government was prepared to improve relations: in February 1966 it concluded a new five-year trade agreement, but the political gesture which immediately preceded it—the dispatch of an ambassador to Tirana to replace the chargé d'affaires—did not temper the diplomatic climate, and in a recriminatory exchange Poland demanded the recall of the Albanian Ambassador. Chinese advice, which had undoubtedly steeled Albania to reject Polish conciliation (and an invitation to its Workers' Party to be represented at the Twenty-third Congress of the Soviet Communist Party in March

[14] Speech in Leipzig by the Chairman of the Soviet Council of Ministers, *Pr.*, 2 Mar. 1965.

1966), was not, however, accompanied by compensatory economic aid. By 1962 China was exporting to Albania as much as the USSR had done in 1960 and during the Albanian Third Five-year Plan (1961–5) had furnished substantial, though decreasing, aid. During April–June 1965 an Albanian delegation in Peking had negotiated a loan for the Fourth Plan, but another mission in March 1966 reportedly failed to elicit any supplementary assistance: this may have helped to modify the Albanian attitude to its neighbours: in February it had agreed increased trade flows with Yugoslavia and in March the first commercial agreement since the war was signed with Greece.

Chinese prompting was also behind an attempt in Mongolia in December 1965 to withdraw that country from Comecon. At a meeting of the Central Committee of the Mongolian People's Revolutionary Party just a year before, the targets of the Third Five-Year Plan (1961–5) had been reduced to meet the decline in its transit dues—as Sino-Soviet trade via the Trans-Mongolian Railway diminished—and the withdrawal of 10,000 Chinese technicians;[15] and in June 1965 the USSR had offered $733 m. aid for a Fourth Plan. When the Committee met *inter alia* to discuss the Plan in December a group, pointing to the country's economic difficulties, explicitly proposed withdrawal from Comecon and realignment of 'the position which Mongolia had taken in the international communist movement'. A pro-Soviet majority rejected the change and expelled from the Committee three 'careerists' for their part in the move.[16] A few weeks later a mission of the Soviet Communist Party, led by a member of the Central Committee Presidium, came to strengthen the majority's resolve. The delegation to Ulan Bator was concerted with two others to fortify the Soviet political position in Asia—mediation between India and Pakistan in Tashkent and a deputation to North Vietnam. Kadar's visit to Mongolia in October 1965 may well have been designed to check the dissension before it reached debate in the Mongolian Central Committee. Avowing historical affinity—the Mongol hordes of the thirteenth century absorbed those Magyars of the Urals who had not migrated to Europe—the Mongolian delegation to Comecon since its admission had regularly relied on the Hungarian delegates for guidance in voting.

[15] *The Times*, 4 Feb. 1965. [16] Ibid. 28 Jan. 1965.

A pro-Chinese faction was the first of many conflicting descriptions of the group behind the abortive coup d'état in Bulgaria in April 1965. Whatever its motivation, the conspiracy reached into the Party Central Committee, in the person of Ivan Todorov-Gorunya, and later in the year the Soviet Union accorded the country further capital aid (and a five-year trade agreement raising exchanges by 70 per cent) for its 1966–70 Plan.

Comecon's attitude to observer status

The intimacy of the Soviet relationship with Yugoslavia has normally been in inverse relation to that with Albania, and, in the past six years, with China. The conciliatory Soviet approach to China involved estrangement from Yugoslavia, and one of the reverberations of the Sino-Soviet rift was the reopening to Belgrade of the door into Comecon.

Yugoslavia had thus ceased receiving invitations to meetings in 1958 and would, no doubt, have not sought re-entry in 1961 had the United Kingdom not been prepared to join EEC. The prospect of exclusion from its most valuable markets by a common tariff embracing both EEC and EFTA (in August the United Kingdom proposed negotiations and in December Switzerland, Sweden, and Austria declared their interest in joining) was clearly the factor determining Yugoslavia to request permanent observer status in Comecon. The Twenty-Second CPSU Congress in October defined the Soviet stand in the dispute with China—the denunciation of Albania led to the break in diplomatic relations within two months. In the three and a half months between the opening of the Congress and the end of January 1962 there were no less than seventy delegations exchanged between Yugoslavia and Comecon members—at the government, commercial, cultural, and trade union levels.[17]

The Comecon Session of December 1961 offered Yugoslavia full membership but refused observer status. At first sight the reason given by the Warsaw Session—that the Charter made no provision for observers—may appear specious, for observers from the three smaller Asian states were around the table, and there had been no Session without some observer since 1955. But it may be that an all-or-nothing attitude was extended to the Asians: Mongolia accepted the

[17] *Survey*, June 1962, p. 22.

'all', and the others 'nothing'. Moreover, only on this occasion did the communiqué name the observers (as had long been the case for heads of member delegations): all three were ambassadors accredited to Poland. Representation by local diplomats in a conference of senior economic ministers made observership a formality. It cannot be said whether the level of representation was dictated by Comecon—to make its point about membership—or by the observers—partially to associate themselves with a Chinese boycott.

Yugoslavia did not formally withdraw its application, but when the next Session met in June 1962 the specific proposals to form a supranational agency would have cooled its interest; and prospect of the revival of Sino-Soviet talks—which began a month later—might have reinforced the Soviet unwillingness to concede. Yugoslavia, in turn, began to explore the possibility of penetrating the rival EEC. In the autumn of 1962 the Yugoslav ambassador in Brussels opened unofficial talks with the Commission, and technical officials came in from Belgrade. After lengthy, and somewhat intermittent, discussions, the stage termed 'pre-negotiation' was completed, but neither side was anxious to enter the more important phase until Yugoslavia had joined GATT as full member and the EEC had achieved its own agreement on agricultural prices and common marketing arrangements. Both objectives had been attained by mid-1966, and the formulation of their respective offers on the Kennedy Round negotiations in GATT provided the basis for the talks under way in 1967.

In 1963, therefore, Yugoslavia was set on a course increasingly distancing it from Comecon, and Rumania—then seeking occasions to demonstrate a similar sentiment—took the opportunity to join with Yugoslavia in a revival of the Iron Gates project explicitly outside the Comecon framework. A technical memorandum having already been agreed by both parties in 1960, the outlines could rapidly be settled by a Rumanian-Yugoslav protocol of 12 June 1963, and a treaty was signed by the Chairman of the Rumanian Council of Ministers, Gheorghiu-Dej, and by President Tito of Yugoslavia on 30 November. Over the years, however, the 1956 proposals had become less ambitious: they had envisaged several power stations generating 35 m. MWh a year, but the 1963 plan was curtailed to two plants aggregating 10·7 m. MWh. Moreover, the June 1963 protocol envisaged the Danube Commission, not Comecon, as the source of further capital,

Yugoslavia and Rumania providing $148 m. each, the remaining $96 m. (of the $392 m. eventual cost) to come from other members. The approach to the Danube Commission stated that the cost of the navigational improvements should be borne by users of the rivers: failing a contribution from the other riparian states, Yugoslavia and Rumania would recoup their investment by tolls. The cost of transport delays in the present state of the Iron Gates, where ships have to be towed upstream, is such that the market would bear a rather high levy.

At this juncture (August 1963) Khrushchev paid a state visit to Yugoslavia and took up the subject of participation in Comecon, accompanied by Lesechko, the Soviet delegate to its Executive. His public statements referred to association in the work of specialization rather than to joint planning. Visiting the Split shipyards, where eight tankers were being built to Soviet orders, he remarked,

> What an opportunity! Socialist countries should be able to agree on what type of ships each one of them ought to concentrate upon.... We are glad to see that the Yugoslav Government has manifested its intention to take part in the division of labour now being organized with the socialist countries.[18]

In other remarks Khrushchev expressed approval of Comecon's long-term plan for Danube improvement and specifically of the Romano-Yugoslav Iron Gates project. No official statement was made on the Yugoslav reaction to the Soviet invitation to join Comecon—although it is almost certain that a place as observer was now on offer. Yugoslavia discussed the possibilities with the Comecon Secretariat in early 1964, and agreement appears to have been reached on the standing commissions which Yugoslavia could attend (see p. 104).

Unlike the Yugoslav case, the Cuban application for association has never been before a Comecon Session, but Cuba has been allowed to attend a number of standing commissions, without—or, doubtless, before—formal acceptance. As an avowedly socialist state with close economic ties with the European members of Comecon, its adherence seems in principle to present no problem. Moreover, while Yugoslavia engages in normal trade throughout the world and has observer status with an alternative grouping (OECD), Cuba not only has domestic and external economic difficulties but no other trading

[18] *The Times*, 26 Aug. 1963.

area, being outside the Latin American Free Trade Area and the Central American Common Market. Its desire for observership, let alone for full membership, is certainly stronger than the Yugoslav.

Cuba was first represented at an agency of Comecon when it attended a meeting of the Standardization Commission in Berlin during March 1963, and has subsequently participated in a number of standing commissions. It seems nevertheless to have been at only one meeting of the Executive, in October 1963, when all the Asian states reappeared as observers and the question of membership was on the agenda. The somewhat massive character of that meeting would imply that the broad attendance was for a *tour d'horizon*, rather than routine business. When the London *Financial Times* reported, in its issue of 10 October 1963, that Cuba's participation in the Executive was due to a discussion on the concert of aid—Cuba had just previously sat in at a meeting of the standing commission on Currency and Finance—*Pravda* (24 October) issued a formal denial. It may nevertheless be imagined that the subject was raised. During 1959–62 development aid pledged by Comecon members to Cuba had virtually reached $300 m. ($200 m. from the USSR, $50 m. from Czechoslovakia, $15 m. each from Hungary and Rumania, $12 m. from Poland, and $6 m. from Bulgaria).[19] In 1962, however, Cuba had begun to incur heavy balance-of-payments deficits with the USSR: it had had a favourable trade balance in 1961 of $10 m., but this turned to a deficit of $190 m. in 1962 and rose to $295 m. in 1963. The deficit was being met by current Soviet credits. It cannot be affirmed whether any decisions were taken at the Comecon Executive of October 1963, but the Cuban trade deficit was rapidly reduced (that with the USSR fell to $135 m. in 1964 and to $130 m. in 1965).[20] The first Cuban *Plano Perspectivo* for 1962–5 had been revised before reaching operational use, and the drafting of a more limited programme was being undertaken in late 1962 and during 1963; according to a Chilean economist on the Seers mission, this was being done in contact with Comecon.[21] Two senior Soviet economists, whose study was completed in mid-1963, gave no figures for the 1963–5 'control figures'

[19] M. Nolff, in D. Seers, ed., *Cuba, the Economic and Social Revolution* (Chapel Hill, NC, 1964), p. 313, and S. Sergeev, pp. 183–6.
[20] L. Tansky in US Congress, Joint Economic Committee, *New Directions in the Soviet Economy* (Washington, DC, 1966), p. 964.
[21] Nolff, p. 285 and pp. 307–8.

but observed that the original draft had envisaged for 1962–5 a gross investment of 2·5 m. pesos—or half the total fixed assets (productive and unproductive) of the entire Cuban economy.[22] Aid offers from Comecon members slowed in 1963–4 ($85 m.), but rose in 1965 ($167 m.); Cuba did not attend any later meeting of the Executive.

It was, however, linked with Yugoslavia in the April 1964 issue of *Voprosy ekonomiki* as one of the two countries which might collaborate with certain standing commissions. Negotiations with Yugoslavia proceeded during the middle months of that year.[23] An agreement of 17 September 1964 admitted Yugoslavia to three general commissions (Foreign Trade, Currency and Finance, and Co-ordination of Scientific and Technical Research) and four sector commissions (ferrous metals, non-ferrous metals, engineering, and chemicals); this entry was subsequently extended to the commission for the radio-technical and electronic industry,[24] and later to that for statistics.[25] The agreement entered into force, after ratification, on 24 April 1965. A Yugoslav observer was first present at the Executive Committee at its meeting of November 1965, and attended regularly thereafter (except at those of June and November 1966, the one concerned with the second Rumanian crisis—see p. 125—and the other with preparation for a Council Session).[26] A Yugoslav observer re-appeared in the Council at the Nineteenth Session (Prague, January 1965).

The contrast between Comecon's treatment of Cuba and Yugoslavia deserves comment. At the 1965 Session, the Havana press reported the presence of a Cuban observer,[27] but he was not mentioned in the official communiqué nor, it would appear, in the eastern European press. While Guevara was in charge of Cuban economic affairs, his opposition to Yugoslav policy must have been the decisive factor

[22] A. Efimov, A. Anchishkin, *Kuba planiruyet natsionalnuyu ekonomiku* (Moscow, 1963), pp. 61 and 72.

[23] They are noted by Korbonski (*Int. Con.*, Sept. 1964, p. 56); initially five commissions were spoken of, then six, and in the event Yugoslavia was admitted to seven.

[24] Comecon Secretariat document, *Informatsia o deyatelnosti SEV v oblasti selskogo khozyaistva* (Moscow, May 1966), p. 3.

[25] It attended the eighth session of the Statistics Commission in Riga (*Iz.*, 21 Sept. 1966).

[26] Initially a member of the Yugoslav Federal Executive Committee, A. Grlickov, attended; thereafter the delegate was the Permanent Representative of Yugoslavia to Comecon, V. Gajinovic.

[27] *Hoy*, 29 Jan. 1965, cited by D. Tretiak, *Cuba and the Soviet Union: the Growing Accommodation* (Santa Monica, Calif., 1966), RAND Memorandum 4935–PR, p. 33. As late as September 1964 Castro was publicly decrying participation in Comecon (*Hoy*, 18 Sept. 1964), ibid. p. 5.

in Comecon discrimination. In an interview in Cairo in April that year, he claimed that 'in Yugoslavia there is a danger of moving towards capitalism and it is imminently to be expected that this economic principle should be reflected in its political position'.[28] Until Guevara's dismissal on 3 October, Cuba seems to have attended only two Comecon Standing Commissions during 1965. Immediately afterwards, however, a Cuban delegation visited the Dubna Institute and attended the exercises of the Warsaw Treaty Organization;[29] during 1966 it resumed participation in Standing Commissions, including at least one on which it had not earlier taken part.[30]

Dispute among members

In 1961 the more industrialized members of Comecon, Poland, Czechoslovakia, and Hungary, were at one with the USSR in anxiety for their markets in the western European groupings. Intra-German trade was protected under the terms of EEC, but this was the very trade which the GDR was seeking to reduce: in 1961—the Berlin Wall was erected in August—it launched a policy to 'assure' its trade with Comecon.

Of the two less-developed members, Rumania had determined on rapid industrialization. It was unwilling to commit itself to the import of manufactures and the export of raw materials that the needs of the more developed members seemed to imply. However amenable Comecon partners could be in negotiating product specialization, the adoption of 1980 as the horizon for plan co-ordination required Rumania to select a long-run pattern of output without knowing upon which goods it would be most rational to concentrate. It claimed that it could not tell, so far in advance, what would be its relative production costs.

Bulgaria might be thought to share this disquiet, but its record in Comecon matters seems to have been with the developed group. Political factors—the traditional alliance with Russia—have joined themselves with advantageous economic terms for any integration. Since the concessions of 1958 (see p. 180), terms of trade with Comecon partners appear to have been particularly favourable, and it has had two large loans from the USSR ($162 m. in 1960 and $300 m. in

[28] *Al-Tali'ah* (Cairo), Apr. 1965, quoted ibid. p. 27. [29] Tretiak, p. 34.
[30] See *Pr.*, 2 Mar. 1966.

1963). Its efficiency is undoubtedly high for the exports upon which it concentrates. Its non-ferrous metals, fruits, and (mainly early) vegetables command a high price because they are largely non-competitive in intra-Comecon trade.

The meeting of Party leaders from Comecon countries in June 1962, on Polish initiative, approved the *Basic Principles*. A key paragraph for Rumania's vast projected steel industry (the Galatz plant of the new plan was scheduled for 4 m. tons) stated:

> International socialist division of labour in metallurgy should stimulate rapid expansion of ferrous and non-ferrous metal production in amounts and grades that meet the growing requirements of the socialist countries and reduce production costs. . . . Integrated iron and steel centres should preferably be set up in countries that are fully, or nearly fully, provided with ore and processed fuel, or at least possess one of the two.

The projected Rumanian plan was geared to imported iron ore and was located far from the areas producing metallurgical coke. Its output was partly intended to support the rapid expansion of engineering (14 per cent per annum) but also intended for export: by 1970 its steel production per capita (372 kg.) would substantially exceed the 1962 Soviet level (345 kg.). The phrase that production should be related to the 'requirements of the socialist countries' thus seemed to deprecate Rumania's plan. Moreover, Soviet steel output was to expand by 1970 to 500 kg. per capita, and the existing steel industries of Czechoslovakia, the GDR, Hungary, and Poland were to develop (indeed these countries were anxious to realize a profit on the burdensome outlays of their Stalinist expansion). The implication of the criterion 'to reduce production costs' was concentration on the already developed steel producers.

It was, however, the Soviet proposals for a central Comecon planning organ which created the major rift. They were set out in an article by Khrushchev originally published in *Kommunist*, no. 12, August 1962 (but given wide diffusion from the international Party information centre in Prague, in the *World Marxist Review* of September 1962) and in his speech of 19 November to the Central Committee of the CPSU. Khrushchev drew from the evolution of the supranational EEC—to which the United Kingdom had just signified its readiness to adhere—the lesson that Comecon should itself establish 'a unified planning organ, empowered to compile common plans and to decide organizational matters'. Although expressed as Soviet proposals, the policy was originally Polish. Concerned by the prospects of a shrinkage of exports to the Common Market, and exasperated by the dispersion of Comecon's capital resources, Gomulka, on the eve of the Thirteenth Session which was to discuss Comecon plans to 1980, had declared to the Polish Central Committee, 'There is no co-operation whatsoever in the important sector of investment: everyone peels his own turnip—and loses by it.'[31] The crux of the new programme for Comecon lay in the rational allocation of investment. Most big capital projects would better serve the area as a whole than the limited market of one country—they could be located near the cheapest or most convenient source of materials, or, subject to the limits of delivery cost, they could profit from the economies inherent in large-scale production. On this the USSR made a major concession:

> International specialization is advantageous not only to small countries, but also to such large states as the Soviet Union. . . . The Soviet Union is even prepared to reduce its output of some kinds of manufactures if it proves more expedient to produce them in other CMEA countries.[32]

Such allotment of investment would firstly require the co-ordination of national plans for a period exceeding that of the construction of the longest projects (the concurrent Soviet choice for its Party Programme confirmed 1980 as the end-year). The second requisite would be capital lending; although all would benefit from cheaper current costs, the burden of construction in each country would not necessarily conform to its investment resources. As Khrushchev put it to Comecon in July 1962:

> When the target is the most efficient utilization of investment, we ought perhaps also to reckon with the need for a certain movement of these resources from country to country. . . . The Soviet government, like those of other CMEA countries, advocates the extension of the practice of joint finance of those industrial transport and other projects which are of international importance.[33]

In order to select the investment projects, there should be sectoral plans, and projects once accepted could, if commonly financed, become common property. Charter amendments to implement this transformation were drafted, at the June 1962 meetings, but the only modifications then admitted were to establish the Executive Com-

[31] *Tryb. Lud.*, 21 June 1960. [32] *Komm.*, no. 12, 1962. [33] Ibid.

mittee and to relax the restriction of membership to European states. The most sweeping of the proposed changes remained in suspense,[34] in face of the Rumanian contention—eventually made public in the Declaration of April 1964—that 'transmitting such levers to the competence of super-state or extra-state bodies would turn sovereignty into a notion without any content'. The amendments accepted by the two Sessions of 1962 are shown in the text of the Statute reproduced in Appendix IV: they all remained unratified, though whether this was due to the absence of Albania or to the non-compliance of Rumania is still unclear; the present constitutional position is described at the end of that Appendix. It is widely believed that, during the November plenary meeting of the Soviet Central Committee, the Rumanian Central Committee sent Khrushchev a letter declaring readiness to leave Comecon if the supranational policy were pursued. Its April 1964 Declaration said:

> Our Party has very clearly expressed its point of view, declaring that, since the essence of the suggested measures lies in shifting some functions of economic management from the competence of the respective state to the attribution of super-state bodies or organs, these measures are not in keeping with the principles which underlie the relations between socialist countries. The idea of a single planning body for CMEA has the most serious economic and political implications . . . undoubtedly, if some socialist countries deem it fit to adopt in the direct relations between them forms of cooperation different from those unanimously agreed upon within CMEA, that is a question which exclusively concerns those countries.

It can hardly be doubted that the protests voiced in the Declaration were the arguments being advanced in early 1963 by Rumania privately in Comecon; that by July the contention was admitted that 'direct relations' should be the rule where full unanimity was not reached. The atmosphere of the February 1963 Executive can be judged from the views expressed by the President of the Czechoslovak National Assembly, Zdenek Fierlinger, on the one hand, and the laconic announcement made by Rumania immediately after the session.

> From the very start Czechoslovakia eagerly supported the CMEA in its efforts to promote economic co-operation. We welcomed N. S. Khrushchev's appeal for the closest economic unity of the socialist countries. That idea is strongly supported by every sincere fighter for socialism and communism. The proposal that the CMEA play a bigger part has met with

[34] P. Slavkovic, *R. pol. int.*, 20 Oct. 1962.

warm response also in Poland. . . . There is much talk about delegating more authority to the CMEA, so that it will be more than a consultative body. We would like to have its recommendations and decisions (unanimously agreed on, of course) binding on all member-states. . . . In short, what we need is the enlistment of the most efficient and competent experts from all member countries. They would act independently of their respective national authorities and be responsible to the CMEA collective leadership.[35]

The Rumanian Party Central Committee met from 5 to 8 March and issued the following communiqué:

The Plenum heard a communication on the February session of the CMEA Executive Committee made by the RPR representative, Alexander Birladeanu. The Plenum unanimously approved the Party and state directives given to the RPR representative and his actions in accordance with those instructions.[36]

At the end of April at the annual plenary session of the ECE, Gogu Radulescu, Rumanian Minister of Foreign Trade, in his speech as retiring chairman, spoke of the need to pursue economic collaboration with full respect for national sovereignty. As national sovereignty has never been questioned in ECE, observers took the reference to be to Comecon. At the same time Polish sources were putting out the line that the Comecon debate with Rumania was already settled. In June the Rumanian agreement with Yugoslavia on the Iron Gates project, bypassing Comecon in favour of the Danube Commission, was concluded (see p. 101).

In June 1963 China joined the polemics. One of the points of difference with the USSR in the Chinese letter restating views for the bilateral Party talks in July was that economic assistance had to be granted on the principle of complete sovereignty, and that the infringement of independence on grounds of the international division of labour was 'Great-Power chauvinism'. In eastern Europe the letter was published only by the Albanian and Rumanian papers.[37] A link of its own policy of 'going it alone' was perhaps intended to be made with the Rumanian standpoint. The Chinese letter stated:

[35] *New Times* (*Novoe Vremya*), no. 12, 1963 (27 Mar. 1963). [36] *Sc.*, 9 Mar. 1963.

[37] *Zer. pop.* (18 June 1963) published the letter in full and reported the Soviet reply (ibid. 20 June); *Sc.* summarized the letter (20 June) and the reply (23 June) in approximately equal length. In the latter issue prominence was given to a meeting of the Comecon Chemicals Commission at which the only observer was from North Korea: that country's press (*Rodong Shinmoon*, 12 June) had qualified its support of the Chinese letter with emphasis on the need for continued economic co-operation.

Relations between socialist countries are international relations of a new type. Relations between socialist countries, whether large or small, and whether more developed or less developed economically, must be based on the principles of complete equality, respect for territorial integrity, sovereignty and independence, and non-interference in each other's internal affairs, and must also be based on the principles of mutual support and mutual assistance in accordance with proletarian internationalism....

If, proceeding only from its own partial interests, any socialist country unilaterally demands that other fraternal countries submit to its needs, and uses the pretext of opposing what they call 'going it alone' and 'nationalism' to prevent other fraternal countries from applying the principle of relying mainly on their own efforts in their construction and from developing their economies on the basis of independence, or even goes to the length of putting economic pressure on other fraternal countries—then these are pure manifestations of national egoism....

In relations among socialist countries it would be preposterous to follow the practice of gaining profit for oneself at the expense of others, a practice characteristic of relations among capitalist countries, or go so far as to take the 'economic integration' and the 'Common Market', which monopoly capitalist groups have instituted for the purpose of seizing markets and grabbing profits, as examples which socialist countries ought to follow in their economic co-operation and mutual assistance.[38]

The Secretary of Comecon, Faddeev, answered the Chinese charges in a journal of the Soviet Academy of Sciences,[39] describing the 'go it alone' theory as 'anti-historical, abstract and dogmatist', and defended Comecon collaboration as a 'major prerequisite' for economic progress. In another article—in *Izvestia* of 15 September 1963—he wrote:

The leaders of the Chinese Communist Party, disregarding the economic laws pointed out by Marx and Lenin, want to discredit the task of intensifying the international socialist division of labour being carried out by the agencies of the CMEA. The CPC allegations that the international division of labour means the imposition of one country's will on others and an encroachment on the independence and sovereignty of the socialist countries are egregious nonsense.

The situation evidently demanded a meeting at the highest level, and recourse was again had to a session of Party Secretaries from Comecon members. They met also, the Mongolian delegate excepted, as representatives of members of the Warsaw Treaty Organization, and the unanimity reached on that agenda contrasted with the diver-

[38] *Hsinhua News Agency*, suppl. no. 11, 17 June 1963. [39] *Mir. ekon.*, Nov. 1963.

sity of view on the other. The fundamental propositions for the central allocation and implementation of capital projects were abandoned. Ulbricht is reported to have commented: 'It is no misfortune that this suggestion was not adopted.... Now it will be up to the party leaderships and governments to determine to what extent they wish to agree on bilateral co-operation in individual sectors'.[40]

The paramountcy of the 'interested party' was established as the working principle of Comecon. The phrase had first been used in the communiqué of 1949, and was embodied in Article IV (3) of the 1960 Charter. The interpretation accorded it in 1963 changed the basis of collaboration from contracting out to contracting in. The new lines of activity now being undertaken comprise, for Comecon itself, improved central consultations to supplement bilateral negotiation at an increasingly departmental level, and for the members, at their option, three modes of collaboration which may be classified as joint investments, the joint enterprise, and the international association.

Within the central structure of Comecon two new foci of consultation appear to have emerged as part of the reappraisal of July 1963: the conference of commission chairmen, and the Bureau of the Executive. According to its communiqué, the Executive Committee meeting of February 1964 heard a report on a conference of the chairmen of the standing commissions and of the directors of Secretariat departments on 'problems connected with the progress of work on the co-ordination of national economic plans for the period 1966–70'. The 'orientational balance estimates' for 1966–70 were presented to the Executive in July, and it is easy to draw a parallel with the conferences of heads of Gosplan divisions in preparing Soviet long-term plans. The Bureau of the Executive Committee for Integrated Planning Problems comprises the deputy chairman of national planning offices, and its task is 'to prepare proposals for co-ordinating the economic development plans of member countries and to give direct assistance in promoting broad co-operation between their respective planning bodies on specific matters'. It is not a 'Bureau' in the usual eastern European sense, i.e. a subcommittee of the members of a given body themselves, such as the Politbureau of a Party Central Committee. The Comecon Executive cannot delegate its powers to the Bureau but can only be advised by it. The creation of the Bureau

[40] Cited by R. Jaster, *The World Today*, Dec. 1963, p. 521.

would thus appear to have been a cornerstone of the compromises reached when the proposals for a central planning body were definitively dropped at the July 1963 conference, which had recognized that 'bilateral consultations... create the best pre-conditions for multilateral plan co-ordination in the CMEA framework'. This was in conjunction with the tacit replacement of the concept of centralized allocation by the statement that 'the co-ordination of long-term economic plans is the basic method of operation of the CMEA'.

The new mechanism for central consultations, as opposed to central plans, was supported by agreements on trade and payments between members. The revision of the 1957 clearing agreement was apparently first taken up by the Executive in September 1962. There was doubtless—to judge by the outcome—some discussion on the treatment of persistent debtors. The western European counterpart, the European Payments Union (EPU), had permitted the carrying over of debts from one year to another, and had thus helped the less-developed members with chronic deficits, notably Greece and Turkey. The Comecon arrangement required an annual equilibrium of payments of each member with the rest as a group: previously—any small swings under the 1957 agreement apart—each member had to balance with each other member. From the start, however, Comecon references included separate allusion to a Bank to be linked with the clearing union, and the possibility was being debated of a lending institution whose loans would offset the deficits in accordance with agreed investment programmes. The need for Soviet capital was freely mentioned. When the Bank was set up, it envisaged loans for joint projects in bilateral, not multilateral, lending: to put it in Washington terms, it represented approval for institutions such as the US Export-Import Bank, and made no move towards an International Bank.

The Executive Committee continued its discussion of transferable settlements and the functions of the proposed bank in December 1962, when the GDR raised the question of revising the price basis for intra-Comecon trade. It was clear that the possibility of converting earnings from one member into the currency of another jeopardized the balance of advantage which each party had built into the negotiated pattern of bilateral trade flows. The more distant possibility urged by Hungary and Poland of some convertibility of the clearing currency into dollars or sterling made the price ratios of intra-member trade and commerce with the rest of the world still more important. The GDR and the USSR jointly proposed that the 'corrected world-market prices of 1957', which had been used since 1958, be replaced by the world averages for 1958–61. They received no support, and eventually the mean of 1957–62, affording better terms of trade to the less-developed members, was accepted as the basis for further study. Two years later discussion was still proceeding and trade was being carried out on the old 1957 prices (see pp. 184–5). To examine the real parity of costs within member economies two working parties were set up within the frame of research—one on prime costs, headed by the Director of the Hungarian Price Office, Csikos-Nagy, and one on price formation, with the head of the USSR Price Office, Pautin, in the chair. The aim of 'Comecon's own price basis' had been part of the Soviet proposals of July 1962 and had been advocated in the USSR since 1959.[41]

The failure to reach agreement on pricing may also be traced to a change in outside circumstances: contrary to the fears of which Poland had been the main exponent, Comecon trade with the EEC had expanded, not contracted. Czechoslovakia explicitly adopted a 'half-open door policy', which required the continued use of world-market prices, and Poland relaxed some of its support for an independent Comecon price system under similar considerations. The USSR, even while a firm proponent of a separate set of prices, had observed on Comecon trade with EEC that 'a policy of economic collaboration concerns relations not only between individual states, but also between economic groups'. The EEC offer in September 1963 of a modest reduction of tariffs on some Soviet goods may have told in favour of world pricing.

Although no decision was reached on prices—and the question was deferred to await the results of detailed cost analyses—a compromise was reached on the International Bank. The clearing union and the associated bank were set up at the October 1963 Executive. So far as joint investments were concerned the Bank was to 'provide substantial help to countries through the concentration of the funds of interested states'.[42] This implied that the Bank could be used as an intermediary

[41] K. Ostrovityanov, *Pr.*, 6 Feb. 1959 (and see the present writer, *Income and Wealth, Series IX* (London, 1961), p. 165).
[42] K. Nazarkin, Chairman of the Board of the Bank, after its first session, *Iz.*, 22 Nov. 1963.

for the sort of joint project in which Poland was primarily interested, but the reference to the 'concentration' of funds only of 'interested states' did not make the Bank itself an international lender. Delegates returning from the October Executive commented, however, that international loans for Comecon projects and to finance exports to underdeveloped countries were possible under the rules of the Bank, but would not be undertaken for some years.

The Rumanian delegate took the chair at that Executive, and afterwards gave an interview which only in the last phrase showed the main continuing feature of dispute in the economic sphere.

> The major question on the agenda of the Executive Committee was the question of preparing measures to carry out the basic decisions of the conferences of 1962 and 1963 on the co-ordination of the development plans of CMEA countries for the 1966–70 period. This is not the first time that work has been done within the framework of the CMEA to co-ordinate the long-term plans of our countries. Such work was done both in 1955 and in 1960, but it essentially related to a narrow field of economic relations among members of the Council—to their mutual trade. . . . The work on co-ordinating plans for 1966–70 will go deeper than before: it will encompass the major economic branches and will be implemented in close harmony with international output specialization and co-operation. . . . Consistent application of the 'Basic Principles of the International Division of Labour', approved by last year's conference, will be facilitated in the co-ordination of long-term plans and the correct determination of economic development proportions for each country.[43]

The point of political contention at that session seems to have been China, and the Rumanian Declaration of the following April made the demand for its admission explicit: 'Since there are fourteen socialist countries in the world, only some of them CMEA members . . . the best way should be found for the participation in CMEA of all socialist countries.'

When the Executive returned to Bucharest in December 1963, chemicals were the main agenda item. A few days before this, Khrushchev, speaking to his Central Committee on 9 December, had quoted 'preliminary' estimates for Soviet imports of chemical-industry equipment from other Comecon members as some $1,000 m. No final plan for chemicals (which obviously interlocks with the equipment needs and availabilities) seems to have been evolved at the meeting. This

[43] A. Birladeanu, *Pr.*, 25 Oct. 1963.

can be inferred from a subsequent statement by the then chairman of the Comecon Chemicals Commission, Walter Schirmer, that he had no official plan for chemicals, and had had to make what projections he could.[44] At the same meeting an agreement was drawn up on a railway-waggon pool; it seems that Rumania initially declined to participate, but subsequently changed its mind.

The Executive in February 1964 evolved what appeared to be a formula for contacts within the framework of Comecon—an 'agreement on the further expansion of economic, scientific, and technical co-operation' which, through bilateral commissions and limited consultations (described below), provides a bypass around any member's objection to specific projects. The Executive session continued its discussions on the 1966–70 plan co-ordination, presumably on this basis.

The arrangements concluded between July 1963 and February 1964 for Comecon's own operations, and the deflexion of investment agreements outside its frame, would seem to have met virtually all of the Rumanian arguments, at least as laid out in the April Declaration. Yet the Declaration was made public in April 1964. It seems possible that the publication was made as a political move rather than as a defence of strictly economic policy. Perhaps to emphasize its political intransigence, Rumania refused at this time to move in step with other eastern European states towards the mutual abolition of visas for their citizens. A plenary of the Rumanian Central Committee was convened on 15 April, just before a session in Moscow of the Comecon Executive (21–25 April) and overlapped the Committee by two days. It is significant that it followed the Rumanian mission of attempted mediation to China, North Korea, and the Soviet Union (March 1964) and the publication in the Soviet press on 3 April of Suslov's denunciation of China at the February Plenum of the Soviet Communist Party, which Rumania had asked should remain private. Suslov had claimed that China intended to break up Comecon and 'would like to be able to give orders in the socialist commonwealth as in her own estate'.[45]

The Rumanian delegate, Birladeanu, was at his own Central Committee and deputed the Secretary-General of the office dealing with Comecon matters, Cioara, to the Executive in Moscow. Some commentators took the more junior level of representation as a slight to

[44] *Chim. Tech.*, Jan. 1964. [45] *Pr.*, 3 Apr. 1964; the speech had been delivered on 14 Feb.

the meeting; Cioara is, in fact, a former Minister of Electric Power (and now of Foreign Trade) and the insinuation was denied in Rumania. *Izvestia's* report of 28 April on the Executive made no mention of attendance and ignored the underlying crisis:

> The CMEA as a collective organ of economic co-operation will be strengthened and developed, creating solidarity and unity of the peoples of the countries of the socialist commonwealth, which under the leadership of the Communist and Workers' Parties are confidently creating socialism and communism. The Executive Committee session reviewed a series of questions of the economic and scientific-technical collaboration of CMEA countries.

Immediately on his return to Berlin, the GDR member of the Executive, Bruno Leuschner, published a long statement of 'Current Problems of Co-operation of Socialist Countries in the CMEA'. He condemned the 'false theories' of the Chinese 'go it alone' policy and mentioned approvingly bilateral projects of every Comecon member except Rumania. Even his phrasing of the Danube scheme avoided naming the riparian states: 'The members of the CMEA on the Danube are working together on the integrated utilization of the water resources of the Danube'.[46] The Rumanians were describing the Iron Gates project in exclusively bilateral terms.[47]

The modest plan for a Fifteenth Anniversary celebration was also an occasion for both sides to snub each other. As for the Twelfth Anniversary,[48] Comecon commissioned a series of articles on its work by leading economists of member countries, including one by Ion Rachmuth, the Deputy Director of the Rumanian Institute of Economics. The April issue of *Planovoe khozyaistvo*, the organ of the Soviet Plan Office, prefaced this commemorative symposium with the statement that the same texts would appear in the Bulgarian, Czechoslovak, GDR, Hungarian, Mongolian, Polish, and Rumanian magazines, but the Berlin *Wirtschaftswissenschaft* omitted Rachmuth's study. The Bucharest *Probleme economice*, Rachmuth's own house organ, relegated the papers to a supplement and ran a normal issue, carrying as counterpoise an analysis of Rumanian trade with non-members, in support of the UN Conference on Trade and Development.

[46] *N. Deutsch.*, 24 Apr. 1964.
[47] O. Goza, Director of the Inst. for Hydro-Electric Projects, *Sc.*, 14 June 1963.
[48] See *Plan. khoz.*, no. 8, 1962, and corresponding issues of eastern European journals.

At that conference, Radulescu, as leader of the Rumanian delegation, not only made his national position clear but drew a link with prewar Rumanian policy.

> The Rumanian People's Republic consistently strives for the promotion of normal economic relations among all states of the world, irrespective of their social system, based on strict observance of national sovereignty, economic independence, equality in rights and non-interference in domestic affairs.... I should like to recall that at a European economic conference held thirty years ago, the Rumanian representative expressed his hope that the day would come when an international conference would discuss the various aspects of economic relations among states, as components of a unique problem of world economy. May I quote a few sentences from the speech, which the former Rumanian Minister of Foreign Affairs, N. Titulescu, delivered in this same place, in Geneva in January 1931: 'Je pense', he said, 'qu'il n'y a pas dix problèmes économiques, mais un seul, et que c'est un problème mondiale'.[49]

Rumania followed its independent line at that conference by voting with Yugoslavia (one of the leaders of the 'less-developed' lobby) for six resolutions on which all other Comecon members abstained.[50]

A pragmatic solution

The statement in the Rumanian Declaration of April 1964 that 'forms of co-operation different from those unanimously agreed upon within CMEA... can be decided by them alone in a sovereign way', with the Comecon agreement of February 1964 on co-operation, epitomize the solution which was found to the dispute. The agreement in essence formalized arrangements for co-operation between the interested parties when accord could not be reached within Comecon. The term 'interested party' has a special connotation, for the Charter states (in Art. IV (3)) that 'Recommendations and resolutions are ineffective in respect of those countries which declare their lack of interest in the matter in question'. If the matter in question is the aggregate 'material balance' underlying the network of production and trade programmes, 'lack of interest' is of course the equivalent of a veto.

[49] Speech delivered on 2 Apr. 1964 (E/CONF.46/STA/70) at the UN Conference on Trade and Development. This reference was supplied by Dr Gh. Ionescu, of the London School of Economics, in the course of an illuminating discussion.

[50] See the Final Act of the Conference (E/CONF.46/L.28). The subjects on which Rumania differed do not fall into any consistent pattern, and were possibly chosen as gestures: they covered the use of funds released by any eventual disarmament, price stabilization, terms of investment financing, the UN Special Fund, a proposal for a regional development fund, and rates of interest.

But the article itself is a provision for contracting out, and in the majority of cases should not have prevented agreement by the rest. The Rumanian position, as its Declaration shows, was that a notification of 'lack of interest' removed the matter from the Comecon agenda. As a clash on this score demonstrated in 1967 (see p. 128), Poland was the most dissatisfied, and has indicated that the compromise represented by bilateral arrangements came from the USSR.[51]

The procedures envisaged by the resolution are along three lines. Where a multilateral problem is concerned, the 'interested parties' may use the Comecon framework for research and negotiation. Thus the July 1964 Executive approved proposals of the Coal Commission 'on the co-operation of interested countries in building new capacity in the coal industry', and of the Oil and Gas Commission 'on the assurance of the requirements of interested members for low-viscosity oils, including transformer oil, for 1966–70'. Where an operational function arises, however, the collaboration is to be effected outside Comecon. In the case of a proposition to set up a programming centre for iron and steel production, Rumania declared lack of interest and the centre could not be subordinated to Comecon (i.e. on the lines of the control office for electric power). Six members (i.e. all save Rumania and Mongolia) therefore set up their own agency, Intermetall, in July 1964 with headquarters in Budapest. At a meeting of Deputy Heads of Government of participating countries on 11 February 1966, the Director of its Bureau, M. Ostatni, reported that Intermetall contracts had expanded deliveries of rolled metal and steel pipe among members above the levels envisaged in the long-term agreements and that capacity-use had been raised; he envisaged in the near future the use of optimal programming techniques for the choice of product-mix.[52] Two other agencies do not embrace all members. Mongolia is not in the Common Waggon Pool because its tracks are broad-gauge; it has no rail link save via the USSR (the latter constructed standard-gauge waggons especially to supply the pool). It is consequently listed as a 'specialized agency' of Comecon by Ciamaga.[53] The Organization for Co-operation in the Ball-Bearings Industry, on the other hand, was intended to be all-embracing and a provisional Standing Commission was created in April 1963, only to

[51] See K. Olszewski, Polish Deputy Minister of Foreign Trade, *N. drogi*, Feb. 1964.
[52] *Pr.*, 13 Feb. 1966. See also A. Sokolov and Yu. Shirayev, *Int. Aff.*, no. 1, 1966, p. 42.
[53] Ciamaga, pp. 97–101. Faddeev, however, does not include it in his official survey.

be liquidated on Rumanian insistence at the end of the year. The other members with a bearings industry therefore set up the separate body in 1964.

Bilateral arrangements are to develop within intergovernmental commissions, both general and sectoral. When visiting Hungary in April 1964 at the height of the Rumanian polemic, Khrushchev linked a determination to 'close our ranks' with the need for 'new forms of organization' among the eastern European countries.[54] A study by the Soviet academic economist most closely concerned with Comecon, Bogomolov, which appeared in January 1964, referred to the alternative of international co-operation between 'a group of interested countries', when observing that 'the evaluations of national and international efficiency could be incorrectly opposed to each other'.[55] In the Fifteenth Anniversary symposium (April 1964), he commented:

> But this system (even if possible shortcomings can be temporarily eliminated) naturally cannot ensure the solution of all the complicated domestic economic problems of each socialist country. . . . Many CMEA states have by mutual agreement set up bilateral commissions (or committees) for economic and scientific-technical collaboration. The terms of reference of these commissions include the organization of co-operative production, agreed management in certain fields, the co-ordination of plans for investment, output, and intra-trade, joint scientific research and the exchange of technology.[56]

The statement of the GDR delegate at the April meeting of the Executive included the observation that

> the ways and means of economic and technical collaboration formerly applied did not nevertheless guarantee their outcome. . . . We wish particular success to the CMEA in undertaking new forms and methods, such as the economic-technical relations of CMEA countries, and the collaboration in the specialization and co-operation of production, together with the important problems of financing and utilizing the results of joint research.[57]

In organizational terms, bilateral co-ordination is now to be run through the intergovernmental commissions started by Poland and Czechoslovakia in 1957. As Chart 4 (p. 120) shows, the network between members other than the USSR was substantially completed by 1962. In late 1963 and early 1964 the USSR linked itself with all the European members and the GDR. The treaty with Rumania did

[54] *The Times*, 16 Apr. 1964. [55] *Vopr. ekon.*, no. 11, 1963, p. 7.
[56] B. Leuschner, *N. Deutsch.*, 24 Apr. 1964. [57] Ibid.

CHART 4

Intergovernmental Commissions on Economic, Scientific, and Technical Collaboration: year of establishment and number of sessions (to February 1967)

	Bulgaria	Czechoslovakia	GDR	Hungary	Mongolia	Poland	Rumania	USSR
Czechoslovakia	1958 (8)							
GDR	1961 (5)	1959 (9)						
Hungary	1958 (6)	1961 (5)	1962 (5)					
Mongolia	—	—	—	1966* (1)				
Poland	1958 (7)	1957 (10)	1960 (7)	1958 (7)	—			
Rumania	1959 (6)	1958 (5)	1963 (2)	1958 (6)	—	1958 (5)		
USSR	1964 (5)	1963 (6)	1965 (2)	1964 (4)	1967 (–)	1964 (4)	1966 (–)	
Yugoslavia	1962 (4)	1963 (3)	1964* (3)	1963 (1)	—	1958 (8)	1964* (2)	1965 (2)

* Date of first session.

not come until October 1966, but that with the GDR was concluded in September 1965. The suicide at that time of the Chairman of the State Planning Commission of the GDR was interpreted as indicative of the division within the government on the treaty and on the cognate agreement on the bilateral relations (notably east German exports of equipment) subsuming the Soviet Five-Year Plan for 1966–70. The commission thus authorized with the GDR met for the first time in June 1966.

Similar bilateral arrangements have been made with Yugoslavia and Mongolia. The Polono-Yugoslav and Bulgaro-Yugoslav relations, however, antedate the present association of Yugoslavia with Comecon: the former were established through a joint committee on industrial planning, authorized in February 1958 (when the Yugoslav example of workers' management was precariously, but enthusiastically, installed in many Polish factories). The committee was raised to a status covering all economic sectors in 1964. The treaty of October 1962 setting up a mixed commission of Bulgaria and Yugoslavia can be seen as a revival of the hopes of 1947. The USSR established a joint committee with Yugoslavia on industrial planning in 1963, and raised it to an Intergovernmental Committee on Economic and Scientific-Technical Co-operation in 1965. Meanwhile, all other Comecon members had signed corresponding treaties; Mongolia signed an agreement on scientific-technical co-operation, and three meetings were held in 1964–6. Hungary—for reasons suggested above (p. 99) —was the first member to convene an economic, scientific, and technical commission with Mongolia (July 1966); the USSR followed in January 1967 (replacing a scientific-technical committee), but somewhat slowly in view of its intimate political relations dating from its treaty of November 1921.[58]

Bilateral committees at the departmental level were started by the Polono-Czechoslovak treaty of 1957, which established a standing joint transport committee (meeting *ad hoc* on a trilateral basis with the GDR on the Danube–Oder canal project); bilateral committees were similarly developed under the other intergovernmental commissions. Here too the USSR did not participate until 1963. Its stated position was that, after its abolition of industrial ministries in 1957, there were

[58] For a brief Soviet review of these relations, see I. Ivanov, *Ekonomicheskoe sotrudnichestvo vzaimopomoshch stran sotsializma* (Moscow, 1962), pp. 188–92.

no formal Soviet counterparts for departmental contact. When industrial committees were fully re-established in November 1962, such arrangements were in fact introduced.[59]

Many of the committees on technical assistance which were among Comecon's first fruits in 1949 still exist as subgroups of the new intergovernmental commissions. Mixed commissions to control the functioning of commercial agreements are also general, and in some instances, e.g. by the Czechoslovak-GDR agreement of 1 June 1960, have terms of reference covering all aspects of trade and payments between the two parties.[60] The network of bilateral contact became, by the additions of 1964, the chief means of reciprocal negotiations on plans, and the main channel for the discussion of economic policy.

The Nineteenth Session, which met in Prague at the end of January 1965, made this relationship clear when it received reports on the conclusion of bilateral agreements for the period 1966–70. The Comecon Secretariat and Commissions are at the service of members for the collation of materials, but the framework for the crucial negotiations are the mixed commissions.

Renewal of dissension

Before the Twentieth Session originally scheduled for July met in Sofia in December, a crisis had arisen in the Warsaw Treaty Organization. The practice of convening meetings of Party Secretaries to discuss the agencies consecutively had been established in 1963 (see p. 110) and a subordinate organizational link may have emerged as early as 1957 (p. 82). Just as the standardization of the national accounts of OEEC members was necessary to determine the economic infrastructure for bearing the shared defence costs of NATO, so plan co-ordination within Comecon must be related to projected participation in military expenditure.

The evolution of the dispute within WTO is, however, of interest as an historical parallel to that in Comecon, pointing to the political tensions that are common to each.

Like Comecon, the Warsaw Treaty was established in the wake of an unsuccessful attempt to create a pan-European system—in this case Soviet calls for a treaty of collective security—and as a public counterstroke to an institutional move by western Europe and the United

[59] K. Olszewski, *N. drogi*, Feb. 1964.   [60] E. Usenko, *Vnesh. torg.*, no. 7, 1962, p. 12.

States—the incorporation of the Federal Republic of Germany into NATO. The signature of the treaty in May 1955—by the same states that were then members of Comecon—took place within a framework of existing bilateral treaties with the USSR—again, as with Comecon in 1949 (see p. 46). For its first six years the Organization had little more than a paper existence, and served only to formalize relations with the dominant partner, who regarded the armed forces of the others as the extension of its own defence system.[61] Measures to integrate the military potential of the treaty were first taken in 1961: the initial resolutions seem to have been passed by its Political Consultative Committee in March 1961, its first meeting of Defence Ministers was held the following September, and its first joint manœuvres in October.[62] In January 1960 the Supreme Soviet had decreed substantial demobilization of the armed forces, motivated in terms of the economic needs by labour shortages, as the smaller cohorts of war-time births entered gainful employment.[63] Khrushchev defended the reduction of military power on the grounds that conventional forces were being replaced by nuclear striking power. This 'modernist' view met with opposition among 'traditionalist' military leaders in the USSR, and the integration of the armed forces of the other Warsaw Treaty members may be seen as intended to appease the 'traditionalist' group by attenuating the effective manpower reduction.[64] Coinciding with serious investment difficulties, the expansion of the industries serving the aero-space sectors presented severe problems of resource allocation.[65] In the Soviet view, this strain could be eased by sharing defence-support costs among other WTO members, and by effectively integrating their armed forces.

In this, as in Comecon, the extreme and opposing views in east Europe were held by the GDR on the one hand and by Rumania on the other. It was the GDR which took the initiative in convening the WTO Political Consultative Committee in January 1965[66] to strengthen the alliance, while it was Rumania which first demonstrated unwillingness to bear the military burden by cutting its nation-

[61] T. Wolfe, *The Evolving Nature of the Warsaw Pact* (Santa Monica, Calif., 1965), RAND Memorandum 4835–PR, p. 3.

[62] Ibid. pp. 7–8. [63] See *Econ. Survey Eur. 1960* (Geneva, 1961), ch. II, p. 37.

[64] Wolfe, p. 12.

[65] On the competition between these sectors and the civilian industries with advanced technologies then chosen for development, see J. Hardt, in Kaser, ed., *St Antony's Papers 19* (Oxford, 1966), pp. 24–30.

[66] According to Kosygin, *Pr.*, 2 Mar. 1965.

al service period in November 1964. In 1965 (and again in 1966) Rumania failed to participate in the annual manœuvres of the Organization (begun in October 1961 in pursuance of integration).[67]

The WTO Political Consultative Committee met just before the Nineteenth Session of Comecon in Prague and a few days after the dispatch of an unpublished letter (dated 4 January 1965) from Gheorghiu-Dej to Brezhnev, in which the Rumanian First Secretary is alleged to have set out his Party's reasons for disapproving the Soviet convocation of the meeting of communist parties on the Sino-Soviet dispute.[68] It revealed that Soviet-Rumanian talks had been held in July–August and in November 1964, that is before and after the replacement of Khrushchev by Kosygin and Brezhnev; it reiterated criticism of 'attempts to integrate the economies of socialist states in ways that would have damaged their independence and sovereignty'. At the WTO meeting, the Rumanian delegation, led by Gheorghiu-Dej, was reported to have sought to moderate the 'new impulse to the struggle against west German militarists and politicians' advocated by the GDR and Poland.[69] Rumania was not anxious to disturb its flourishing trade with the Federal Republic by inflammatory declarations.

The renewal of the 1945 Polono-Soviet Treaty of Friendship and Mutual Assistance, which fell due in April 1965, included the guarantee 'to take jointly all possible measures against the threat of aggression by west German militarism', but provided that the parties would 'consult with each other on all the most important international questions which concern them'.[70] The clause had not figured in the pact of twenty years earlier, and could be seen as a stage in the revision of the Warsaw Treaty towards a genuinely common formulation of policy.

This evolution did not go far enough for Rumania, which, in May 1966, circulated a note to other WTO members calling for the termination of contributions for the support of Soviet troops in eastern Europe and for the withdrawal of such troops; the parallel with French policy on NATO was widely drawn.[71] The First Secretary of the Rumanian Communist Party, Ceausescu,[72] came near to doing so

[67] It nevertheless sent an observer mission in Sept. 1966.

[68] Reported by E. Crankshaw, *The Observer* (London), 15 May 1966.

[69] Report in *The Times*, 21 Jan. 1965; the quotation is from Ulbricht's speech on return to Berlin after the meeting.

[70] Ibid. 13 Apr. 1965. [71] Ibid. 17 and 18 May 1966; *The Sunday Times*, 22 May 1966.

[72] Who had succeeded Gheorghiu-Dej on the latter's death; the title of the Party had also been changed.

himself in a speech in June, advocating the abolition of both WTO and NATO. Just as in the dispute centred on Comecon two years previously, China supported the Rumanian position,[73] and Czechoslovakia sided with the GDR and Poland. In his speeches at the Twenty-third Czechoslovak Party Congress in late May–early June, Novotny stressed that co-operation with the USSR was 'the core of the defence of the entire socialist camp' and Brezhnev the need to accelerate economic specialization and the socialist division of labour.

The division of interests in both Comecon and the WTO brought the GDR and Hungary to a new level of intimacy. The First Secretary of the Hungarian Socialist Workers' Party, Kadar, led a party and government delegation to Berlin in June for discussions which resulted in a joint declaration that the two governments

> stress the objective necessity of enlarging the role played by CMEA and of enhancing the effectiveness of its activity. They affirm their conviction that a higher stage must be reached in organizing voluntary economic co-operation by interested fraternal countries. . . The two sides will make every necessary contribution to further strengthen the WTO as the most important factor for securing the peace of Europe.[74]

The two countries had already tightened their economic collaboration as a consequence of the first crisis in Comecon—by an agreement of May 1964—which had been further fostered by the deterioration of Hungaro-Rumanian relations (over the status of the Magyar minority in Transylvania).[75] Hungary and the GDR are complementary in that the former can work up labour-intensive components or semi-manufactures for those branches of engineering and chemicals which require the heavy outlays of research and skilled manpower which the latter can provide.[76]

Consecutive meetings of Heads of Government and Party First Secretaries took place in Bucharest in July on WTO and on Comecon. The latter's Twentieth Session was postponed until December 1966, but the presence in Bucharest of all but one of the members of the Executive implies that a meeting was held of that body.[77] The com-

[73] Cf. speeches of Chou En-lai during his visit to Rumania in June (ibid. 18 and 21 June 1966).
[74] *Foreign Affairs Bulletin* (of the GDR Ministry for Foreign Affairs), 4 July 1966, p. 150.
[75] 8·4 per cent of the population of Rumania according to the 1966 Census (*Sc.*, 18 Sept. 1966).
[76] On the excessive range of exports in the GDR and Hungary, see I. Vajda, *The Role of Foreign Trade in a Socialist Economy* (Budapest, 1965), pp. 230–2.
[77] See lists of delegations in *Sc.*, 8 July 1966.

muniqué of the 'summit meeting' on Comecon was terse: it said nothing more than that the countries had resolved to co-operate

> in accordance with the principles of full equality of rights, of respect for national sovereignty and interests, of mutual advantage and of comradely aid, and to contribute thereby to the further consolidation of proletarian internationalism and of the unity of the countries of the world socialist system.

But while Ceausescu, at a conference reception, would go no further than a dry statement that there had been 'the occasion for a useful exchange of views on economic collaboration', Ulbricht, in a responding speech, claimed that

> We are happy that our conversations in Bucharest closed in a very friendly mood, and we promise our Rumanian friends that on our return to our countries we will do everything so that our understanding here should be correspondingly achieved.

The conflict of interest was unresolved,[78] and re-emerged at the next WTO meeting (February 1967), after Rumania had opened diplomatic relations with the Federal Republic, in defiance of the GDR.

Shift of authority

But, while statesmen and Party leaders skirmished along their divergent paths in the international political arena, they were divesting themselves of many of their powers over their home economies. The reforms of management which all save the Rumanians ratified during 1964–6 allowed much wider authority in the allocation of current resources to enterprise associations, in a form of state cartelization. Central governments retained considerable powers over the appropriation of investment funds, but even here decision-making was being transferred to the state banking system and to the associations themselves. Conforming to this trend, economic collaboration outside the formal structure of Comecon is increasingly taking the form of the international enterprise or association.

The oldest form of international capital flow was the government-to-government loan: although the credit was usually envisaged for itemized projects, the recipient accepted no responsibility towards the

[78] See particularly a Polish commentary on the October 1966 meeting of the Executive Committee in *Zyc. gos.*, 6 Nov. 1966.

donor for their viability. Repayment was to be from general government revenues. The GDR-Polish agreement of 1957 broke this tradition, with the donor earmarking funds for individual enterprises and the recipient assuring amortization and interest from profits (paid not in cash, but in the product of the plants themselves). Poland was the chief mover in this scheme and subsequently participated in more joint investments than any other Comecon member.

After its pioneering investment of German and Czechoslovak funds in its coal-mining and sulphur, it took a $125 m. credit from Czechoslovakia in 1961 to develop copper-mining and chemicals production. In the other direction, it is investing $77 m. in fertilizer plant in the USSR (for potash and, with Bulgaria, GDR, Hungary, and Poland, phosphate).[79] Czechoslovakia has an investment in Bulgarian copper-mining and a substantial stake ($280 m.) in Soviet non-ferrous mining under a 1960 agreement, but its major investment is of $550 m. in Siberian oil (with repayments in oil) arranged in 1966; other members of Comecon were considering in early 1967 similar loans for the development of Soviet raw materials,[80] demanded by the USSR for supplies to continue after it had accepted serious price cuts for its primary exports to members (see p. 185). The price of Soviet oil delivered to Czechoslovakia is now down to the c.i.f. price of Arabian crude. An arrangement for the USSR to process Hungarian alumina involves no international finance.

In all joint investments the plant developed remained the property of the recipient. An entirely novel form is represented by the joint enterprise, the ownership of which is pooled. In this field Hungary has been the leader with the Hungarian-Polish Haldex Corporation (a joint-stock company in Katowice since 1959) to briquette coal slack. In December 1964 Hungary set up two joint enterprises with Bulgaria. Agromash, with head office in Budapest, operates engineering plants for the manufacture of equipment for market gardening, viticulture, and fruit-growing. It has an autonomous Board which, 'differing from other similar organizations, does not recommend, but takes decisions which are compulsory for the two countries.'[81]

[79] See H. Unger, *Der Handelsdünger im Comecon* (Kiel, 1965), p. 20.

[80] *Soviet News*, 11 Jan. 1967. Simunek's report on this agreement (*RP*, 20 Jan. 1967) envisaged Czechoslovak investment in other members' deposits of aluminium, copper, lead, tin, and zinc.

[81] B. Berec, Hungarian Deputy Minister for Engineering, *Rab. delo*, 28 May 1965. For details of both companies see ibid. 23 Dec. 1964.

Intransmash is not a producer, but a design and supply agency for intra-factory transportation and hoisting equipment. A similar joint design office—though without the brokerage functions—has been established by Poland and Czechoslovakia to develop new tractor designs.[82] Such joint enterprises led to a willingness to entertain similar propositions from western corporations, stopping short only of equity participation. Although the first and biggest project—that of Krupps in Poland—fell through, a number of schemes seem likely to materialize: in a visit to London in 1966 the Rumanian Deputy Prime Minister, Birladeanu, emphasized that his government would welcome such offers from western firms.[83]

On a still larger scale, though without merging ownership, 'interested' Comecon members have set up international associations. Intermetall was originally conceived as a programming centre for Central European rolling mills: it came to life in 1964 as a capacity-allocation agency of all Comecon members save Rumania and Mongolia. Poland led the majority resistance at the twenty-fifth session of the Ferrous Metals Commission (January 1967) when Rumania protested at the inclusion on the agenda of an Intermetall scheme for joint investment. The Polish delegation termed this 'an arbitrary interpretation of the Charter', and pointed out that Rumania might wish later to co-operate on some specific question in spite of not showing previous interest.[84] The Organization for Co-operation in the Ball-bearing Industry, also set up in 1964, similarly rationalizes the use of capacity: its operation has permitted Hungary to reduce the sizes and types of ball-bearings it produces by two-thirds. It has recently formulated a corresponding scheme for roller bearings. If Rumania (and Mongolia) were to participate the association could be formally within the agency, but, under present conditions, this is unlikely for production plants. One brokerage agency was, however, created in 1963, the Bureau for the Co-ordination of Ship Charters; and the more optimistic members hope that it might prove possible to 'organize collective foreign-trade agencies to co-ordinate CMEA countries' activities in the world market.'[85] Reporting to the Sejm on Comecon affairs, the Deputy Chairman of the Polish Committee for Foreign Economic Relations observed that 'the new conditions in socialist markets . . .

[82] Sokolov and Shiryaev, *Int. Aff.*, no. 1, 1966, p. 44. [83] *The Times*, 10 Feb. 1966.
[84] Inferred from J. Cierpikowski, Radio Warsaw, 7 Feb. 1967.
[85] Sokolov and Shiryaev, p. 44.

require the establishment and strengthening of direct contacts between industrial and commercial organizations on concrete matters.'[86] The emergence of the big firm within Comecon members is not only significant as the form of international co-operation typical of a Common Market; it mirrors the enterprise and its environment in the countries themselves.

[86] K. Olszewski, *Tryb. Ludu*, 29 Jan. 1967.

Part II

ACHIEVEMENTS AND PROSPECTS

VII
TRADE

Output and trade

COMECON's first choice on the direction of its trade was registered in its founding communiqué: 'to establish . . . wider economic co-operation between the countries of people's democracy and the USSR'. Autarky as a group was partly dictated by the international tension which marked the first five years of its existence, but within the association trade seems to have developed rather less rapidly in relation to the growth of production than in any other of the world's economic groups. The national index-numbers of industrial production cannot be certainly compared with those of western Europe, but if Comecon's share of world industry in 1962 (when it faced its major crisis on integration) was about 30 per cent, the rise in their official index-numbers since 1949 implies that when Comecon was established, their aggregate was just on 16 per cent. Comecon members then had 7 per cent of world trade, and in 1962 11 per cent. There are some reservations on trade values which indicate that the rise would be less if measured at the prices ruling in the rest of world trade. The inflation—relatively to measurement in the indices for the rest of the world—of industrial growth doubtless exceeds the discount properly applicable to the trade figures, but not to the extent of showing a trade rise for Comecon as fast as for the rest of the world relative to the industrial growth of each. Of the turnover amounting to 11 per cent of world commerce, two-thirds was among Comecon members themselves, and the group's trade on other markets was hence less than 4 per cent of the total.

The international comparison of production is obviously more difficult than that of trade, but some indication of the magnitude of Comecon production is necessary to describe the degree of its dependence on trade. Estimates of the two standard aggregates of output of industry and gross national product for the world other than Comecon and the Asian socialist countries have for some years been made by the United Nations Statistical Office.[1] In 1964 it also pub-

[1] UN, *Yb. of Nat. Accounts Statist. 1965* (1966), pp. 493–503.

lished an estimate of industrial production in Comecon. Two sets of estimates may also be made for Comecon national products in values roughly comparable with those for the rest of the world. The first is based upon estimates of the gross national product (GNP) of each country in local currencies converted at the official exchange rate applicable to tourist transactions (which is intended, without much accuracy, to reflect purchasing-power parity for common consumers' goods and services). The second procedure follows a Hungarian technique (pioneered by Janossy) of fitting physical indicators of the level of consumption in eastern Europe to the relationship of such indicators to GNP in western countries.[2] Each method—and refinements thereof—has been used by both eastern and western statisticians; their results diverge considerably in their comparisons both with western levels and among Comecon members. Some description of the measures and of their widely different results is hence necessary as a preface to the tentative conclusions on trade dependence.

A standard of comparison outside the group is needed to assess the degree of trade dependence not only for alignment with western ratios, but because all members show their commerce at 'world market' prices, i.e. roughly those ruling between capitalist countries. Relationships within the group are particularly significant in assessing the obstacles to integration set by differences in economic development—a problem examined in Chapter X.

Direct comparison of official national accounts is inhibited in the majority of Comecon countries by restriction of published data to net material product (NMP), falling short of GNP by allowances for depreciation and by the value of 'non-productive services.'[3] Within this Marxian definition of national income, the Central Statistical Administration of the USSR has computed Soviet product per head in 1964 as $885, converting its rouble value at the official exchange-rate (at what it terms 'comparable prices', its estimate was $1,013). Using the same definition, a Czech adaptation (published by Novozamsky) of Janossy's method, avoiding rouble valuations, has shown

[2] For the calculations in the present chapter the starting-point for the first method was a Soviet estimate of product (NMP) in dollars (published annually in the official statistical abstract), and for the second, F. Janossy, *A gazdasagi fejlettseg merhetosege es uj meresi modszere* (Budapest, 1963).

[3] Practice varies among Comecon members on the definition of NMF; for reviews of these, and comparison with western practice, see the present author in, *Income and Wealth*, IX (London, 1961); and *Econ. B. Eur.*, xi/1.

Soviet income for the same year as $630.[4] A 40 per cent margin thus separates the results of the two techniques when applied to the USSR. The two basic methods have been applied to eastern European statistics within the production boundary of GNP by Ernst and Beckerman respectively.[5] Ernst calculated GNP for six countries of eastern Europe

Per Capita Income in 1964
(*Dollars*)

	Ernst	*Novozamsky–Janossy*	
	GNP	*NMP*	*Enlarged to GNP**
Bulgaria	690	469	..
Czechoslovakia	1,470	813	960
GDR	1,400	844	1,080
Hungary	1,020	513	610
Poland	890	498	590
Rumania	680	423	570
USSR	1,184†	630	770
FR Germany	1,980	..	..

* By application of percentage of depreciation and non-productive services to NMP for latest available year estimated in the following sources: T. Alton, *Czechoslovak National Income and Product, 1947–1948 and 1955–1956* (New York, 1962), pp. 74 and 234 (18 per cent margin in 1955); W. Stolper, *The Structure of the East German Economy* (Cambridge, Mass., 1960), pp. 418 and 419 (28 per cent margin in 1957); T. Alton, *Hungarian National Income and Product in 1955* (New York, 1963), p. 93 (19 per cent margin in 1955) and *Polish National Income and Product in 1954, 1955, and 1956* (New York, 1965), pp. 58 and 95 (19 per cent margin in 1956); M. Kaser, 'An Estimate of the National Accounts of Rumania Following Both Eastern and Western Definitions, *Sov. Stud.*, July 1966, pp. 88–89 (34 per cent margin in 1961); A. Bergson, *The Economics of Soviet Planning* (New Haven, 1964), pp. 365–6 (23 per cent margin in 1960).

† Cohn, *New Directions*, p. 108 ($1,289), adjusted to Ernst's West German standard on respective estimates of FR Germany.

[4] J. Novozamsky, *Pol. Ek.*, no. 8, 1966, p. 731. He points out that the estimate is 'closer to national income utilized than to national income produced'. The Soviet figure for income produced (cited above) exceeded that for income utilized by less than 1 per cent (*Narodnoe khozyaistvo SSSR v 1964 godu* (Moscow, 1965), pp. 89 and 578). The difference is thus almost wholly attributable to the techniques of measurement.

[5] M. Ernst, in US Congress, Joint Economic Committee, *New Directions in the Soviet Economy* (Washington, D.C., 1966), pp. 873–916 (this source is subsequently cited as *New Directions*); W. Beckerman and R. Bacon, *Econ. J.*, Sept. 1966, pp. 519–36, based on techniques (developed independently of Janossy) set out in W. Beckerman, *International Comparisons of Real Incomes* (Paris, OECD, 1966). Ernst confined his estimates to eastern Europe, but a corresponding calculation for the USSR by S. Cohn was also published in *New Directions* (pp. 99–132) following accounts set up by M. Bornstein, *Soviet National Accounts for 1955* (Ann Arbor, Mich., 1961).

(other than the USSR), converting the branch components of production valued in national currencies to the purchasing power of the western German Deutschmark in 1955. Comparison of Ernst's results with those of Novozamsky–Janossy requires enlargement of the latter by the value of depreciation and non-productive services. While the adjustments shown in the table on p. 135 are subject to considerable reservation, the latter fall short of the former by between one-third and one-fifth.

A final comparison may be made between estimates of eastern European consumption also in relation to western Germany. Ernst's calculations were of commodity samples in physical units weighted by west German prices. Beckerman's method was the same as Janossy's, save that he regressed physical indicators on the values of real consumption in selected western countries derived on the Gilbert–Kravis method.[6] Beckerman's results show a lower per capita consumption in Hungary in 1960 than those of Janossy (who, as stated, regressed on values compared at official exchange-rates), and are both lower and more dispersed than those of Ernst:

Comparative Levels of Personal Consumption per Capita in 1960

(FR Germany = 100)

	Ernst	*Beckerman*
Czechoslovakia	63	58
GDR	68	44
Hungary	49	24
Poland	42	26

The wide disparities between measures of Comecon production in relation to that of the rest of the world hence furnish a severe caveat on the comparisons which follow; the difficulties of deflation add to the

[6] M. Gilbert and I. Kravis, *An International Comparison of National Products and the Purchasing Power of Currencies* (Paris, OECD, 1954). The Gilbert–Kravis method has been used by Ya. Kotkovsky and others, *Sopostavlenie urovnei ekonomickeskogo razvitiya sotsialisticheskikh stran* (Moscow, 1965), whose results are close to those shown by J. Smilek, *Hosp. nov.*, no. 29, 1966, p. 3; neither, however, provides a link with a western country and their results here are shown only in Table 7 (on intra-Comecon comparisons). Kotkovsky, *Vopr. ekon.*, no. 8, 1966, pp. 80–91, has reviewed in detail work in Comecon on international comparisons, particularly that of its Working Parties on National Income and on Accounting, and conferences in Budapest in 1961 and in Moscow in February 1966. See also A. Mod, L. Drechsler, D. Silady, *The Standard of Living: Some Problems of Analysis and of International Comparison* (Budapest, 1962).

caution with which aggregated national time-series can be used. On the growth rate shown in the official statistics of Comecon countries, industrial production in Comecon states in 1949 would have been almost 16 per cent of the world total; the countries of the Commonwealth (both independent and colonial) made in 1948 some 17 per cent of world output. At the same time OEEC could aggregate 26 per cent of world industry. The two groups which were to become the EEC and EFTA almost divided OEEC industry between them: the Inner Six (EEC) accounted for 11 per cent of the world total and the Outer Seven (EFTA) produced almost 12 per cent, the United Kingdom alone representing just under 10 per cent of world output. Comecon industrial production was thus smaller than that of OEEC, but considerably more than that of the future EFTA, and almost half as much again as that of the eventual Common Market. The USSR by itself would have been producing as much as the EFTA group.

The 1962 share of Comecon members was some 30 per cent (on the UN estimates, 27 per cent in 1958). The rise in the share would not be as fast if the output index of the USSR (vastly the biggest industrial contributor to Comecon) were computed by alternative methods. If the end-year proportion is valid, but the index working it back to 1949 is exaggerated, the Comecon share at its creation would have been higher than the 16 per cent suggested above.

Soviet industrial output—on the official index—rose 3¾ times between 1949 and 1960 (from a world share of an estimated 12 per cent); that of the other members of Comecon was in aggregate faster—just over 4½ times—but from a world share of, say, 4 per cent. In sum, their proportion was thus brought up to about 29 per cent of world industry in 1960. During that period the Commonwealth share dropped to 13 per cent, and in Europe the output of EEC—the most dynamic—expanded to 15 per cent, while EFTA, largely because of slow British development, declined to 10 per cent.

These calculations take Comecon as it stood in the period covered, thus ignoring the replacement of Albania by Mongolia in 1962. The 'world', moreover, excludes China (and North Korea, North Vietnam, and Mongolia) because output data are not available.

The United Nations Statistical Office has also computed, for the world other than the socialist group, estimates of gross national products in 1958 at the foreign-exchange rate to the United States dollar.

The shortcomings of such figures are, conceptually and statistically, much greater than those of the industrial-production aggregates from the same Office. The Soviet statistical administration has published a calculation apparently on the same basis, but the relationship of its domestic prices to the exchange rate exaggerates its share. With the GNPs of other Comecon members converted at tourist exchange-rates (in a reflexion of purchasing power which does not hold good for the commercial rates), Comecon's share of world GNP would have been 21 per cent in 1958. On an alternative calculation—based on Janossy's method which, as stated, avoids prices so far as the Comecon magnitude is concerned—the 1960 aggregate was only 13 per cent. The United Nations estimates for 1958 show for the two largest trade-preferential areas, the Commonwealth and the EEC, shares of approximately 13 per cent. The less-than-1 per cent of world output attributable to the EEC Associates—then, the independent states of the former French colonial empire plus the Congo and Somalia—would edge that group slightly above the Commonwealth, but the estimates are too uncertain for such fine ranking. EFTA was well behind with 8 per cent of world product.

The Comecon proportion in the United Nations estimate of industrial output and the analogous procedure for GNP is without doubt inflated, but its greater share in world industry than in production of all goods and services—in 1960 estimated at 29 per cent for the former and 22 per cent for the latter—is obviously attributable to governmental policies driving ahead with industry and neglecting agriculture. That industrialization which Stalin directed was, moreover, one of autarky.

> Our industry is based on the home market. In this respect the economic development of our country resembles that of the United States, whose industry grew up on the basis of the home market, in contrast to Britain, whose industry is primarily based on foreign markets. There are a number of branches of industry in Britain forty or fifty per cent of whose output is for foreign markets. America, on the contrary, still relies on its home market, exporting to foreign markets not more than ten or twelve per cent of her output. The industry of our country will rely upon the home market—primarily the peasant market—to an even greater degree than American industry does.[7]

[7] J. Stalin, 'On the Economic Situation of the Soviet Union and Party Policy' (speech of 13 Apr. 1926), *Works*, viii. 131.

An examination of the extent to which this injunction still holds involves, in addition to the vast uncertainties of international output comparisons, the slighter problems of trade valuation. As Chapter IX shows, Comecon intra-trade has never been carried on in exact concordance with world prices. No documented assertion is possible (by the recalculation of Comecon trade at world unit-values) because the national commodity breakdowns by group of trade partner are not available for all countries and for all years (least of all for 1950–5). From 1949 until 1956 or 1957, exchanges within the group almost certainly took place at below the world level; since 1958 they have probably been higher. Thus Comecon's rise is somewhat overstated in the comparisons made below between 1949 and 1960 or 1962, which assume equality of prices in intra-trade, East–West trade, and trade among non-members. The rough calculations of trade dependence in a recent year (1960–2) also show percentages for Comecon members which are higher than they would have been if intra-trade had been priced at the level ruling in their outside trade. Finally, the analysis of the direction of Comecon trade reflects a somewhat inflated value of intra-trade.

A useful indicator of trade dependence is the percentage of GNP represented by the sum of imports and exports (viz. trade turnover). It provides some way of assessing the importance of foreign transactions in the domestic economy, but its significance will vary from country to country with the proportion of re-exports to exports and with the degree to which imports are worked up for export. If the relative price inflation in the value of Comecon trade was 10 per cent —and the few demonstrations that have been made do not show a margin less than this magnitude—the trade turnover of members other than the USSR was in 1962 about one-third, and of the Soviet Union about one-eighth, of GNP at the lower of the two estimates noted above. Thus, at most, the trade dependence of the area, excluding the special case of the USSR, was close to that of the EEC (33 per cent in 1962) and less than that of EFTA (39 per cent, but 48 per cent if the United Kingdom is excluded). The Comecon traded share thus shown is an upper limit, but a more realistic figure cannot be determined.

TABLE I

Foreign Trade per Capita in Comecon, EEC, and EFTA

(US $: imports *plus* exports)

Countries ranked by 1962 order

*Comecon**	*1950*	*1955*	*1961*	*1962*	*1965*
Soviet Union	17	32	54	61	71
Rumania	28	50	86	94	115
Poland	52	67	105	117	145
Bulgaria	34	64	166	194	287
Hungary	68	115	200	223	299
GDR	47	135	259	276	376
Czechoslovakia	113	148	292	308	379
Total	28	49	87	100	121

EEC	*1962*	*1965*	*EFTA*	*1962*	*1965*
Italy	209	282	Portugal	107	162
France	317	417	Austria	395	510
FR Germany	469	599	UK	442	530
Netherlands	842	1,127	Norway	722	979
Belgium and Luxembourg	931	1,297	Sweden	798	1,080
			Denmark	814	1,081
			Switzerland	925	1,120
Total	399	533	Total	486	621

* Albania: 1961–71, 1964–90.
Mongolia (excl. imports on credit): 1960–169.

Sources: 1950–61: J. Novozamsky, *Vyrovnavani ekonomicke urovne zemi RVHP* (Prague, 1964), p. 101 (imports and exports at 'frontier parity'); 1962–5: UN, *Statist. Yb.* 1963 and *Monthly B. Statist.*, June 1966 (imports c.i.f. and exports f.o.b.).

From Table 1 it may be seen that the spread between the least and the most trade-dependent is slightly wider in Comecon (Czechoslovakia is 5 times the USSR) than within EEC (the Belgium–Luxemburg Economic Union is 4½ times Italy); it is narrower than that shown inside EFTA (Switzerland is 7 times Portugal), although if Portugal is excluded EFTA forms a more homogeneous group with a spread of 2·2.

For Comecon as a whole, the average trade per capita is brought down by the low trade dependence of the USSR; the membership changes of 1962—withdrawal of Albania and entry of Mongolia—would raise the average (see note to Table 1). A more significant group, given the special situation of the USSR, would comprise the present European members: their turnover per capita in 1962 was \$190—that is, rather less than the trade of the USA (\$202), which embodies relative external autarky with intensive internal commerce. When Comecon was founded, its members' share of industrial output, on estimates certainly inflating the proportion, was 16 per cent: their share in world trade was 7 per cent—or about the same as it had been before the outbreak of war (8½ per cent in 1938). By 1960 Comecon's share was 29 per cent in industry and 22 per cent in total world output (on the overstated United Nations figures), and 13 per cent on a minimal calculation: its trade was 10 per cent; in the year when regional autarky was being seriously pressed on Comecon its percentage was 11 per cent of world trade.[8] For the centrally-planned economies as a whole, the still greater autarky of China (\$6 trade turnover per head in 1959, the latest available year), widens this divergence: a 1960 share of 37 per cent in industrial production was accompanied by one of 9 per cent in all trade and of 10 per cent in trade in industrial goods. The latter comparison makes some allowance for the smaller share of farm produce in Comecon trade—partly because of the continuance of large rural populations and partly because agricultural self-sufficiency is deliberately sought. The inclusion of China is appropriate, given the contemporary exports to it of machinery and other manufactured goods by Comecon members. The 10 per cent of world trade in manufactures flowing within the socialist group (Comecon plus the four Asian states), compares with 66 per cent taking place within the industrially-developed countries. These market economies produced all but 10 per cent of the remainder of world output.

One of the factors within the strictly economic mechanism making for this self-sufficiency has already been discussed in Chapter III—namely, the intrinsic preference for domestic supplies under 'material-balance' techniques. Chapter IX describes the difficulties of measuring

[8] The trade statistics in this section were derived from the same sources as for Table 1, together with UN, *Yb. Internat. Trade Statist., 1960*; OECD, *Overall Trade by Countries*, Feb. 1962; and OEEC, *Statist. Bs*, Series 1: *Foreign Trade*.

comparative costs when the set of home prices used by planning offices and by enterprise managers far from coincides with the pattern ruling in foreign trade.

Trade expansion within Comecon

Paradoxically, the present state of Comecon affairs may be attributable more to its success in fostering the expansion of production than to its shortcomings in finding ways of optimizing the share of trade in that growing output. The absolute freedom of technological intercourse must have been an important contributor to the rise in industrial output. Measurements of the effect of technical progress are still in an exploratory stage, but the figures quoted below (pp. 156–7) for exchanges of technical documentation imply that benefit was gained by all.

This facet of Comecon's achievement is taken up in the next chapter, but even within the trade aspect, Comecon's record is by no means one of failure. The domestic policies ruling in 1949 were evidently an obstacle to 'organizing wider economic co-operation between the countries of people's democracy and the USSR' which the founding conference had set as Comecon's chief aim, but the cuts in trade with non-members were more than replaced by intra-regional flows. In 1948 45 per cent of Comecon trade was among member countries themselves. From then until 1954 this intra-trade rose 3·12 times in value and, if price experience was the same as in western Europe (a decline in unit value to 87 per cent of the 1948 level), 3·58 times in volume. An exact breakdown among all Comecon members will not be possible until Soviet and Rumanian data for the period are published, but, on the basis of statistics from the other countries and an estimate for Soviet-Rumanian trade, the value of trade between members rose 3·3 times from 1948 to 1954, and, on the same price assumption, 3·8 times in volume. Trade with western Europe reached a peak in 1949 but thereafter was rapidly retrenched: exports from Comecon members were by 1952 at a nadir of three-quarters of that peak (well below a third of the 1938 volume).

By comparison, within a substantial expansion of trade with the rest of the world, exports among OEEC members in the same period rose 2·25 times in volume and in Europe other than Comecon intra-trade rose 1·96 times. Over the same period world exports other than from Comecon members[9] increased only 1·48 times. Intra-Comecon dynamism continued after 1954 when East–West trade was increasing and when, as described in Chapter IV, Comecon resumed an active part in trade policy. In the second six years—1954 to 1960—intra-trade rose 1·75 times in value (1·71 times in volume if the 2 per cent western European unit-price rise was paralleled in Comecon transactions), and 1·80 times (1·76 times in the constant prices assumed above) if trade with the USSR is excluded. These increments are proportionately greater than was shown for trade within Europe other than Comecon (1·63 times in volume), within OEEC (1·61 times), or for the world other than Comecon (1·47 times).

For the period as a whole, that is from the year preceding Comecon's foundation to the latest available year, 1965, trade with other members has risen 9 times in current prices, against a sextupling with all partners (see Table 2, p. 144). Quantum index-numbers compiled by Ernst show that by 1964 Bulgaria, Czechoslovakia, Hungary, Poland, and Rumania imported considerably more in relation to their national products than before the war, but that the GDR was less dependent on trade than in the corresponding area of the German Reich in 1936, if allowance is made for intra-national commerce. For all these states the postwar increase in trade dependence dates from around 1955.[10]

The expansion of commerce within Comecon can fairly be attributed to the existence of the agency itself, since governments from the very first chose its Sessions to negotiate long-term trade agreements and, from as early as its Fourth Session (1954), discussed production specialization. Significant progress in intra-product specialization—agreements to divide Comecon production of types of a given product—started at the Seventh Session (1956) and is further examined in the next chapter.

Direction of Comecon trade

Three tables illustrate the salient features of the group's trade. Table 2 shows the distribution by the trading regions most important for Comecon. Exchanges with other members rose from the 45 per cent of their total turnover already cited for 1948 to a peak of 65 per cent

[9] As elsewhere in this chapter, 'world' excludes China, North Korea, and Mongolia because full trade and output data are not available.

[10] Ernst, p. 900.

TABLE 2

Direction of Comecon Trade, 1948–65

(US $ m.: exports f.o.b.)

Year	*Comecon partners*	*China &c.**	*Intra-German trade*	*EEC*	*EFTA*	*USA*	*Under-developed areas*	*World*
1948	1,405	150	†	330	600	115	195	3,170‡
1950	2,535	490	79	235	440	85	231	4,220
1951	3,240	705	35	280	590	70	165	5,380
1952	3,750	860	33	300	550	40	175	6,100
1953	4,340	1,080	70	275	460	37	170	6,850
1954	4,650	1,190	105	350	485	41	260	7,500
1955	4,750	1,190	136	435	625	60	385	7,990
1956	4,830	1,210	154	580	650	65	470	8,590
1957	5,930	1,010	205	635	665	55	570	9,800
1958	6,060	1,220	211	695	620	70	710	10,310
1959	7,380	1,520	230	820	770	75	690	12,230
1960	8,080	1,380	241	930	880	78	830	13,220
1961	9,000	800	219	1,040	970	79	1,390	14,340
1962	10,170	630	210	1,130	940	79	1,560	15,980
1963	11,050	580	242	1,240	1,010	89	1,820	17,220
1964	11,960	560	264	1,330	1,140	105	1,890	18,740
1965	12,520	690	315	1,430	1,250	135	2,070	19,945

* Mongolia, North Korea, North Vietnam.

† Not available in either UN or German statistical abstracts.

‡ Excl. intra-German trade; a rough estimate is included in the index computed in the text (p. 143), based on ECE calculations in *Econ. B. Eur.*, i/3, p. 43.

Note: In Tables 2 and 3 entries for groups of countries (and for the UK in Table 3) are rounded to the nearest $5 m.

Source: UN, *Statist. Ybs 1948* to *1965*.

in 1953. This subdivides in almost equal proportions into a rise from 24 to 31 per cent for intra-trade other than with the USSR and from 26 to 40 per cent for members' trade with the USSR (the peak for which was 42 per cent in 1954). The share of exchanges with the Soviet Union varied inversely with the degree of industrialization: at this time Albania, Bulgaria, and Rumania reached maxima of Soviet orientation at around 60 per cent of their trade, whereas Czechoslovakia, Hungary, and Poland never exchanged more than 40 per cent of their turnover with the USSR; by reason of its political dependence, the GDR share was higher than that of the latter group, attaining a peak of 47 per cent. Trade with the rest of the world comprised an increase with China and a decrease with western Europe and the United States, in all cases both absolutely and relatively. Trade with the underdeveloped areas fell off less rapidly to 1953 because Comecon remained dependent on these areas for raw materials. Between 1953 and 1960 all major groups of partners took more of Comecon trade. Despite fears about the effect of the Common Market—formally expressed by the USSR in 1957 and which contributed in themselves to the Comecon policy of separate integration—exports to both EEC and EFTA have continued to rise. In 1960 the Sino-Soviet dispute led to a decline in trade with China, and the efforts of the GDR to free itself from dependence on the Federal Republic brought a fall in intra-German commerce. On the other hand, a very rapid rise, substantially financed by credits, took place in exports to underdeveloped countries. In 1963 64·2 per cent of their exports went to other members, but this proved to be the peak. In 1964 the share of intra-trade began to decline and in 1965 was 62·8 per cent.[11]

The reverse flows of trade, i.e. imports into Comecon, are not tabulated. Two groups of partners have had unbalanced trade by virtue of loans. Soviet credits began to be made to underdeveloped countries of Asia and Africa in 1954 and, as just observed, these, together with loans from other Comecon states, have risen rapidly in recent years. The USSR financed deliveries to China by loans in 1950 and 1954, but since 1957 repayments have swung the balance of trade in the opposite direction and by the end of 1965 China had repaid its debts. Trade is also unbalanced within the Sterling Area (see Table 3). Exports from Comecon to the United Kingdom are largely to finance purchases from the rest of the Sterling Area—notably rubber from Malaysia and wool from Australia. Comecon turnover in 1962 with the United Kingdom separately was 2½ times that of 1948. Table 4 (p. 147) provides a detailed breakdown of United Kingdom and United States trade by Comecon member.

As is evident from Table 2, the fall in trade with China has been drastic. According to the Peking *People's Daily* in July 1963, the Soviet Union on 16 July 1960 suddenly notified the Chinese government of its decision

to withdraw all the 1300 and more Soviet experts in China within a month,

[11] For a discussion of this in connexion with similar trends in EFTA and EEC, see the present writer, *The World Today*, Mar. 1966, pp. 100–6.

TABLE 3

Comecon Trade with UK and Sterling Area, 1948–65

(US $ m.: exports f.o.b.)

Year	*Exports from Comecon to*		*Exports to Comecon from*	
	UK	*Rest of Sterling Area*	*UK*	*Rest of Sterling Area*
1948	220	65	85	195
1950	185	60	70	170
1951	255	70	45	205
1952	240	45	45	105
1953	210	45	45	125
1954	225	45	70	140
1955	305	80	105	145
1956	290	145	125	175
1957	305	215	160	265
1958	275	260	125	275
1959	330	210	170	395
1960	390	220	215	425
1961	440	335	295	405
1962	430	380	315	490
1963	465	540	340	580
1964	530	570	280	710
1965	580	590	315	700

Source: UN, *Statist. Yb.* and direct communication from UN Statistical Office.

to scrap the hundreds of agreements and contracts it had signed, and to discontinue supplies of many important items of equipment and materials [which] inflicted incalculable difficulties and losses on China's economy.[12]

Contrariwise, *Pravda* at the same time claimed that

The statistics show that in the course of the past three years the Chinese People's Republic cut the volume of its trade with the countries of the socialist community by more than 50 per cent. Some socialist countries felt the results of this line adopted by the Chinese comrades with particular sharpness. The actions of the Chinese leadership stand in glaring contradiction not only to the principles of mutual relations between socialist countries, but in many cases even to the generally recognized rules and norms which should be observed by all states.[13]

The same considerations affected the curtailment of Comecon exchanges with Albania, which switched its imports from the USSR to China; as described above (p. 99), China came to the same im-

[12] *Peking R.*, 26 July 1963 (J. Gittings, *The Sino-Soviet Dispute, 1956–63*, Chatham House memo. Feb. 1964, p. 52). [13] *Pr.*, 14 July 1963.

TABLE 4

Comecon Members' Trade with UK & USA, 1962

(US $ thous.: imports c.i.f., exports f.o.b.)

	Exports from Comecon to		*Exports to Comecon from*	
	UK	*USA*	*UK*	*USA*
Albania	355	124	60	—
Bulgaria	9,342	1,166	3,407	33
Czechoslovakia	37,053	9,935	36,153	6,992
GDR	18,489	3,003	20,133	1,698
Hungary	13,371	1,678	18,992	835
Poland	107,768	45,589	90,862	94,415
Rumania	19,801	609	23,461	802
USSR	235,524	16,357	117,443	20,062
Total	441,703	78,461	310,511	124,837

Source: OECD, *Statist. Bs*, Series C, Suppl. Jan.–Dec. 1962.

portance in Albanian trade as the Soviet Union had previously occupied. The Albanian Finance Minister claimed at the end of 1962 that 'it is perfectly clear that the economic blockade against our country created a series of problems for our foreign trade. But in general our economy has secured imports of all the materials and commodities we needed.'[14]

The origins of the trade cuts with Albania and China were strictly political, but the economic repercussion has been to heighten Comecon interest in sales of the type of goods in demand by underdeveloped countries.

Commodity composition

In commerce with western Europe, Comecon members as a group chiefly sell raw materials for industry to the EEC and EFTA. The predominance of this product-class is larger in exports to the former than to the latter, because EFTA has, notably in Sweden, a more parallel, and hence competitive, resource endowment. The return flow from the western groups is almost as heavily weighted by manufactures, especially machinery and equipment, but the position of the two western groups is reversed, with the share of this class of goods higher

[14] *Zer. pop.*, 26 Dec. 1962.

in EFTA exports to Comecon than from EEC to Comecon. Foodstuffs are the same large share of Comecon exports to EEC as to EFTA, and, unlike the other two major product groups (shown in Table 5, p. 151), exhibit virtually no return flow from the west within the same commodity class.

The elimination of all internal tariffs within EFTA (at the beginning of 1967) and EEC (in 1968) should, in principle, little affect the dominant commodity pattern of East–West trade. Only a very few primary goods (assimilated to the manufactures group) are covered by the EFTA reduction, the participants of which moreover have an incentive to reduce existing tariffs on materials in order to gain competitive advantage within EFTA on manufactures incorporating imports from outside the group. The EEC Common External Tariff will effect a net reduction in the average duty on raw materials. The common agricultural policy in effect permits the conclusion of bilateral quota agreement with individual eastern European countries on foodstuff imports, an arrangement which for manufactures is reserved to the Community under the 'EEC Clause' in existing treaties (other than French) with eastern Europe. Within the widened markets of both EEC and EFTA, the enhanced competitiveness of the capital-good sectors should ensure better terms of trade for a Comecon wishing to continue the present commodity-exchange pattern.

In the long run, however, such perpetuation is neither desirable nor feasible on the part of Comecon. Growing industrialization is altering product availability (in cost and resource terms) towards the western European pattern of predominant exports of manufactures and imports of foodstuffs and raw materials. An American calculation demonstrates the proximity of eastern and western percentage shares of industry and construction in GNP:

	1964		*1963*
GDR	54	FR Germany	53
Czechoslovakia	52	France	48
Soviet Union	43	United Kingdom	47
Poland	41	Italy	44
Hungary	40	Japan	42
Bulgaria	39	United States	37

Sources: Ernst, *New Dimensions*, p. 878, and Cohn, ibid. p. 110.

A recent Czechoslovak study by Smilek describes the difficulties arising from an industrialization process, the leading sector of which has been engineering, in the following percentages for 1964:

	Industrial output in NMP	*Engineering in industrial output*
Bulgaria	46·2	15·5
Czechoslovakia	65·7	31·4
GDR	65·0	35·6
Hungary	63·6	27·5
Poland	52·0	24·6
Rumania	47·8	28·2
Soviet Union	53·3	26·0

Source: J. Smilek, *Hosp. nov.*, no. 29, 1966, p. 3.

In 1950 the engineering percentages had been as low as 2·9 in Poland, 9·2 in Bulgaria, and 13·3 in Rumania. Thus the members who were initially least developed rapidly increased their sales of engineering goods on the markets of the more developed—an exchange promoted by Comecon specialization agreements. The lag in the corresponding expansion of primary products (agriculture and the extractive industries) diminished the scope for trade in such goods, and, in all but two countries, reliance on fellow-members for these classes of commodity has declined, as the following data show.

	Percentage share of			
	Engineering goods in total exports to other Comecon members		*Raw materials in total imports from other Comecon members*	
	1955	*1965*	*1955*	*1965*
Bulgaria	2·8	29·9	39·9	45·0
Czechoslovakia	51·1	56·3	75·6	59·3
GDR	53·6	58·6	82·9	78·6
Hungary	37·6	42·8	74·6	59·2
Poland	17·4	48·7	50·8	48·0
Rumania	6·1	24·5	50·5	51·5
Soviet Union	17·3	18·0	47·7	31·6

Source: Smilek, p. 3.

The USSR has in effect 'rescued' the rest of Comecon from the consequences of this trend.[15] Smilek states that the net Soviet exports to other European members of Comecon of foodstuffs and raw materials rose from $284 m. in 1955 to $1,655 m. in 1965, but at the same time its absorption of Comecon exports of equipment rose from a net $253 m. to $1,082 m.

Future trade

The disposition of the fruits of industrialization, and the acquisition of its necessities, will be the crucial problems of Comecon in the medium term. The rate of growth of intra-Comecon trade has been shrinking as difficulties emerged within the group and as diversion outside became more possible and attractive: in 1950–5 trade among members rose by 85 per cent, in 1955–60 by 71 per cent, and in 1960–5 by 55 per cent; the increase foreseen for 1966–70 is 49 per cent.

Yet the present gap between east and west Europe in external dependence suggests an increasing propensity to trade in the planned increments of output. Such a forecast is particularly supported by the present reform of decision-making within each Comecon economy.

The new approach to prices as a component of planned management, described in Chapter IX, will tend to introduce the factor of relative cost—in international trade or domestic production—into the initial decisions on the pattern of output. Although likely exports will remain an integral part of the plan forecasts, they are put on a par with the gain from imports. The prospect of advantageous purchase thus comes to determine the output pattern as much as does that of a potential sale. Greater liberty for enterprises in choosing the detail of their production profile is an expected concomitant of value planning. Such devolution is taking place in all the European members of Comecon save Rumania.

A multiplicity of enterprises seeking to achieve a planned profit is patently more conducive to trade than are the efforts of a few central agencies to assess sector-wide proceeds. Still more, the possibility of financing purchases in one country by sales in another relaxes the con-

[15] The view of Soviet partnership as a 'rescue' is that of Montias, who, in the three papers cited in ch. IV (n. 46), has closely examined these movements. Studies of the 'engineering goods problem' are treated by a Soviet and a Czech writer, E. Matvievskaya and J. Novozamsky respectively, in the proceedings of a conference of the International Economic Association, M. Kaser, ed., *Economic Development in Eastern Europe* (forthcoming).

TABLE 5

Commodity Composition of Comecon Trade with the Rest of Europe in 1962

(US $ m.: imports c.i.f., exports f.o.b.)

Commodity group	Exports to				Imports from			
	EEC	*EFTA*	*Other*	*Total*	*EEC*	*EFTA*	*Other*	*Total*
I. *Food, beverages, & tobacco*	*289*	*258*	*70*	*617*	*87*	*63*	*91*	*241*
Livestock & products	121	92	18	231	31	36	14	81
Grains & products	67	73	19	159	31	6	—	37
Fruit, vegetables, & tobacco	66	31	4	101	18	1	53	72
II. *Raw materials*	*751*	*481*	*296*	*1,528*	*420*	*242*	*134*	*796*
Timber & products	173	135	16	324	1	18	46	65
Other agric. products	120	70	22	212	70	44	48	162
Mineral fuels	271	179	154	604	2	2	2	6
Base metals	145	60	80	285	341	168	28	537
III. *Manufactures*	*159*	*208*	*175*	*542*	*659*	*511*	*283*	*1,453*
Machinery	38	26	68	132	367	298	87	752
Transport equipment	9	12	35	56	49	42	100	191
Chemicals	43	34	29	106	125	77	12	214
Other manufactures	68	136	43	247	118	94	85	297
Total (incl. unspecified)	1,203	950	544	2,697	1,171	830	508	2,509
of which Albania	1	—	1	2	5	—	1	6

Note: Comecon includes Albania but not Mongolia (for which data not available).

Source: Econ. B. Eur., xv/1, Tables 23 B & C.

strictions of bilateral compensation. The latest multilateral procedure in Comecon (see Ch. VII) still starts from a round of bilateral negotiations among members, but it is complemented by the concerted examination of trade possibilities, while the extension of the clearing union to payments with non-members is in perspective.

The direction of this coming trade expansion is less clear. Comecon's technical commissions have continued to meet in full membership and to report discussion of plan co-ordination in their branches for 1966–70, despite the rift with Rumania. The crux of that dispute

—as Chapter x shows—was between those who sought maximum efficiency within the group, thus largely concentrating output on existing producers, and those—notably Rumania—who would postpone that aim until all members had reached roughly similar levels of industrialization. It may be suggested that a *modus vivendi* has been reached in which each country formulates its own long-term plans in accordance with its cost projections. If no prospective buyer can be found for the planned exports proposed by each member, the producer must assume an export to a third country. Trade within the group can still gain by intra-product specialization, and the standing commissions are undoubtedly working on this. Where inter-product planning—that is, the division of product branches, not just of types of product—is admitted (the more so where joint finance of the required investment is involved), bilateral procedures are introduced. The opposition to establishing a Comecon price-list to govern its own trade in favour of the continued use of world prices supports these inferences.

The devolution of domestic planning may well involve the mutation of the central foreign-trade corporations towards the role of liaison (as in Hungary today), but not to that of an autonomous commercial enterprise (as in Yugoslavia).[16] The novelty of domestic-price criteria for foreign-trade choice may thus be accompanied by the admission of different agencies to the exercise of that choice. The two innovations imply that East–West trade could thus respond, more than at any time in the past, to the initiative of western business.

[16] P. Kalensky, *Pravni otazky rizeni zahranichniho obchodu clenskych statu RVHP* (Prague, 1966) advocates the uniformity of foreign-trade corporations in Comecon states as a necessary adjustment to the new management systems.

VIII
TECHNICAL CO-OPERATION

Exchange of expertise

COMECON may be modified both by an increase in its trade on other markets, and by the decentralization of its constituent economies; most of its technical activities should continue, and be extended, in their present form. Under the conditions to be expected, nevertheless, they must involve wider contact with the rest of the world. A limited start to intercourse with western Europe has already been made through its commissions and the technical committees of the ECE; Comecon's new Institute of Standardization is to make an, as yet undefined, alignment with the International Standardization Organization; and its International Bank of Economic Co-operation was authorized in October 1965 to review the possibility of clearings with convertible-currency areas.

The interchange of expertise has unquestionably been one of Comecon's most successful objectives: as just observed, the diminution of trade dependence can be regarded as the consequence of rapid industrialization as much as of the slower development of trade: Comecon can take credit for the supply of knowledge which generated the new industries. The gratuity of this aid, under its 1949 recommendations, was a practical expression of the injunction of communism: 'from each according to his ability, to each according to his needs'. Comecon members have already done much to extend such service to other, poorer economies. At the beginning of 1963 some 22,000 workers were being trained at enterprises under construction overseas by Comecon states; in 1962 those states sent over 7,000 experts to the underdeveloped areas; in the same year over 10,000 Asians, Africans, and Latin Americans were studying in member countries.

Technical collaboration is one of the Comecon activities which can be expected to ramify—but in forms more open to western participation. A reciprocal trade in patent licences is growing up between eastern and western Europe—the Soviet Union purchase of synthetic-fibre processes from the United Kingdom and its sale of turbo-drilling technology to the United States are widely-known examples. The Comecon member buying a patent (or equipment at a price including a charge for incorporated new technology) would *prima facie* be less ready to present it to a fellow member; those contracts under licence would, of course, preclude such transfer. Members now have enough processes to dispose of to have set up specialized selling agencies (e.g. Litsenzintorg, created by the USSR in 1962, or the Czechoslovak Polytechna). By mid-1966 the Soviet agency had sold licences to firms in twelve western countries; its most important sale has been of a new process for continuous steel pouring, purchased by concerns in France, Italy, and Japan.[1] The new trade brings the temptation of charge for licences within Comecon, and something of this has in fact emerged by the conclusion of inter-member commercial contacts for research and development.[2] In addition, within a generally-co-ordinated programme of research for 1966–70 (comprising 200 projects), two bilaterally-financed research agencies have been set up, the Soviet-Czechoslovak Scientific Research and Design Office and the Polono-Czechoslovak Joint Research Centre for Tractor Development. The commercialization of East–West technological exchange stopped the ECE, in 1960–2, from adding the subject of chemicals to its technical committees (all of which have their origin in the period 1947–56).

Within Comecon, the activities springing from its founding aim of 'extending technical aid to each other' are too numerous and specialized to enumerate, but it must be stressed that the achievement is remarkable for a Secretariat which until recently had a very modest staff. In the period during which most of these technical services were set up the headquarters staff in Moscow does not appear to have exceeded 100—inclusive of all grades.[3] Each of the offices servicing a Standing Commission in other cities had (and still have) a staff of some twenty apiece. In 1962 the authorized establishment was sharply increased.[4] Recruitment rapidly expanded—in 1963 the staff reached 200 and the following year 500[5]—through completion of the full establishment (shown below in comparison with the corresponding

[1] *Financial Times*, 6 June 1966, quoting V. Salinovsky, Director of Litsenzintorg.

[2] Faddeev, *Iz.*, 3 Nov. 1966; Bogomolov (*Komm.*, no. 18, 1966) advocates licensing 'at world prices'.

[3] There has been much western exaggeration on staff. Knorre (p. 15) cited a Swedish report of 1950 of 'over 2000' and believed that it was in fact of the magnitude in 1960.

[4] When a new organizational structure was set up, including specialized technical departments (see B. Miroshnichenko, *Vopr. ekon.*, no. 9, 1963).

[5] P. Jaroszewicz, *Zyc. gos.*, 26 Jan. 1964; Korbonski, p. 20, cites 420 during 1964.

1964 data for other European economic agencies) was hindered by the inability of member governments to release the officials requested (and not by the conditions of service).[6]

	Comecon	*EEC*	*OECD*	*ECE*
Total establishment	700	2,136	1,150	179
—of which posts in the professional categories	350	647	340	85

Note: Translators are not included in data for ECE and EEC, because these agencies have, respectively, three and four working languages (against Russian alone in Comecon). ECE figures also exclude the administrative services of staff of the European Office of the UN.

Comecon methods for the exchange of technical documentation, training, or the supply of specialists correspond to those used by the United Nations Technical Assistance Office—the parallel was in fact drawn by the Executive Secretary, Pavlov, in 1955—or by the European Productivity Agency. Both for this work and for the standing commissions established from 1956 onwards, Comecon could draw upon a fund of national experts who had had virtually no chance of discussion with foreign colleagues (save perhaps under the duress of war) for a decade and a half. Just as the enterprise directors seized upon international fairs (Leipzig, Poznan, Brno, and Plovdiv) as a means of contact with their fellows, so Comecon's requests corresponded to a real demand for foreign contacts. In 1961 alone more than 10,000 specialists were reported as working in some way or other for the organization.[7] Like WHO in its expert panels or the ECE or OECD in their technical committees—similarly serviced by staff small in relation to the volume of technology collated and analysed—Comecon has depended largely upon international expert groups. The list in Appendix VIII (see p. 257) shows, though not precisely, the present extent of this practice: there are known to be more subcommittees than have here been noted from reports in the east European press, and some *ad hoc* working parties may have been disbanded. The

[6] Staff members receive a 25 per cent expatriation allowance. For a survey of conditions of service and training see *N. Deutsch.*, 3 and 29 May and 2 June 1964; the Secretariat has been allotted flats in one of the best modern blocks in the new Cherëmushki district of Moscow, and an impressive residence for short-service staff and delegates has been built adjoining the new headquarters in the Prospekt Kalinina redevelopment zone.

[7] *N. Deutsch.*, spec. issue published for the Leipzig Spring Fair, 1961; E. Hoffman, *Comecon: Der Gemeinsame Markt in Osteuropa* (Opladen, 1961).

novelty Comecon introduced in this field can best be termed 'national reference groups'. Under this system, an institute or ministry is allotted a problem for study: it analyses the technical literature (of Comecon members or from outside), receives written comments from corresponding agencies in other member states, and prepares a draft report on its own responsibility; the latter is then of course submitted to the appropriate Comecon group. The USSR, for example, has 10 such reference groups, with a membership of 70 experts, working for the Agricultural Commission.[8] The use of these groups is facilitated by the existence in each member country of a national parallel to each Comecon commission, subcommittee, and working party, the delegate to the Comecon body normally being the chairman of the relevant national committee.

The secondment of technical, as opposed to administrative, staff for international service, or their detachment from normal duties to work in a national reference group is also somewhat easier with all industries nationalized than in a largely private-enterprise economy. Nationalization—substantially complete, save only in agriculture, in eastern Europe by the end of 1948—has also brought advantages in the exchange of expertise. In accordance with the recommendation of the Second Session (1949), each member supplies each other with free licences for technological processes and charges only for the cost of making copies of plans, working drawings, blueprints, etc. Not only does the social system of each member obviate trade secrecy—it makes a positive virtue of the 'exchange of advanced experience'. During 1960–2 alone more than 38,000 sets of scientific and technical documents were exchanged within Comecon (to 1958 the cumulative number was 14,700); 30,000 workers from member countries visited others to study industrial methods or to acquire skills; and 700 research, planning, or designing agencies of Comecon states co-operated on approximately 3,500 specific projects.[9] The exchange until recently exactly reflected levels of industrial development. Between 1948 and 1960 Czechoslovakia and the GDR dispatched more sets of documentation to the USSR than they received in return; Bulgaria,

[8] Art. by the secretary to the Soviet delegation to the Agricultural Commission, *Mezh. sels zhur.*, no. 2, 1964, p. 5. On two such national reference groups appointed by the Comecon Economic Commission, see the present writer in *Income and Wealth, Series IX*, pp. 169–70.

[9] 1960–2 data from the Comecon document *Information on Economic Co-operation*, p. 10. Cumulative total to 1958 from *Vopr. ekon.*, no. 2, 1959, p. 95.

Hungary, and Rumania received more than they sent, while for Albania the flow was all inward.[10] In 1962, however, even Czechoslovakia and the GDR obtained more Soviet sets than they forwarded; Mongolia sent one 'technological document' to the USSR and received 144 sets of material in return.[11]

In this interchange, the value of the central planning of research activities—under which all national institutions operate (within their Academies of Sciences or under state co-ordination committees)—is also exploited. The comparison of annual research plans can serve to eliminate duplication. The specialized subcommittees of the Commission on Engineering thus examined 9,000 research projects during 1956–61 and recommended the exclusion of no less than 4,000. Other, more homogeneous, commissions created subcommittees expressly for the co-ordination of research (Agriculture, Electric Power, Light and Food Industries). From 1958 to 1962 the Economic Commission was responsible for the general oversight of scientific and technical research, but in the radical reorganization of the Sixteenth Session, June 1962, a Standing Commission on the Co-ordination of Scientific and Technical Research was constituted and met for the first time in Moscow in December that year. Among its plans for 1964–5 was the 'elaboration of a theory of automated administration' (information theory).[12] Comecon organized its own Symposium on Information Systems (entitled 'Inforga 65')following the world-wide 'Interdata 65' organized by the IFIP.[13] Many research institutes, hitherto financed from public funds, were made self-supporting under the management reforms of 1966–7. The new problem of sharing such outlay was taken up by the bilateral Intergovernmental Commissions: the GDR and the USSR, and Poland and Hungary, for example, divided costs in profit-centred research at sessions in early 1967.[14]

The Commission on Research Co-ordination is one of the very few from which Rumania, at the height of dissension, seems to have been absent: it did not appear at a study group arranged by the Commission in Prague in April 1964 (it also went unrepresented at the Agricultural Commission in Sofia in December 1963). Generally, however, technical co-operation within the commissions was maintained in the

[10] From detailed statistics in Novozamsky, p. 131. [11] Ciamaga, p. 199.

[12] T. Azarov (Comecon Secretariat), *Plan. khoz.*, no. 4, 1964, pp. 39–40.

[13] *Pol. ek.*, no. 11, 1965. [14] *Foreign Affairs Bulletin*, 25 Jan.; *Nep.*, 10 Feb. 1967.

immediate aftermath of the dispute.[15] Subsequently China was the only observer to cease participation, but individual members pursued technical collaboration on a bilateral basis. Thus in September 1966 the Polish Committee for Foreign Economic Relations approved 'protocols on scientific and technical collaboration' with China, Korea, and Mongolia:[16] Cuba seems to have suspended virtually all contacts at this level in 1964 and 1965 for the reasons already described (p. 105).

Common experimental services

Although the major intergovernmental experimental project is outside the Comecon structure (the United Institute for Nuclear Research), Comecon has provided some useful common services. Perhaps the best arranged have been the international trials of farm machinery run by the Agricultural Commission, which between 1959 and 1965 tested 683 types of equipment for farming and for forestry. In the first year tractors were tested and the appropriate models recommended to the Engineering Commission for standard production; no trials were held in 1960, but they were resumed in 1961. In 1962 they were so numerous—vegetable cultivators, beet diggers, broiler-fowl equipment, manure spreaders, two-phase wheat harvesters, mowing machines, and potato lifters—that the trials were spread over three countries, the USSR, Hungary, and the GDR. Comecon's stud-book of pedigree bulls available for artificial insemination (including photographs of the animals for service) has been regularly reissued since 1961.[17] Field trials were made in 1962 on pesticides and insecticides. As a result of these tests 37 preparations were recommended, of which 15 were Czechoslovak, 7 Polish, 6 Soviet, 5 German, 3 Bulgarian, and 1 Rumanian.

A scheme for the exchange of selected seeds was one of the Agricultural Commission's first recommendations (at its second meeting in May 1957). In the following agricultural year, 1957–8, 96 sorts of

[15] Attendance at technical meetings—in this sample, the two months after the crisis of mid-April 1964—is also of interest in indicating the extent of participation by observers (Rumania was present at all): in April Ferrous Metals, Warsaw (China, N. Korea, Cuba); Grid Control Office, Prague, and Common Waggon Pool Council, Brno; in May Light Industry, Prague; in June Electric Power, Leningrad; Food, Varna (N. Korea, Cuba); and Standardization Commission, Berlin (N. Vietnam, Cuba). Attendance was not apparently published for the Board of the Standardization Institute, Moscow, or the Geology Commission, Prague, both held in May.

[16] *Tryb. Lud.*, 18 Sept. 1966.

[17] Faddeev, p. 50.

seed were shipped to the USSR from other Comecon members and 154 went in the reverse direction; by 1961–2 the exchanges had reached 368 and 945 respectively. Under the Commission's auspices delivery contracts for seed-potatoes have been established: during 1966–70 28,000 tons per annum of high-quality seed potatoes will be delivered by the GDR and Poland to Bulgaria, Hungary, and Czechoslovakia. Rumania's absence from such arrangements is not surprising since it is not a major consumer, but it failed to co-operate in the 1966–70 delivery plans for maize seed, of which it is the largest producer. Bulgaria, Hungary, and the USSR are to ship annually 33,000–36,000 tons of hybrid-maize seed to Czechoslovakia, the GDR, and Poland. Other long-term seed contracts relate to wheat, sunflower, clover, lucerne, and sugar-beet. Payment for seed is covered by the normal trade agreements, but seeds sent for experimental purposes are exchanged without charge: thus in 1965 the USSR dispatched 561 seed types to other members and received 143 types in return. Rumania has participated in this form of co-operation and, in a three-year plan for seed selection (1964–6) drawn up by the Agricultural Commission, undertook experimental work on 18 seed types (other commitments being Bulgaria 7, Czechoslovakia 28, GDR 37, Hungary 29, Poland 36, and the USSR 39). In May 1965 the Commission approved a joint research plan for 1966–70 distributing 23 major projects among member countries.[18]

None of these projects involved much international finance: the exchange of documentation was free, and the cost of training of experts, research, the work of national reference groups and the running of field trials were borne by the country in which the activity took place. Since the developed countries in the event did more of this than the less developed, the process was of aid provided without the formalities of loan or grant. The national services called upon to extend this aid did not until recently (see p. 157) themselves need compensation since they were supported by the public exchequer.

Statistical uniformity

The Statistical Commission was also set up at the Sixteenth Session and started work at the same time and place as that on Research Co-

[18] The information on the work of the Agricultural Commission was taken from recent issues of its organ, *Mezh. sels. zhur.*, and Comecon Secretariat document, *Informatsiya o deyatelnosti SEV v oblasti selskogo khozyaistva* (Moscow, May 1966).

ordination; it complements the other's efforts by promoting uniformity in the data employed.[19] The creation of the commission seems, however, to have been long delayed by the singular insularity of the Central Statistical Administration of the USSR. It had been criticized at the Twentieth Party Congress in 1956, but, despite an expanding publications programme, its isolation from the research needs of the domestic economy continued to be a live issue,[20] and it is clear that its contacts with statistical offices in Comecon states were more tenuous still. Comecon's statistical work in its first decade—virtually its sole duties in 1951–2—was entirely in foreign-trade statistics (compiled in the USSR by the Ministry for Foreign Trade), and the slowness to co-ordinate these with a classification of domestic activities may well have been due to the unwillingness to participate of the Central Statistical Administration. For long that Administration undertook no international representation whatsoever: the Soviet delegate to the UN Statistical Commission was the head of the Statistics Department of the Institute of Economics; an official of the Planning Office participated in the Conference of European Statisticians; and still others attended the International Statistical Institute. In this time of alienation, the only work on statistical methodology within Comecon was done through its Economic Commission.

It would be unfair to blame the Soviet statistical authorities alone, for even in the pioneering field of foreign-trade statistics in Comecon, co-ordination is still far from complete. The USSR, for example, records its imports by country of origin, i.e. ignoring re-exports by third countries, whereas all other Comecon states[21] follow western European practice in showing the country of dispatch. Thus the Soviet trade abstracts show Malaysia as a supplier of natural rubber even when this is bought on the London Rubber Exchange, but Hungarian statistics in such a situation give the United Kingdom as the origin. The case is important because London transactions are substantially used by Comecon members for primary commodities both as buyers

[19] Before the Commission was formed, however, three *ad hoc* conferences of statisticians met during 1961: they drafted, first, a uniform classification of economic activities, second, a minimum list of indicators of the level and rate of economic development, and third, a comparable nomenclature for industrial and agricultural products (to unify output, procurement, and trade statistics).

[20] See esp. Academician Nemchinov's criticism in *Vopr. ekon.*, no. 4, 1959, p. 34.

[21] Mongolian practice is not known: its sole statistical abstract does not provide breakdowns by country and commodity.

and sellers. Again, the Soviet Union values its imports f.o.b. while other members use the standard c.i.f. All employ f.o.b. frontier for exports (although Hungary deviated by using contract price during 1952–6).

The delay in beginning work on statistical classification has been more serious than a mere failure to provide neat international tabulations for statistical abstracts, though this was striking enough.[22] A common basis of data was essential for joint planning. When in 1962 the Sixteenth Session 'decided that its main field of activity should be the co-ordination of the national economic plans of member states',[23] the unification of the reporting and projections for those plans could no longer be put off and the Statistical Commission was created. The growing availability of electronic data-processing machines[24] and the increasing awareness of the scope for the application of mathematical methods in planning,[25] gave added pressure for statistical uniformity. This connexion was made coincidentally apparent in the negotiations to bring Cuba into the co-ordination of 1966–70 plans: within a month of the arrival of a delegation of the GDR Planning Office at the Cuban Juceplan in Havana, a mission of the Cuban statistical office was in the Soviet Central Statistical Administration in Moscow.[26] Similarly, as Yugoslavia drew closer to Comecon on the exchange and discussion of plan drafts, it was admitted to the Statistical Commission, its presence on which had not been envisaged in the agreement of September 1964. North Korea's increasingly pro-Soviet policy in the Sino-Soviet division was similarly reflected in its presence, with Yugoslavia, at the 1966 meeting of the Commission at Riga, convened to define the components of a statistical balance of the national economy, to revise the classification of production branches and to elaborate a common methodology and form for input-output tables.[27]

Intra-product specialization

The *Basic Principles* have already been quoted on the fostering of

[22] See the present writer in *Sov. Stud.*, Jan. 1963, p. 335.
[23] Statement by the Comecon Secretariat in its *Information on Economic Co-operation*, p. 12.
[24] The Comecon states have been active contributors to the working party of the Conference of European Statisticians on this equipment.
[25] See, among a number of recent studies, the ECE paper 'A Note on the Introduction of Mathematical Techniques into Soviet Planning', *Econ. B. Eur.*, xii/1; and A. Zauberman, *Sov. Stud.*, July 1962, pp. 62–74 and *Economica*, Aug. 1965, pp. 323–9.
[26] Respectively *N. Deutsch.*, 24 Apr. 1964, and *Pr.*, 2 June 1964.
[27] *Iz.*, 21 Sept. 1966.

specialization by type of product in the absence of the country allocation of whole branches of production. Although it was the Fourth Session (1954) which initially discussed specialization, the first practical results within Comecon came at the Seventh Session (1956) which benefited from the work of the *ad hoc* technical committees, put on a permanent footing at that session. One example of the type of decision made is probably enough (the Twelfth Session, 1959): the country allocations for rolling-mill equipment gave large-scale mills to Czechoslovakia and the USSR, small-scale mills to the GDR and Poland, and wire-drawing plant to the GDR and Hungary; oil-drilling and refinery equipment went to Rumania[28] and the Soviet Union; excavating machines to the GDR, Czechoslovakia, and the USSR; and among special machine-tools for roller-bearing production 10 models went to Czechoslovakia, 40 to the GDR, 12 to Poland, and 55 to the Soviet Union.[29] Since Bulgaria and Albania did not happen to be on this list it is as well to observe that they were, for example, later allocated telpherage and agricultural equipment and certain types of glassware respectively. To date, intra-product specialization has covered three major industries—engineering, metallurgy, and chemicals—but every standing commission for an industrial branch has made some recommendations.[30]

Since 1964 agreements on intra-product specialization have also been made in the bilateral commissions for economic, scientific, and technical co-operation. It is not, however, clear whether these represent obligations additional to those entered into through Comecon, or whether they prepare for (or follow) multilateral negotiations in the multilateral framework. Thus a meeting of the Polish Committee for Foreign Economic Relations[31] in September 1966 accepted the agreements reached in the mixed commissions with the USSR, the GDR, Czechoslovakia, Yugoslavia, and Bulgaria.[32] Because the specific items mentioned as for specialization had not previously been listed in Comecon announcements, the agreements apparently preceded

[28] Czechoslovakia was subsequently also allocated oil-refinery equipment.

[29] R. Fidelski and M. Paszkowski, *Rocznik polityczny i gospodarczy, 1959* (Warsaw, 1960), pp. 1201–9.

[30] Shurshalov, p. 290. For a list of specialization agreements to 1959 see Klinkmüller and Ruban, pp. 180–90.

[31] The terms of reference of which cover both Comecon and the bilateral commissions; see Art. 6 of its Statute of 2 Sept. 1962, in *Rada Wzajemnej Pomocy Gospodarczej* (Warsaw, 1964), p. 273.

[32] *Tryb. Lud.*, 18 Sept. 1966.

multilateral discussion.[33] This seems to be the new way to overcome the inadequacy of multilateral recommendations. 'Until now', wrote a Soviet observer in January 1967, 'many of the same types of product have been made concurrently in virtually all CMEA members. Obligations arising from the recommendations taken have not always been fulfilled'. Furthermore, bilateral negotiations on specialization for 1966–70 took place while the plans were still in draft. 'In past years . . . each CMEA member elaborated its draft, had it approved by its highest authorities and, only after the plan had been enacted with the force of law, tied it up with the similarly-confirmed plans of other countries.'[34]

Under such conditions, it is not surprising that effective specialization fell far short of what is feasible under economic integration. Only Bulgaria seems to have done well out of it. Between 1951 and 1964 it has enjoyed the highest rate of industrial growth in Europe, and its rise of national product has been exceeded only by three countries. Its rate of growth of GNP has been 5·9 per cent per annum, against 6·3 per cent in the USSR, and 4·9 per cent for members other than the Soviet Union); its relative expansion was exceeded in western Europe only by western Germany and Greece (6·8 and 7·0 per cent respectively).[35] The growth of guaranteed trade with other Comecon countries has played a considerable part in this rapid development. Some of the expansion was in traditional produce, notably fruit and vegetables. In the year in which, at the Twelfth Session, members agreed to make specified purchases of Bulgarian produce annually to 1965, their imports of its fruit and vegetables were 591,000 tons. On average over 1961–4 those imports rose to 932,000 tons (i.e., by 58 per cent) and further agreements envisage imports of 1,350,000 tons by 1970. Imports of such fruits have transformed the pattern of Soviet urban fruit sales, which previously had comprised virtually no early varieties and few soft fruits. The Bulgarian figures include—in fresh equivalent—canned and dried produce and preserves; the growth of food processing has assisted industrialization.

[33] The items were components for telephonic, automatic, and electronic equipment with the USSR and condensers and semiconductors with the GDR; references to the other agreements were insufficiently detailed (products of the tractor industry with Czechoslovakia, of the motor-making industry with Yugoslavia, and of shipbuilding with Bulgaria).

[34] Sokolov, pp. 99–101.

[35] *New Directions:* Ernst, pp. 880–3, Cohn, p. 105, and J. Noren, p. 281.

Comecon specialization has also fostered the development of Bulgarian non-ferrous metallurgy, but manufacturing industry has benefited from Comecon's assured markets for Bulgarian engineering goods. In 1964 and 1965 such products reached 25 per cent of Bulgaria's exports, against 12 per cent in 1959 (and 3 per cent in 1955). In the Bulgarian decree of 11 June 1965 reorganizing the engineering industry into amalgamated enterprises, explicit provisions were made for plants operating under Comecon specialization contracts, and further agreements with members were reached at the session of the Comecon Engineering Commission in Warsaw that month.[36]

Rumania was initially offered much the same formula as was accepted by Bulgaria, viz. expansion of raw-material exports, both traditional—e.g., maize, oil, and timber—and newly-developed—e.g., methane and chemical raw materials—and development of specified engineering capacity. Its rejection of the role of raw-material supplier has already been described in Part I, but it also seems to have accepted, but failed to execute, some of its commitments on intra-product specialization in engineering. A Czech writer, for example, has stated that Rumania was apportioned the production of 4-ton lorries under such a scheme, but that, when the capacity was in operation, the Rumanian authorities decided to allocate the entire output to supply the domestic market, thus breaking the agreement to sell some to other members and correspondingly to buy the lorries of other dimensions, *inter alia* from Czechoslovakia.[37]

Rumania claimed that balance-of-payments difficulties precluded its execution of both the export and the import consequences of the specialization agreement. At about the same time—the second half of the 1950s—Rumania switched some of its agreed imports of engineering products from Czechoslovakia to the GDR and the Soviet Union because the latter were prepared to purchase more Rumanian equipment than was Czechoslovakia. Despite an agreement in 1956 to discontinue production of 6 types of tractor, by 1964 only 2 had in fact been discontinued; in place of the 17,700 tractors agreed in 1956 to be produced by the GDR by 1960 and 6,000 by Rumania, actual output that year was 17,102 in Rumania and 9,076 in the GDR. In 1963 a

[36] It is worth noting that a Soviet study of eastern European trade attributes only the growth of food exports to Comecon specialization; that of engineering exports is commended without discussion; see Zolotarev, pp. 130–2.

[37] Machova, pp. 155 and 201, quoted by J. Montias, *J. Int. Aff.*, no. 1, 1966, p. 62.

Hungarian writer calculated that only 3–5 per cent of total engineering output corresponded to the specialization agreements of Comecon.[38]

Inter-product specialization

The allocation of an entire product among members gave rise to still greater difficulties: it was not until 1962 that the Soviet Union admitted the possibility that it could forego the output of any good in order to import it more advantageously.

The Seventh Session (1956) which began intra-product specialization in engineering also laid down those guide-lines for primary commodities which natural endowment indicated—Polish coal or Bulgarian non-ferrous metals for example—but the process was soon faced with obstacles. First, there were very few commodities where one country had absolute advantage, or patent lead, over another. Albanian and Bulgarian soft fruits were in fact the prime beneficiaries. Secondly, where resources permitted many members to engage in substantial production—as in most branches of agriculture, and in coal-mining—the cost calculations needed to define the relative advantage (net of transport costs) were protracted and often unconvincing to the state prospectively renouncing (on the coal specialization discussions, see p. 79). Moreover, specialization in the products of mining was held by the agrarian countries to be a hindrance to their industrialization, while the developed were by no means ready to reduce their existing outputs.

In manufacturing, the allotment of an entire product to one or two countries could either merely confirm the existing concentration or require the present producers to slacken the expansion which their lower costs would have justified; in the case of a new product (the Rumanian development of oil-drilling equipment was novel for the group outside the USSR), allocation to a less-developed economy implied higher costs than in an industrialized country. No production lines seem to have been curtailed as a result of inter-product specialization, but members with a developed industry were faced with a limitation on intra-Comecon sales of their manufactures at the same time as the growing needs of raw materials by the new producers (and their inability to invest in export commodities simultaneously with

[38] Montias, p. 68, quoting respectively C. Murgescu, *Viata economica*, no. 23, 1964 and A. Balassa, *Koz. Sz.*, no. 11, 1964, p. 1274.

manufacturing) dampened the supply of materials and foodstuffs which they needed to import. Montias, in describing this situation, understands that the less-developed countries pressed their efforts for this specialization to the point where they sought bilateral balancing by broad commodity group, notably of manufactures.[39] He adds two complementary criticisms from Czech sources. First, that the developed countries themselves inhibited the growth of industries suited to agrarian economies by setting up parallel enterprises in their own underdeveloped regions (notably by the Czechoslovak authorities in Slovakia).[40] Secondly, the less developed members imported from the more developed precisely those machines which the exporters were efficient at making for their own industry and which enjoyed especially large economies of scale. Isolation from western technology in the fifties reinforced in engineering 'the creation of parallel, superfluous, and at times unprofitable production in a few socialist countries'.[41] By 1961 the proportion of imported equipment in Comecon-member consumption was only 6·4 per cent, against an estimate of 24 per cent in the EEC.[42]

Rivalry in standardization

Intra-product specialization demands common technical standards; the predominance of trade among themselves would in any case impose standardization—components and spare parts, for example, have to be manufactured to equal tolerances. Superficially the need is so obvious that it is difficult to believe that formal work on standardization, like research co-ordination and statistical classification, remained untouched until the Party Meeting and Sixteenth Session of June 1962. The problem, not fully resolved by their decisions, was the existence of two parallel and highly-developed sets of norms, the TGL standards of the GDR and the GOST of the USSR.[43] Standardization was first discussed—for engineering, the main field—in bilateral talks between the GDR and USSR in Moscow in May 1957, and at the end of the month there was a conference in Berlin, attended by all Comecon

[39] Montias, *J. Int. Aff.*, no. 1, 1966, p. 64.

[40] Ibid. p. 65, citing G. Aptauer (a member of the Czechoslovak mission to Comecon), *Plan. Hosp.*, no. 1, 1965, p. 72.

[41] Ibid. p. 66, citing Vanek, p. 219.

[42] Ibid. pp. 67–8, citing Novozamsky, p. 113.

[43] The TGL (*Technische Normen Gütevorschriften Lieferbedingungen*), first authorized in 1950, were developed from the all-German DIN (*Deutsche Industrie Normen*); the GOST (*Gosudarstvennye obshchesoyuznye standarty*) began to be issued in 1925.

members, on modular co-ordination in building. A Soviet hope for a commission on standardization was expressed in early 1959,[44] but the technicians of both countries continued to defend their national systems; a certain amount of conversion of TGL into GOST nevertheless began to be made. When the drive for integration was launched in 1961,[45] there should in principle have been no more procrastination. In early 1962, moreover, the idea of a technological *Wirtschaftsgemeinschaft* with the Soviet Union was gaining currency in the GDR.[46] The Comecon decision of July 1962, however, had something of the division of Solomon, for a Commission on Standardization was established in Berlin under a German director, and an Institute of Standardization in Moscow under a Soviet director with Polish and Czechoslovak deputies; the Comecon Headquarters Division on Standardization was also located in Moscow. The Commission set to work more quickly than the Institute—the former, in June 1964, was holding its sixth session in Berlin a few days after the Board of the Standardization Institute convened for the first time in Moscow. The division of work has not been made clear: the Berlin meeting, for example, was reported to have ratified a number of recommendations on standards in ferrous metals, chemicals, and mechanical, radio, and electrical engineering, while the Institute drew up a plan for the co-ordination of norms during 1966–70. A session of the Council of the GDR Standardization Office on the eve of the Berlin meeting was stated to have worked on adaptation required by new international standards and by the reform of the domestic planning system. At its meeting in February 1964 the Executive

> required all CMEA organs to concentrate their attention on recommendations for the unification of standards, assuring the realization of measures for the specialization and co-operation of production, and promoting the increase of product exchanges among CMEA members.

In August the Institute submitted to all Standing Commissions a programme for unifying standards in their fields between 1966 and 1970: some thousand groups of standards were to be covered.[47]

[44] *Vopr. ekon.*, no. 3, 1959, p. 38. [45] A. Lange, *Wirts.*, no. 7, 1961.
[46] Zauberman, *Industrial Progress*, p. 299, citing R. Brauer, *Wirts.*, no. 2, 1962.
[47] The various reports on the Institute and Commission are in *Iz.*, 7 Feb. 1964, and *N. Deutsch.*, 13 and 14 May, 2 and 8 June, and 17 Aug. 1964.

Technical co-operation with non-Comecon agencies

Comecon has formal relationships with those agencies of socialist countries listed in Appendix IX, and its Standardization Institute is required to be in touch with the International Standardization Organization (Geneva). Of other international bodies, however, Comecon's main contact has been with the ECE;[48] a Comecon Secretariat delegation first went to Geneva in October 1955 and an ECE mission returned the visit two months later. The Secretariat was first represented at the ECE plenary session in 1958 and continued each year to send a delegate; ECE has not been invited to Comecon Sessions. Comecon has participated regularly at the ECE technical committees on agricultural problems, electric power, gas, coal, housing, steel, inland transport, and trade (the first at which it appeared) and at the Conference of European Statisticians.[49] In fact, the only Committee to which an official is not sent is that for timber, because there is no corresponding Comecon sector department (the Timber Commission having been abolished in 1958). Although the ECE Secretariat is not reciprocally invited to the Session or to the Executive Committee, it has recently been represented at the Comecon Commissions for Electric Power, Coal, Steel, and Statistics, and at certain special conferences (e.g. on housing in 1964 and on automation in 1965), but not, unfortunately, at the Commission for Foreign Trade.

Comecon was invited to the United Nations Conference on Trade and Development (March–June 1964); this proposal was accepted by the Executive at its meeting of February 1964. The Secretary, Faddeev, attended a number of the Conference sessions, and the permanent representative was the Deputy Minister of Foreign Trade of the GDR, Willi Hüttenrauch. The Conference, apart from the manifestations of intra-Comecon differences it occasioned, was the first major international meeting at which Comecon's policies were scrutinized, in the context of 'the implications, for trade and development of the developing countries, of economic groupings and preferential trading arrangements among developed states'. The EEC (and the Franc Zone), EFTA, and the Commonwealth Preference System were also

[48] UN, *Fifteen Years of Activity of the ECE, 1947–1962* (1964), p. 31; *Information on Economic Co-operation*, p. 6; these contacts are termed by the ECE 'on a working level' and by Solodovnikov (p. 296) as 'non-official'. Faddeev (p. 52) observes that Comecon's proposal 'for closer contact with EEC . . . did not receive a positive decision'.

[49] Sponsored jointly by the ECE and the UN Statistical Office.

examined. It has subsequently been represented at the United Nations Board for Trade and Development.

Its Commission for Atomic Energy also has contacts with the International Atomic Energy Agency.

Article IX of the Comecon Charter states that 'in carrying out their duties, the Secretary of the Council, his deputies and the Secretariat staff shall act as international officials'. Aware of this, the Federation of International Civil Servants' Associations requested the collaboration of Comecon staff in a study 'to achieve a major step towards the fuller realization of a true international civil service'.[50]

Clearing unions

The technical collaboration so far described has been for the benefit of members, though some has been shared with other European states through the ECE. Multilateral clearing within Comecon may appear to have the same objective, but the latest of its two procedures promises also to develop East–West trade. The first scheme was agreed in Warsaw in June 1957, the second in Moscow in October 1963.[51] The former agreement was formally denounced by Article 12 of the latter, but—largely because recourse to its arrangements was optional—it had never become significant. During its six-year life it cleared only 1·5 per cent of intra-trade.[52] The 1963 agreement was ratified by all contracting parties (with that of the Soviet Union on 25 January 1964) and the Bank came into operation on 18 May.

Both agreements designated a clearing agency in Moscow—in 1957 the USSR State Bank, in 1963 a new International Bank of Economic Co-operation—on which each Comecon member had drawing rights. No participant can by right remain in debt to the clearing agency beyond 31 December—the persistent-debtor situation of the EPU is thus excluded. Under Article 3 of the 1957 agreement,

> the total amount of payments through the multilateral clearing by each of the parties to the present Agreement in any calendar year shall be equal to the total amount of such country's receipts from other countries parties to the agreement over the same period.

[50] Res. of Council of FICSA, 4 Oct. 1963.

[51] *Ved. Verkh. Sov. SSSR*, nos. 5 and 7, 1964. Sources used other than those listed below were *Ek. gaz.*, 11 Jan. 1964, and *Nepszava*, 19 Aug. 1963.

[52] A. Zwass, *Finanse* (Warsaw), Oct. 1963, p. 5. The trend was a declining one, since in 1961 it had cleared only $38 m., or 0·5 per cent of intra-trade (Novozamsky, p. 126).

M

By the 1963 agreement, 'each contracting party, in concluding trade agreements, is to ensure a balance of receipts and expenditure in transferable roubles within the calendar year with all the other contracting parties as a whole'.[53] Both agreements set limits to swing credits permissible during the calendar year: the first allowed up to 3 per cent of the value of the country's total exports made the previous year to contracting parties; under the second the credit is at the discretion of the Bank. Both arrangements levied a higher interest rate the larger the debt. At the end of each year the 1957 agreement permitted the carry-over of 25 per cent of its maximum debt (viz. $\frac{3}{4}$ per cent of its standardized exports) for three months, during which debtor period it lost its right to further credit. Under the 1963 scheme the Bank is endowed with a capital of 300 m. roubles ($333 m.)—that is, 3 per cent of mutual exports at the time—but after a 20 per cent deposit in the first year, the demand is statutorily at the discretion of the Bank. Interest-bearing credit will be permitted for a maximum of a year. The amount of credit is explicitly not related to that of a member's paid-up share in the Bank's capital; if repayment is delayed, further credits may be withheld—though this is optional, not mandatory, as under the 1957 treaty.[54]

The 1957 system distinguished between normal bilateral clearing and the multilateral accounts: transfers from the former to the latter were made by agreement with the parties. This was a major difference from EPU, under which all payments had to be declared for multilateral clearing (at the Bank of International Settlements). The 1963 agreement requires all payments between contracting parties to be made through its Bank but ensures annual compensation by obliging each party to plan for equilibrium in its balance of payments with the rest, including settlement of any debit balance at the Bank. This provides an important innovation: after the usual round of bilateral trade protocols, the parties meet in multilateral negotiation to realize supplementary exchanges. In 1964 these multilateral negotiations took place in Moscow in May.[55] All Comecon observers, China, North

[53] A. Birladeanu, chairman of the session of the Executive Committee at which the agreement was signed (*Pr.*, 25 Oct. 1963).

[54] The Statute of the Bank is, *inter alia*, in *Rada Wzajemnej Pomocy Gospodarczej*, pp. 245–6 and its first report is available as *La Banque Internationale pour la Coopération Économique 1964* (Moscow, 1965); among eastern European commentaries see esp. L. Frei, *Mezhdunarodnye rascheti i finansirovanie vneshnei torgovli sotsialisiticheskikh stran*, 2nd ed. (Moscow, 1965), pp. 205–11, and Ciamaga, pp. 88–97.

[55] The 1967 meeting was in February (with Cuba, Korea, Vietnam, and Yugoslavia).

Korea, North Vietnam, and Cuba, participated, and the possibility thereby arose of trilateral deals with them, settled by the transferable roubles of any two members, or of calling on the Bank (under Art. 9 of the 1963 agreement) to effect the settlement directly.

Under both agreements the rouble was made 'transferable' between members, but not 'convertible' to outsiders. The 1957 agreement laid down that debts not redeemed in the time-limit for swing credits had to be repaid within one month by deliveries of scheduled goods (14 such goods, all raw materials or semi-manufactures, being set out in Annex D of the agreement).[56] Under EPU all required settlements had to be made in gold. Poland proposed for the 1963 treaty that under certain conditions a debtor would have to repay partly in gold (or convertible currencies) and that a creditor would hence have a right to some gold drawings. Hungary (the original promoter of the scheme, as early as 1958) and Poland also suggested that the 300-m.-rouble capital be partly composed of gold.[57] In this manner payment obligations with the rest of the world could be incorporated into the scheme. It was agreed to reopen discussion after a year's operation and the Polish proposal was duly tabled at the session of the Bank Council in October 1965, having previously been through the Comecon Finance and Currency Commission (at Kiev in May) and the Executive Committee (at Leningrad in June). According to the official communiqué, the Council authorized the Board of the Bank to approach the central banks of 'developed capitalist countries' to negotiate arrangements for the conversion of transferable roubles and to open similar negotiations for the otherwise inconvertible currencies of 'other socialist countries' (presumably, Cuba, North Korea, North Vietnam, and Yugoslavia) and of developing countries.[58] Bank clearing of these latter would be of considerable significance, since each member tends to deal in about 40 inconvertible valuta (even more in the GDR whose trade is almost wholly in such currencies). It would, moreover, facilitate joint foreign-trade programming among members along the lines of the Kronsjø scheme

[56] Hard coal, synthetic rubber, motor tyres, sawn timber, diesel fuel, fuel oil, rolled steel, aluminium, zinc concentrates, potassium salts, grain, sugar, meat, and tobacco.

[57] The proposals were first reported by H. Kotlicki, the Polish delegate to the Bank (*Tryb. Lud.*, 25 Oct. 1963); they were reiterated by the Polish member of the Comecon Executive, Jaroszewicz, in *Wld Marx. R.*, Mar. 1964, p. 7, and by the Hungarian member, Apro, in *Tars. Sz.*, no. 3, 1964.

[58] *Den. i kr.*, no. 12, 1965.

(see p. 194), and eliminate recourse to the rather cumbrous ECE Compensation Procedure (see p. 174). The Bank has made arrangements with some commercial, but not yet with any central, banks of countries with external convertibility. Nor did it accept in full the cognate Polish proposal that debtor balances be paid in gold or convertible currency in a rising proportion increasing with time. Thus, for example, during the first period 10 per cent of the indebtedness would be so payable, and an additional 10 per cent would be levied until 100 per cent convertibility was reached. This would put pressure on members to expand intra-Comecon trade and to export to the others goods of a quality comparable with those sold on western markets. The preferential allocation of exports in volume and quality to western markets was cited as a factor inhibiting use of the transferable rouble,[59] and it has been suggested (though not confirmed) that proceeds from exports which could have been sold for convertible currency or in short supply within Comecon have been balanced separately in the Bank's books. This corresponds to the 'hard' and 'soft' items implied by the 'scheduled goods' of the 1957 agreement.[60] Poland, 'with millions on its account,'[61] was without recourse against its debtors; in its view, 'to judge from many statements and publications, the Polish proposal found support among the other countries of the People's Democracies. The Soviet Union's attitude on this problem is so far unknown.'[62]

The Polish authorities were not satisfied[63] by the concession that part of the subscription should be payable in convertible currency, each member drawing against its own quota 'without a reason being assigned'.[64] In 1966 the Board of the Bank set a 10 per cent gold and convertible tranche for immediate subscription, with a further 20 per cent to be subscribed by the end of the year, viz. to 90 million roubles.[65]

[59] Wyczalkowski, *IMF Staff Papers*, July 1966, p. 192, analysing the Polish scheme as reported in Kotlicki, *Tryb. Ludu*, 27 Apr. 1965, and S. Albinowski, *Glos Pracy* (Warsaw), 5 May 1965.

[60] Thus one of the criticisms of Rumania must have been that its export increment of 'hard' goods in 1960–2 to other members was only 1 per cent (but 29 per cent to non-members), against 30 per cent in 1958–60 (Montias, *Slav. R.*, Sept. 1966, p. 436).

[61] *Glos Pracy*. 8 May 1965.

[62] *Zyc. War.*, 8 July 1965; ibid. 14 July said that the USSR had not rejected the scheme. Soviet support for the 'gradual introduction of convertibility' was unofficially indicated by Bogomolov in *Komm.*, no. 18, 1966.

[63] See Kotlicki, *Zyc. War.*, 20 July 1965, who there outlined both schemes.

[64] Reported in *The Economist* (London), 18 June 1966, as accepted by the Bank Council in October 1965, though not figuring in the communiqué in *Den. i kr.*

[65] R. Malesa (Polish member of the Board), *Zyc. gos.*, 3 July 1966.

Jaroszewicz, the Polish representative to the Comecon Executive Committee, observing that the Bank had only gone this very short way, regretted that it had so far been unable to 'modernize financial relations'; it could 'more fully assist multilateral accounts if partial payment in gold or foreign currency could be introduced.'[66]

The prerequisite for the full convertibility of the Bank's rouble is, however, that prices reflect the relative scarcities in member economies, and perform some role in domestic allocation decisions. Even if the trade monopolies were relaxed (as appears possible in some states), the external unit of account does 'not represent a general claim on goods in any member country'.[67] Cognate pricing problems are discussed in the next chapter.

It is envisaged that direct compensation might be arranged with banks in non-member countries—which would introduce a Euro-rouble alongside the Euro-dollar—and that the Bank might employ its reserves as export credits to underdeveloped countries. As a separate operation, the Bank, 'on the instructions of the countries concerned, shall finance and supply credit for joint construction projects and for the reconstruction and operation of industrial enterprises and other projects, against funds set aside by these countries'.[68] A report prepared for submission to the Comecon Executive (at its fourteenth session, convened for October 1964) proposed to raise an investment fund for such purposes of 250–500 m. roubles ($275–550 m.).[69] The suggested incidence of this investment capital is compared below with the quotas for the clearing fund under Article 3 of the 1963 agreement (in percentages):

	Statutory capital (1963 agreement)	*Investment capital (1964 draft)*
Bulgaria	6	4
Czechoslovakia	15	11
GDR	18	8
Hungary	7	7
Mongolia	1	0
Poland	9	11
Rumania	5	8
USSR	39	51

[66] *Tryb. Lud.*, 17 May 1966. [67] Wyczalkowski, *IMF Staff Papers*, July 1966, p. 191.
[68] Comecon statement, *Information on Economic Co-operation*, p. 16.
[69] *Financial Times*, 25 Aug. 1964. Bogomolov (loc. cit.) commended such a plan in Dec. 1966.

The disparities in purchasing power of the various Comecon currencies at the established exchange-rates were shown by the experience of the ECE Multilateral Compensation Procedure set up in 1957. In nine years 77 compensation circuits were arranged, involving \$30·5 m. from Comecon members, \$30·8 m. from EPU–EMA members, and \$50·2 m. from other countries; as the figures below show, use of the arrangements virtually ceased after the 'market' had settled in 1960; thereafter currencies with a higher purchasing power were not offered, and those with a lower were available but were not taken up.[70] The revival since 1963 is due to increasing use of the scheme by developing countries, whose currencies are generally inconvertible; its role in East–West trade has continued to decline.

	Number of circuits	*Value of compensations (\$ m.)*
1957–8	18	22·0
1958–9	11	18·1
1959–60	7	15·9
1960–1	4	6·7
1961–2	5	8·0
1962–3	4	3·7
1963–4	11	11·9
1964–5	5	9·4
1965–6	12	16·0

Source: ECE, document E/ECE/629 of 27 July 1966. Data are for years ending 30 June.

Some indication of the divergence of purchasing power and exchange rates may be obtained from data on the Czechoslovak crown. The official rate for non-commercial transactions (intended to reflect parity for a basket of consumer's goods and services) is 9·65 crowns to the rouble; at the cross-rate of the rouble to the U.S. dollar, the same category of transactions would be 8·00 crowns to the rouble.[71] A study of the Gilbert–Kravis type carried out by the Research Institute of the USSR Gosplan showed 14·50 crowns to the rouble on the Soviet consumption pattern and 10·70 crowns on the Czechoslovak

[70] See G. Curzon, *Multilateral Commercial Diplomacy* (London, 1965), p. 297, and J. L'Huillier, *Problems relating to the Expansion of Trade between Free-enterprise and Collectivist Economies: report to the International Chamber of Commerce* (Paris, 1960), p. 14.

[71] *Hosp. Nov.*, no. 36, 1966, p. 12 (7·20 crowns to the US dollar and \$1·11 to the rouble).

consumption pattern.[72] Finally, the rate used by the Research Institute of the Czechoslovak Planning Commission for comparisons of industrial output with the United States was 14 crowns to the dollar.[73]

[72] Kotkovsky, *Vopr. ekon.*, no. 8, 1966, p. 87.
[73] Novozamsky, *Pol. ekon.*, no. 8, 1966, p. 737.

IX
PRICING

Prices in the transition from bilateralism to multilateralism

THE Director-General of the Polish Ministry of Finance, a delegate to the Comecon Executive meeting which signed the multilateral clearing scheme, just described, stated on his return to Warsaw:

> We are aware that multilateral balancing of payments will be a difficult task in view of the existing bilateral trade agreements, different levels of prices for various commodities, and so on. Some time will pass, no doubt, before we learn how to take full advantage of the potential of the new accounting system.[1]

This chapter is devoted to the pricing problems which have arisen within strictly static assessments of the efficiency of inter-member trade. Since the share of Comecon in total world trade is small, the evaluation of exchanges with non-members must largely be a comparison of domestic costs with world-market prices. Even if Comecon were to act as a common negotiator in each of the western European trading groups (a function it is unlikely to fill despite occasional such hopes, chiefly expressed in Hungary),[2] it would have greatly to expand its sales in the West in order to influence prices. During 1959–65 it sold a steady 7 per cent of its exports to EEC and an equally steady 6 per cent to EFTA: in 1965 these were a mere 2·8 per cent of total EEC imports, 4·0 per cent of EFTA imports, and 2·9 per cent of OECD imports. Nor has Comecon any major commodity to export to the West in which its size of sales can, within the foreseeable future, make it a price-leader. The questions treated here are hence of the transition from two-partner barter deals to multilateral trade between economies when the terms of trade are given, but which could place no reliance on their measurements of domestic cost. Comecon members have only recently assured themselves of comparability of their present costs: they could now, with some confidence, begin to employ their prices to allocate production between domestic use and foreign

[1] Kotlicki, *Tryb. Lud.*, 25 Oct. 1963.

[2] See statements by the Hungarian Foreign Minister, J. Peter, and by the President of the Hungarian Economic Association, I. Vajda, in *The Times*, 3 July 1965 and 4 Mar. 1966 respectively.

trade. The economic reforms being gradually introduced in most member countries during 1966–8 have been—or are being—underwritten by price reforms which primarily permit domestic enterprises to conduct rational trade among themselves. By the same token, the foreign-trade monopolies (or, as devolution proceeds, producing enterprises) can adjudicate between home and foreign markets.

An altogether different problem is presented by pricing problems under dynamic conditions, that is, when the comparative costs of each member alter with economic growth. A country optimizing its long-term production plan with respect to foreign trade must project for itself and its partners the income elasticity of demand and the production possibility curve of each good traded, and must specify the differential between its planned rate of growth and those of its partners.[3] For most prospective partners it must rely on market analyses of world trends—an aspect with which Comecon could properly be more concerned.[4] When each partner is willing to confront and co-ordinate long-term plans with others—and Comecon is the only trade bloc which sets this procedure as its goal—the planned rates of growth are known, and, in principle, the relevant costs and propensities can be projected. It has already been observed (p. 105) that one of Rumania's complaints in the disputes of 1962–4 was its inability to define realistic trends for branches which it was only beginning to develop. Even where industries are adequately established, there is inevitably much less certainty about a planned than about an actual cost.

Although the Rumanian reservations on plan co-ordination went beyond the technical aspect of projection to the specific choice of international specialization, pricing can be seen as a problem, viz. that of planning the terms of trade among members for the horizon year of a long-term plan. This, the crucial choice in the integration process of centrally-planned economies, is discussed in Ch. X.

The static choice of intra-trade, as Comecon members evolved from the virtual barter of residuals in 'material balances', was the assessment of bilateral advantage: an optimal two-partner exchange would (as Ch. III pointed out) follow Ricardo. When trilateral deals are concluded, the cross-rate implicit in the cost-relatives characteriz-

[3] When the only known relationships are of each elasticity to unity and of the production possibility curve to the rate of growth, a majority of cases are indeterminant even in a simplified two-country, two-good model. See F. Pryor, *Oxford Economic Papers*, Mar. 1966, p. 54.
[4] See J. Rudzinski, in Kaser, ed., *St Antony's Papers 19*, esp. pp. 100–3.

ing the trade of two of the states would not necessarily correspond to the rate at which the same goods would exchange directly with the third. By 1956 the trilateral arrangements initiated in 1954 had been written into 'practically all trade agreements between the Soviet Union and the people's democracies' and some trilateral settlement was being effected by 'all countries members of CMEA'.[5] Proposals to convert these arrangements into a multilateral clearing were already under discussion,[6] and the agreement described in the previous chapter was signed on 20 June 1957.

With neither centralized negotiations nor a free market to bring these prices into equilibrium, each partner could be assured of an equitable balance of advantage only if both trade and payments were strictly bilateral. The multilateralization of either—even marginally, as by 1957—could cause the yield of the sale of a given product to differ in terms of imports from alternative partners. Certain intra-Comecon conventions purported to standardize prices in reciprocal trade: since present east European writers cannot agree on a description of these conventions, it may be assumed that they were of limited application. It is common ground that at Comecon's foundation intra-trade was carried on approximately at world-market prices, and at exchange rates which were not inaccurate reflexions of the purchasing parity of traded goods. Traffic with the USSR was the main exception. Quite apart from deliveries on reparations account or from the Soviet share of the mixed companies, certain prices were bluntly inequitable. The case of the price paid for Polish coal during 1946–53 has already been mentioned; one of the counts in the 1949 trial of Traicho Kostov, Bulgarian Deputy Prime Minister (now posthumously rehabilitated) was his attempt to negotiate fairer prices in Bulgaro-Soviet trade. Similarly, while, for example, the Polish zloty was until 1950 reasonably valued *vis-à-vis* western and most Comecon currencies, at 400 to the dollar, it was seriously undervalued at 75 to the rouble. Strategic stockpiling and other consequences of the Korean War disturbed world-market prices: thus the average value of United Kingdom imports in 1950 was 15 per cent and in 1951 just on 50 per cent above 1949, while its export values rose by only 5 and 20 per cent. They were abandoned by members for their own trade either in 1950 or in 1951,[7]

[5] 'Multilateral Payments among Socialist Countries', *Vnesh. trg.*, no. 2, 1957. [6] Ibid.

[7] The variant interpretations of the history of intra-Comecon prices are in V. Cerniansky, *Ekonomika socialistickeho zahranicniho obchodu* (Prague, 1961) and an extensive review of the

in favour of so-called 'stop prices' which were—the histories conflict—either world prices of the first half of 1950 or those of that period averaged with those of 1949 as a whole. One report has it that these 'stop prices' operated only to 1953, and that 'corrected world prices' were used until 1959: world prices were more or less stabilized (over the 1953–9 period the mean unit-value of United Kingdom imports was never more than 6 per cent, or less than 3 per cent, from the 1953 average), and the 'corrections' were intended to adjust for market imperfections or crises (such as at the time of the Suez invasion in 1956). Another record states that the Korea-emergency prices ran until 1956, that in 1957 the price basis was the world market in 1956, and that 1957 prices ruled from 1958. A further statement contends that in 1953–7 the mean used was of the 1951–2 world-price 'plateau', and that the price basis from 1959 was that of 1958. Each of the variants (1956, 1957, and 1958) reflects, no doubt, the predominant set of prices at which a country traded; in fact, most trade protocols for 1957 deliveries seem to have specified 1956 prices, and the basis subsequently most widely used appears to have been that of 1957. The Comecon Standing Commission on Foreign Trade, set up in 1956, appointed a group of experts to make general recommendations. The group's report, presented in 1957, proposed that simple averaging need not apply to commodities subject to wide fluctuation during the chosen base year, nor to those for which a clear world market did not operate. It affirmed as a principle that intra-Comecon prices should be those of the preceding year in world markets, that is, annually revised.

When this advice was presented to the Foreign Trade Commission, the Bulgarian delegation argued that it was tantamount to subordinating the socialist economies to capitalist world monopolies. Although the imperfection of competition is a distorting factor in some prices, the real problem was the terms of trade for primary producers. Bulgaria, to identify one of its practical complaints on the proposal, demanded a price for zinc concentrates well above the London quotation. The Ninth Session (June 1958) accepted the Commission's general rule that prices should be established 'on the basis of average

---

book by E. Georgiev, *Vnesh. torg.*, no. 5, 1963, esp. p. 59; see also W. Trampczynski, *Zyc. War.*, 19 Apr. 1957. Agoston, p. 27, understands that the introduction of 'stop prices' was made by a Comecon Session, but there is no published statement to this effect.

world market prices on the principal market for the commodity in a clearly defined period', specifying that the 1959 trade agreements should be based on 1957 prices. Köhler adds that the onus of documenting a 'world price' is on the seller, though the buyer can furnish counter-materials and that each trade agreement specifies which principal market shall be regarded as price-determining. He observes that this documentation was a lengthy procedure and some agreements were made with 'provisional prices' (which are, however, unenforceable under the commercial law of Comecon members). To obviate this, a 'price court' was suggested, but does not appear to have been accepted.[8] Of itself this choice of 1957 favoured primary producers against exports of manufactures, although the high oil price-mean was excluded as attributable to the Suez crisis. Rumania thus did not gain the benefit of the world market level for all its exports to other members, whereas Bulgaria did. There were, moreover, special concessions for strategic materials (including Bulgarian non-ferrous metals), for some farm produce (again notably that exported by Bulgaria), and for new developments involving high initial cost. Adjustments were also authorized where monopolistic or speculative activity had distorted the price which would have been formed under normal competition. The Session agreed equally to divide between partners the difference between the freight cost included in a world market quotation, c.i.f. to a Comecon member, and the transport charge actually incurred in delivering the commodity from a Comecon supplier.[9] Thus, if hides were imported from the USSR instead of from South America, half the transport differential should be included in the Soviet c.i.f. price. On balance, Hungary found that this arrangement worked to its disadvantage, but it was insufficiently important for it to press for a change. The scheduled annual revisions never took place, and 1957, or in some instances 1958, prices were used until 1964.

Pricing as the instrument of a preference area

The intra-Comecon market was thus separated from that available outside by procedures having the same result as a customs union.[10]

[8] H. Kohler, *Economic Integration in the Soviet Bloc* (New York, 1966), p. 185.

[9] Kohler (p. 184) quotes a proposal (not then proceeded with) of a common basing point system; he also cites some perverse results of the system adopted.

[10] These points are fully argued by F. Holzman, *R. Econ. Statist.*, May and Nov. 1962; see also K. Svendson, *Stats. Tid.*, no. 1, 1961.

Members agreed to pay each other somewhat higher prices than those ruling in world trade—sometimes by reason of the fact that world prices fell after 1957, sometimes because a 'strategic mark-up' was added to the 1957 set. The ECE concluded at the time that 'there is plentiful evidence that sellers of goods that are particularly scarce within the region frequently manage to obtain more than the "basic world market price" '.[11] This 'scarcity' would have arisen either because strategic controls prevented adequate purchases from the West or because development was required on strategic grounds. Under this reciprocal price preference, Comecon is distinguishable from a formal customs union (EEC) or free trade area (EFTA) by depending for its discrimination not on a tariff wall against outsiders (though this came in Hungary and the USSR in 1961) but by agreements to disregard outside offers. Members of EEC and EFTA protect those of their industries operating at costs higher than world costs by imposing a duty on non-member supplies; members of Comecon do the same by acting as if a duty were applied. It is this practice which gives rise to the contention of non-members that Comecon is a trade-preference area and should be treated as such. They claim that although most of them grant Comecon members most-favoured-nation treatment, thereby permitting Comecon sales to be competitive with those of any other country, their own exporters do not enjoy corresponding access to Comecon markets. On the other hand many non-members maintain discriminatory practices against the Comecon states, notably in quotas, licences, and payments control. Such discrimination is not in accord with most-favoured-nation treatment. This study is not the place to rehearse the many arguments in the case, but it seems clear that a compromise solution lies in an agreement on effective reciprocity, whereby non-discrimination in quota arrangements and the like towards Comecon members would be balanced by an import-expansion guarantee by them. This was the consensus of the ECE *ad hoc* group of experts which discussed the problem in 1963.[12]

EEC and EFTA are permitted, under GATT rules, to give within each group preferential treatment (leading eventually to zero tariffs),

[11] *Econ. Survey Eur. 1957*, ch. vi, p. 28.

[12] These proposals are analysed by R. Nötel, *Economia internazionale*, no. 4, 1965, pp. 10–17, and by F. Holzman, in H. Rosovsky, ed., *Industrialization in Two Systems: Essays in Honor of Alexander Gerschenkron* (New York, 1966).

which they do not accord to GATT members or countries afforded most-favoured-nation treatment. A study of the two areas, prepared by the USSR Institute of World Economy and International Relations, observed:

> The Soviet Union and other socialist countries reject the discriminatory policy of closed economic groupings. They uphold the most-favoured-nation principle which has recommended itself over a long period as a universal and generally-accepted principle of international trade. The countries of socialism demand observance of this principle, incorporated in commercial treaties with capitalist states, including those forming closed economic groups.[13]

In line with this contention, Hungary and the USSR introduced two-column tariffs in 1961, the lower rates to apply to countries conceding most-favoured-nation treatment as defined by them; Bulgaria did the same, but has not yet applied the higher rates.[14]

The effect of pricing within Comecon

It has been pointed out that Comecon members thus discriminate in favour of each other within their 'customs union'. It has been suggested that the price practices involve discrimination by one member against another. Thus Mendershausen calculated the unit-values of trade within Comecon with those in East–West trade.[15] He concluded that the USSR was exploiting the others: he did not, however, take account of the price discrimination against Comecon members in East–West trade, if measured by intra-West commerce. Holzman found that if the USSR had been able to sell the 24 comparable commodities which the United Kingdom bought from western Europe at the prices paid to western Europe, it would have gained 3 per cent, and that if other Comecon members had sold their 48 comparable commodities which the United Kingdom similarly purchased in western Europe, they would have obtained 9 per cent more at the latter's prices. He confirmed this effect from Belgian trade, and observed that, as imports are valued c.i.f., the higher transport cost embodied in the unit-values for Comecon partners makes the discrimination higher.[16]

[13] *Pr.*, 26 Aug. 1962.

[14] The implications are fully studied by the ECE Secretariat in *Econ. B. Eur.*, xiv/1, pp. 52–58.

[15] The best review of eastern practice and western analysis is by J. Wilczynski, *J. Pol. Econ.*, June 1966, pp. 250–64; the basic papers are by H. Mendershausen, *R. Econ. Statist.*, May 1959 and May 1960, and F. Holzman, ibid. May and Nov. 1962. For briefer summaries see Svendson, *Stats. Tid.*, no. 1, 1961, and G. Adler-Karlsson, *Econ. Plan.*, Sept. 1963, pp. 146–8.

[16] Holzman, *R. Econ. Statist.*, Nov. 1962, p. 497.

Furthermore, the 1957 price set comprised raw materials in a falling time-series, while manufactures—though less rapidly—were on an upward trend. In the world unit-values as measured by the United Nations Statistical Office, manufactures showed a slight recession in 1958–9 and were above the 1957 level by 1961; raw materials fell quickly in 1958, then declined more slowly, and rose in 1963. Exporters of primary products thus gained better terms by selling to Comecon partners than to others. Bulgaria certainly benefited from this ratio: Holzman's calculations show that while there is mutual discrimination between Bulgaria and the USSR, the former appears to discriminate more heavily than does the USSR against other Comecon partners. Another statistical analysis, by Pryor, of the terms of trade of the USSR with each other Comecon partner implies that those of Bulgaria and the GDR during 1955–8 were consistently more favourable than the average for all members, while Czechoslovakia, Hungary, and Rumania got worse terms; Poland was favoured during 1955–7 but disfavoured in 1958. In only one instance was the deviation from the average as much as 10 per cent, but it is of interest that the ranking (if the GDR is excluded because the sample for that country was too small) also shows that Bulgaria, the least developed member (Albania was not examined), obtained the best terms. The size of the samples in total trade with the USSR over the four years ranged from 26 per cent (Bulgaria) to 61 per cent (Czechoslovakia) for exports and from 4 per cent (GDR) to 33 per cent (Rumania) for imports; in 1958 the GDR sample was as low as 1·6 per cent.[17]

The reservations made above on the comparison of prices in East–West trade with those in intra-Comecon trade by no means imply that members would not, on the whole, do better by trade with the rest of the world. The concern of their foreign-trade ministries to maintain East–West trade is evidence at least that the reverse does not apply—namely, that the higher level of prices within Comecon is not uniformly advantageous. Probably because of this, the introduction of a multilateral payments scheme in 1964—and the possibility of its clearing some non-member (convertible) currencies in 1965—was accompanied (for agreements covering 1964 and 1965) by a proposed revision of Comecon intra-trade prices to the average of 1957–61. This would have almost eliminated the overall differential between

[17] Pryor, *Communist Foreign Trade System*, p. 146.

East and West, as may be seen by comparing the indices for all exports in columns 1, 2, and 6 of Table 6, but entirely at the expense of primary producers who would have lost the mark-up they enjoyed by the use of 1957 prices for their exports. The GDR had proposed the average of 1958–61, which would have improved its own terms of trade but would have been still more to the disadvantage of primary producers, and was rebuffed. The December 1962 Executive accepted the mean of 1957–62[18] which proved to be a little worse for primary producers than the original proposal (see Table 6). Possibly because of the divergence of interest, the recommendation was not implemented and the *status quo*, i.e. a 1957 price basis, was used for trade in 1964, and, somewhat amended, in 1965. Bulgaria's apparent satisfaction with Comecon may perhaps suggest that it was to retain more favourable terms of trade than it could derive from commerce outside (compare column 3 with columns 6 and 7 in Table 6). Alternatively, the loan granted by the USSR at its usual very low rate of interest (viz. well below the rate of return on the investment it finances), may in part offset the terms of trade loss. This would correspond to the proposals of compensatory finance put up by underdeveloped countries to the United Nations and other international agencies of 'western' countries in 1962, and still under discussion. If Rumania did not obtain similar terms, it is

TABLE 6

Price Index-Numbers for World Exports other than by Comecon Members

(1958=100)

	1957	*Av. 1957–61*	*Av. 1957–62*	*Av. 1958–61*	*Av. 1959–63*	*1963*	*1964*	*1965*
	(1)	(2)	(3)	(4)	(5)	(6)	(7)	(8)
Primary commodities	106	99	98	97	97	100	103	100
Manufactures	101	101	101	101	101	103	104	106
All exports	103	100	100	99	99	100	102	103

Note: China, N. Korea, and N. Vietnam also excluded.
Source: UN, *Monthly B. Statist*, June 1966, p. xvi.

[18] *Vnesh. torg.* (no. 3, 1963, p. 42), however, quotes 1957–61 as the decision.

easier to explain its Declaration of April 1964 that it 'develops its economic links with all states irrespective of their social system', and its informal contacts with other preference groups (GATT itself and the EEC) during the United Nations Conference on Trade and Development in March–June 1964.

For the 1966–70 plans the average prices of 1959–62 were taken as the first basis of discussion, but as 1963 prices became available, the proposition had become in mid-1964 the mean of 1959–63. The averages were in fact the same as those in the abortive GDR proposal. They implied poorer terms of trade than primary exporters could gain on a world market for which their goods were reaching a peak (see column 7 of Table 6). Since the prices were to be used to value the repatriation in kind of capital and interest on joint investments, their repayment burden, negotiated when 1957 prices ruled their intertrade, would be raised at a stroke.

A compromise was reached at the Executive in December 1964 and approved by the Nineteenth Session: some alterations to the 1957–8 prices were to be made for 1965 trade, but 1966–70 exchanges would approximate the world average for 1960–4. Some products, however, would be valued on as long as an 8-year mean and others on as short as a 2-year mean; there were some products for which a single base year was taken, and a few 'unplanned goods' for which the world market price was ignored and the traded price left to the negotiation of the partners concerned.[19] In consequence, the unit-value of USSR exports to other members fell sharply in 1966, and as a *quid pro quo* (see p. 127) the main beneficiaries agreed at the Twentieth Session (December 1966) to invest in Soviet raw materials.

Trade and domestic prices

The net effect of the use of multiple price bases has not been revealed, although it may be assumed from progress of long-term trade agreements[20] (notably at the Executive Committee meetings of December 1965 and April 1966) that concessions were made to the primary ex-

[19] The first reference to this procedure seems to have been by P. Nosko, *Vnesh. torg.*, no. 7, 1964, pp. 28–31. K. Popov (ibid. no. 11, 1966) supports such 'corrected' world prices.

[20] The trade-agreement network does not appear ever to have been completed for the preceding plan period. There were 25 bilateral agreements on trade for 1961–5 (E. Usenko, *Vnesh. torg.*, no. 7, 1962, p. 7); for all seven members to be mutually linked 28 agreements would be necessary. Formal discipline may not thus have been fully ensured by quotas, but a Bulgarian reports (*Vnesh. trg.*, no. 7, 1961) cites the import and export targets of each member with the rest.

porters. The sharp change in world terms of trade during 1965 should enhance the interest of that group in Comecon prices, since outside prices for their products have fallen while those of the manufactures they buy have risen. Their import-substitution programmes or manufacturing lines started under Comecon specialization in turn appear more profitable when valued at world prices.

For the more industrialized members, the rise in the prices which they could obtain by sales outside the group by the same token diminishes their desire to rely on intra-trade. To some extent of course the assurance of outlets within Comecon will be considered worth a few percentage-point changes on world markets. A Polish economist concludes:

> It is difficult directly to assess the significance of this particular point of view on the international co-operation of production and specialization in the CMEA. The most important obstacle to the capitalist international division of labour is access to markets, the hindrance to developing countries entering the international market. Long-term agreements between CMEA members securing firm markets for specialized production therefore establish the bases for utilizing the advantages arising from the deepening of the international division of labour.[21]

Countries put at too great a disadvantage by the margin might, however, break rank. In 1958 a Czechoslovak economist specializing in questions of foreign-trade efficiency observed: 'If some socialist country continually asks and obtains higher prices for a good than those on the main world market, it must necessarily lead, sooner or later, to the socialist purchaser's buying the good on the capitalist market.'[22] Since then, Comecon members have improved their knowledge of domestic-cost patterns. When their foreign-trade corporations adhered fairly strictly to the rules of intra-trade, they were cushioned from realization of the potential loss or forgone gain in alternative directions by two factors.

In the first place, the corporations were, for many years, making windfall profits from an overvalued exchange-rate. Sales of imports on the home market, or purchases of exports from home producers, brought an inevitable profit.[23] Corporations could in theory be instructed to ignore this profit as a measure of their acumen, but, in fact,

[21] K. Laski, *Ek.*, no. 1, 1964. [22] V. Cerniansky, *Auss.*, nos. 4–5, 1958.

[23] See Nove, in A. Nove and D. Donnelly, *Trade with Communist Countries* (London, 1960), pp. 23–24.

the actual profit as a percentage of that planned (irrespective of its origin) was used by the Ministry of Foreign Trade of the USSR as the criterion for the payment of managerial bonuses. The elimination of this profit was the avowed objective of the devaluation of the rouble on 1 January 1961 (more than reversing the deliberate break with cost-levels in 1950); the Bulgarian lev was devalued exactly a year later. In the GDR where, according to Köhler, use of these spurious profits as a basis for calculating trade efficiency 'has been conducted with the greatest vigour', the overvalued margin was, with effect from 1 January 1959, recalculated at an estimated 'purchasing-power rate'.[24] At a conference of foreign-trade economists in Sofia in January–February 1964, this differential was said to be 'calculated for all commodities regularly, not less than once a year, in virtually all the member states of Comecon'.[25] Its validity depends upon the correspondence of the exchange rate used with external purchasing power and upon the conformity of domestic prices to some rational criterion.

Such reform of home prices has been the second of improvements to Comecon trade appraised over recent years. Wholesale prices are now everywhere intended to reflect the pattern of production costs, and by the end of 1967 will incorporate a charge for capital in all member countries save Rumania.[26] The gain from trade can thus be measured by a simple comparison of domestic and foreign prices. A round of wholesale-price reform began in Hungary and Czechoslovakia in 1959, in Poland in 1962, in Rumania in 1963, and in the GDR in 1964. The earlier changes were overtaken by radical policy shifts towards decentralizing industrial management: Czechoslovakia decided to introduce new pricing procedures under which a few goods will not be subject to any price control and many more will be negotiable with the price-setting authority. In Hungary a similar attempt to make prices a variable mechanism is envisaged for 1968 and in the GDR the reform of the price pattern is seen as a continuing process in which adjustments will be made to reflect both supply and demand variations. In the Soviet Union regular postponements of a wholesale price reform were brought to a head by the changes in industrial

[24] Köhler, p. 161; in assessing the suitability of this profit, for which he uses the German term, *Preisausgleich* (PAG), or 'price equalization payment', he belittles the information that it can provide under price reform and valid exchange rates. In rejecting the GDR 'purchasing power rate' (ibid. p. 373), he does not discuss the manner of its computation.

[25] E. Georgiev, *Vnesh. torg.*, no. 7, 1964, cited by Köhler, p. 192.

[26] The position in Mongolia is not known.

management announced by Kosygin to the Party Central Committee in September 1965, for implementation by 1968: the bases for a new pricing pattern to be effective on 1 July 1967 were announced in September 1966 by the Chairman of the Committee on Prices,[27] but were accompanied by influential calls for flexible pricing.[28]

Comecon's recent discussion on pricing foreign-traded goods has thus been accompanied by an improvement in the reflexion of relative costs in the domestic-price structure. The evolution of Soviet domestic policy is instructive. For the period until 1957 the Soviet industrial user was isolated from choice between high- and low-cost sources by profit-and-loss compensation arrangements by the producing ministry. The Soviet gradual elimination of subsidies (started by Voznesensky, reversed in 1950, resumed in 1955) did not extend to intra-product pricing until the industrial ministries were broken up in 1957. The new regional agencies (*sovnarkhozy*) on which some of their powers were devolved, were required to close down workshops producing high-cost components; it was forbidden for profits earned on low-cost output in another industry to be transferred to compensate the loss in high-cost plants retained. The parallel between the ministerial autarkies within the Soviet Union, disbanded in 1957, and the corresponding trend in intra-Comecon trade is, of course, striking.

Even under the *sovnarkhozy*, however, the principle of marginal-cost pricing was restricted to certain semi-manufactures and never affected final products.[29] The majority of transactions remained at prices corresponding to the nation-wide average cost plus an arbitrary mark-up entitled 'profit'. Any enterprise operating at cost exceeding that mark-up was subsidized; profits, an insignificant automatic retention apart, were subject to central reallocation and furnished of themselves no incentive to expand low-cost capacity. When the industrial ministries were re-established in October 1965, the Soviet government emphasized that no return to 'ministerial autarkies' was envisaged; because the effective definition of component production has much widened since 1957—under schemes for 'specialization and co-operation' among factories—marginal costing was tacitly retained

[27] V. Sitnin, *Komm.*, no. 14, 1966, pp. 37–46.

[28] e.g. A. Bachurin (a deputy Chairman of the State Planning Committee), ibid. no. 11, 1966, pp. 40–52, and Academician L. Leontief, *Pr.*, 31 Aug. 1966.

[29] On the evolution of the debate on pricing final products see M. Bornstein, in US Congress, Joint Economic Committee, *New Directions in the Soviet Economy*, pp. 65–77.

for a not inconsiderable volume of output. The list to come into effect on 1 July 1967 is intended finally to eliminate prices which are below the average cost of a product, and to convert the arbitrary mark-up into a capital charge (at a mean for producers' goods of 15 per cent of fixed assets).[30]

This practice of pricing (with the exceptions already noticed in Czechoslovakia and Rumania) is now uniform throughout eastern Europe, and the domestic price-relatives facing the foreign-trade planner reflect average costs. But the price-relatives for export goods and import substitutes are interpreted as marginal costs, because the planners evaluate the incremental receipts from exports and the incremental cost of imports. A procedure for formalizing this relationship to guide planners in dynamic choice (i.e. in which export lines or import replacements capacity should be expanded by investment) was proposed by the Polish Mixed Commission for Evaluating Methods of Investigating the Efficiency of Foreign Trade.[31]

Some members have begun to adapt the relative scarcities represented by labour and capital costs to reflect a combined pattern of domestic demand and plan priorities, but these are quite unsystematic even within countries.[32] Yet it is precisely those features of consumers' and planners' preferences which are evoked by the prospective importer (or final end-user): here again a comparison of domestic and foreign-trade price furnishes no rational guide to the composition of exchanges.

The optimization of trade in consumers' goods is further complicated by the insertion of heavy rates of turnover tax between wholesale and retail prices. In the first place, price competition between imported and home products is largely ruled out because both are sold at the same price and differences are absorbed by turnover tax.[33] Where the quality of the import significantly exceeds that of the nearest comparable domestic item, a more than commensurate tax margin is frequently added. In the second place, rates vary widely between products and still more widely between countries. Turnover tax is levied to ensure an overall balance between consumer purchasing

[30] Sitnin, *Komm.*, no. 14, 1966.

[31] *Gosp. plan.*, no. 4, 1963. For the scheme as implemented see W. Trzeciakowski, ibid. no. 8–9, 1966, pp. 10–15.

[32] For a review of eastern European reforms see Wyczalkowski, pp. 157–88, and, on progress of the Soviet reform, N. Baibakov, *Pr.*, 4 Nov. 1966.

[33] Adler-Karlsson, *Econ. Plan.*, Sept. 1963, p. 146.

power and retail availabilities, not necessarily to clear the market for any specific product. While households have adapted their spending to the prevailing prices,[34] those prices are not expressive of inter-product preferences, and cannot be used directly in foreign-trade computations. Indirectly, retail-price elasticities are of significance for forecasting import demand and the release (or absorption) of domestic power by importing lower (or, in the other case, higher) taxed goods. There is an obvious instance in tropical fruit and cocoa imports which, given high demand elasticities, and high rates of tax, can siphon off more purchasing power than most domestic output or other imports. The goods which show a high tax are on some occasions imports from other Comecon countries. This has evoked some criticism from the exporting partners, who consider the situation unreasonable. A proposal was reported to have been made to the Executive to establish a committee on consumer-good prices to work towards some degree of harmonization.[35] The lack of concordance in retail-price patterns from one Comecon member to another is notorious, and governments are likely to be persuaded towards some improvement by the buying sprees on which tourists from one country to another engage to take advantage of such price discrepancies.

The concordance of foreign-trade prices

The problem of evaluating comparative costs (i.e. as reflected in domestic wholesale prices) in terms of foreign-trade prices does not arise in a free-trade market economy, for the producer is indifferent whether he sells to or buys from a native or a foreigner, and competition equates the domestic price and the world price. In a protectionist market economy, the producer's choice is weighted by any export subsidy (or 'drawback' on excise duty) which may lead him as seller to favour the foreigner, and by customs duties which would cause him, as buyer, to favour the home producer. This concordance of free-trade competition may be simulated in a planned economy, logically, in any of three ways: first, domestic prices may be made to coincide with foreign prices; second, foreign prices (i.e. in this instance, those within the control of Comecon) may be made to con-

[34] See J. Chapman, *Real Wages in Soviet Russia Since 1928* (Cambridge, Mass., 1963), App. B, for examples of the radical adaptation of Soviet consumer expenditure to changes in the price and availability pattern.

[35] *Financial Times*, 25 Aug. 1964.

form to domestic prices; third, coefficients to transform the one into the other may be invented. The effect of export subsidies and a tariff wall can be brought about by direct instruction by Foreign-Trade Ministries to export and import corporations or by quota arrangements with partners engaged in similar planning.

Only three countries seem not to have participated in the exploration of export efficiency—Albania, Rumania, and Mongolia. In the sphere of efficiency calculation, Albanian and Rumanian economists have been concerned with the domestic returns to investment.[36] Mongolia is keenly interested in the gain to be got from trade, but does not need sophisticated techniques. Export prospects at its present stage of development are clearly determined by its mineral deposits, the extent of its pasture, and its high trade dependence on the USSR (which in 1962 supplied 65 per cent of its imports and took 75 per cent of its exports).[37] Where research has gone on in the other six members, all but one country (Bulgaria, which has reproduced a Polish procedure) has made a distinctive contribution.[38]

When the pioneers in this field, the Hungarian economists Liska and Marias, pointed out—in 1954—that 'the real results of foreign-trade policy ... are considerably distorted by the present price system', they did not advocate new sets of prices—domestic or foreign—but a set of coefficients relating one to the other with respect to each traded commodity.

> It is not without interest to work out a critical average foreign-exchange return per unit of wage costs, above which it is by and large advantageous to export, and below which it would be better to import. . . . Moreover, when measuring the real prospects of achieving an optimal return, the amount of capital immobilized has to be measured. If, disregarding this factor, we were to come to a decision solely on the basis of indices of labour productivity, we should be heading towards a type of production which, though accompanied by a considerable saving in labour would, in this case, also entail the immobilization of an excessive amount of fixed and circulating capital.[39]

They did not provide numerical coefficients themselves, and the first to appear—in early 1957—was the 'last-phase' index of the Economic

[36] See, notably, P. Bollano, *Ek. pop.*, no. 4, 1963, and I. Desmireanu, *Prob. econ.*, no. 5, 1963, and C. Marinescu, ibid. no. 8, 1966, respectively.

[37] Sh. Tseveen, *Plan. khoz.*, no. 4, 1964.

[38] There are summaries in English of research and practice in this field by the ECE in *Econ. B. Eur.*, xi/1, pp. 70–71, and by Zauberman, *Economica*, Feb. 1964, pp. 5–12.

[39] T. Liska and A. Marias, *Koz. Sz.*, no. 1, 1954, pp. 85–92.

Research Institute of the Polish State Planning Commission.[40] This relates the wage costs incurred in the 'last phase' of production to export proceeds reduced by the world-market value of the inputs of intermediate materials; by using world prices for inputs it reflects relative capital intensity in the economies with which it trades. A Czechoslovak 'global' index related cumulated wage costs (i.e. incurred at all stages in the production of an export good) to the foreign proceeds net of the cost of imported materials.[41] This 'global' index was developed for international use (to determine Comecon specialization) by the Czechoslovak Viliam Cerniansky and the German Rudolf Brauer. Each country would rank its indexes for each product: those at the top of each national set would be chosen for concentration of Comecon output.[42] Köhler has analysed the many variants of these indexes, and records that in some form they were used in Bulgaria, China, Czechoslovakia, the GDR, Poland, Rumania, the USSR, and Yugoslavia.[43]

From this stage, developments went in three directions—one sought to fill the main lacuna, the restriction of these indexes to current (labour) outlays by assessing capital consumption, another employed linear programming to evolve a coefficient, and a third tried unsuccessfully to convert current and capital outlays into non-monetary units.

Coefficients and other measures of capital efficiency equivalent in some way or other to an interest rate were already being explored as a separate study;[44] the link with trade efficiency could, however, be made only if a single rate of interest was used. As stated above, such uniformity within each economy is likely to be achieved (save only in Rumania) by 1968. The Polish 'last-phase' index embodied some reflection of capital intensity, because the world prices used to measure the inputs at that phase were formed on foreign (interest-paying) markets. The initial work on linear programming in foreign trade by

[40] *Gosp. plan.*, no. 2, 1957. The formulation is from the ECE study cited.

[41] J. Navratil, *Za vyssi efektivnost zahranicniho obchodu* (Prague, 1958), p. 55, also as formulated by ECE, ibid.

[42] V. Cerniansky and R. Brauer, *Wirts.*, no. 7, 1960; see also Cerniansky, *Ekonomica socialisticheho*, and comments by Zauberman, *Economica*, Feb. 1964, and Pryor, p. 221.

[43] Köhler, pp. 171–7.

[44] Among many studies see 'A Note on the Introduction of Mathematical Techniques', *Econ. B. Eur.*, xii/1, pp. 65–7; *Wld Econ. Survey, 1960*, ch. 3; Zauberman, 'The Soviet and Polish Quest for a Criterion of Investment Efficiency', *Economica*, Aug. 1962, pp. 234–54; N. Spulber, *Soviet Strategy for Economic Growth* (Bloomington, Indiana, 1964), pp. 89–93; and A. Nove, *The Soviet Economy* (London, 1961), pp. 209–17.

Witold Trzeciakowski, of the Polish Ministry of Foreign Trade, evolved a marginal price in domestic currency paid for a unit of currency of another country, but ignored capital intensity: 'Since investment outlays concerning current production capacity have already been made in the past... [they] cannot affect the decisions concerning the choice of an optimal solution.'[45]

The Polish commission (under the chairmanship of Michal Kalecki) on trade efficiency, already briefly referred to, proposed that export goods should be ranked in terms of foreign currency earned per zloty of domestic cost. The point at which import needs indicated minimum export proceeds should serve as the maximum permissible cost of a unit of foreign exchange.[46] For this to be used (as the commission envisaged) for long-run trade planning, a uniform rate of interest is essential for the cost calculation. Alternatively, since the cut-off point of the ranking shows the marginal, and not the equilibrium or average, exchange rate, a uniform exchange rate could be postulated, from which could be calculated the multiple interest rates implied to expand capacity to the level at which the domestic cost of the various products would meet the exchange rate. Kalecki's own approach, when serving as Economic Adviser to the Polish Planning Commission to draw up a Fifteen-year Perspective Plan (1960–75), was to calculate long-term export earnings, from which, by iteration of an input–output matrix (since exports required imported materials), the limit of raw-materials imports could be determined. With other constraints (notably of labour supply and discontinuities in incremental capital-output ratios), a global investment requirement and an overall growth rate were established.[47]

Hungarian mathematical economists have taken a stage further the research work of Trzeciakowski, and of the Swedish econometrician Tom Kronsjø.[48] Working on data for cotton textiles, Andras Nagy and Tamas Liptak produced a model of 'the optimum com-

[45] W. Trzeciakowski, 'Model of Optimization of Foreign Trade in a Planned Economy and its Applications', *Prace i Materialy Zakladu Badan Koniunktur i Cen Handlu Zagranicznego*, no. 1 (Warsaw, 1962), and in T. Barna, ed., *Structural Interdependence and Economic Development* (London, 1963). See also his comments on the report of the Polish 'mixed commission for evaluating methods of investigating the efficiency of foreign trade', *Gosp. plan.*, no. 11, 1963, and the report itself, ibid. no. 4, 1963.

[46] See Wyczalkowski, p. 181.

[47] See in particular S. Wellisz, *The Economies of the Soviet Bloc* (New York, 1964), pp. 113–19. He rightly describes the draft plan (which was not adopted) as 'the most carefully worked out long-range project within the Soviet camp'.

[48] T. Kronsjø, *Econ. Plan.*, Apr. 1963.

modity composition and market allocations of cotton fabric exports from the point of view of economic efficiency, considering the production capacities available for the purposes of export and the given features of our export markets'.[49] The converse optimization has been examined by Marton and Tardos who set up a linear programming model for the short-term distribution of imports given the volume of goods available for export.[50] The subsequent 'Two-level' planning model of Liptak and Janos Kornai set out the foreign-trade components with other branches of the economy and notably under a single rate of interest.[51] The two-level model (which owes its name to the separation of the feasible allocation patterns, chosen by central planners, from the feasible shadow price systems facing the mutually independent sectors) was the first attempt to evolve an optimization procedure for the entire planned economy (production, imports, exports, capital utilization, and formation, etc.). The Hungarian models are of matrix programming, but more recently a number of Polish economists, basing their models on a general instruction on investment efficiency promulgated by the Planning Office in 1962, have returned to coefficient comparison, though in a form suitable for determining an international optimum.[52] The combination of labour coefficient comparison with an investment-efficiency norm was reported in 1964 to be under study by the Comecon Commission on Economic Questions.[53]

All these optimization procedures take foreign supply and demand conditions as given, but a joint study by the Ministries of Foreign Trade of the GDR and Poland, with the collaboration of the University of Birmingham (and there, notably, Kronsjø) is working on a model applicable to two (or more) Comecon members in their relations with the rest of the world. The number of variables is large not only because of the numerous products traded (or tradeable) but because many payments are in inconvertible currencies: in East–West trade only sterling and Swiss francs are effectively convertible, since bilateralism through commercial-diplomatic channels is exercised

[49] A. Nagy and T. Liptak, ibid. Sept. 1963, pp. 117–40.
[50] A. Marton and M. Tardos, ibid. no. 2, 1964, pp. 76–87.
[51] J. Kornai and T. Liptak, *Econometrica*, Jan. 1965, pp. 141–69. All the preceding sources provide detailed references to the Polish and Hungarian papers.
[52] Z. Knyziak, *Gosp. plan.*, no. 5, 1964; he refers in detail to the previous Polish work.
[53] V. Shastitko and V. Terekhov, *Wirts.*, no. 1, 1964, pp. 144–51, quoted and analysed by Köhler, p. 188.

with respect to other currencies. The maximand ceases to be in terms of prices which cannot be influenced by national planning (world market prices), when it is capable of international negotiation (e.g. in Comecon's own price system, envisaged in the *Basic Principles*).

The third, and final, group of studies in which two Soviet economists seem to have played a catalytic role build on much work on physical productivity comparison by Comecon commissions.[54] The best-known procedure, that of Terekhov and Shastitko, evaluates capital intensity per unit of output in different countries separately for materials and labour. They weight the materials in the prices of a second country (the Gilbert–Kravis method of 'real' national income comparisons) and wage inputs in national currencies converted at the exchange rates applicable to non-commercial transactions. These non-commercial rates fluctuate partly with the reciprocal tourist flows, but also—though not adequately—reflect purchasing power of wages.[55] Materials and wages are then aggregated in their nationally-priced proportions.[56] In a later article the same authors have concluded that physical productivity indicators have proved too contradictory for unambiguous use.[57] Another form of 'material indicator' avoiding domestic prices and converting at world prices has been used in the GDR.[58] The construction of input-output tables in man-hours (i.e. which can be used to show the amount of cumulative labour input for each unit of output) has been suggested as a complement to this approach, but is likely to involve too many methodological difficulties.

The Soviet authors go on to comment:

> Plainly the time has come when it has become necessary to conduct, perhaps within the framework of the CMEA, a comparison of the price systems in the socialist countries. The results of this laborious and intricate

[54] Pryor (*Communist Foreign Trade System*, p. 219) lists seven such parameters (including, e.g., steam needed per cubic metre of concrete production) used by the Standing Commission on Construction. GDR work in this field is important; on aspects of capital efficiency (which this comprises) see G. Friedrich and L. Rouscik, *Wiss. Z.H.O.*, no. 3, 1958. East European propositions were discussed in *Vnesh. torg.*, nos. 1, 3, and 5, 1962.

[55] The procedures for calculating these non-commercial rates are described in *Nova Mysl*, no. 6, 1964, and, more briefly, in *Prace* (Prague), 19 May 1964. See, however, the discussion above, ch. VIII (pp. 174–5).

[56] *Wirts.*, no. 1, 1964; see Köhler, p. 189.

[57] V. Terekhov and V. Shastitko, *Plan. khoz.*, no. 11, 1961. Their approach (as re-expressed in *Mir. ekon.*, no. 7, 1963) was strongly condemned by Vajda (*The Role of Foreign Trade in a Socialist Economy* (Budapest, 1965), p. 223), as a 'lack of value-mindedness'.

[58] For details see Köhler, pp. 169–71.

work will be of great significance not only for comparing value indicators of the efficiency of investment, but also . . . for establishing the world socialist market's own price system.

An independent Comecon price system

The idea of adapting prices paid within Comecon to (presumably, marginal) wholesale prices of members, once such prices reflected commonly-accepted criteria of labour and capital remuneration, is of course grounded in good economics. The proportions of capital to labour, and of each to natural endowment are not the same as in the rest of the world. Moreover, Comecon nations form a fairly homogeneous group between the industrialized western societies and the underdeveloped areas. Intra-trade prices could reflect the pattern of 'productive forces'—Marx's term—in the Comecon group. Such a scheme would be well grounded in Marxist ideology because it would be planned, in contrast to the 'spontaneity' of market—and capitalist—conditions. Such planning would be the more attractive on the view that 'in the world market monopoly prices play a governing role'.[59]

Khrushchev allied himself with this view in his article of August 1962 by calling on Comecon

> to find economic instruments to stimulate the interest of socialist countries in increasing co-operation and specialization, in developing mutually advantageous trade. . . . This purpose might be served by, for example, preferential prices for output produced under specialization.[60]

The *Basic Principles* of Comecon (App. VI) reflected this.

> Every encouragement [must] be given to the production in all the countries of the materials scarce in the socialist camp, taking into account natural and economic conditions. . . . It is necessary continually to perfect the system of price formation on the world socialist market in keeping with the requirements of the planned extension of the international socialist division of labour, steady expansion of trade, and accelerated development of the world socialist economy, while creating conditions for the gradual change-over to an independent price basis.

Bulgaria, as the country with the lowest labour productivity, wanted man-hours as the basis for the independent prices. An estimate

[59] O. Tarnovsky, in Stupov, p. 57. The ideological view, expressed by Tarnovsky, is that eventually prices in intra-socialist trade will 'wither away' (he uses Marx's phrase) but that for the present their function must be enlarged. On the theory of independent pricing for Comecon, see Agoston, pp. 129–30, and I. Schweitzer, 'International Literature on the Socialist World Market's Own Price Basis', *Koz. Sz.*, no. 3, 1963.

[60] N. Khrushchev, *Komm.*, no. 12, 1962.

made in the GDR for 1958 shows the following ratios of labour productivity in industry, with Czechoslovakia as base.[61]

Bulgaria	57	Rumania	88
Hungary	57	GDR	90
Albania	58	Czechoslovakia	100
Poland	84	USSR	120

Such a price basis would give those with low productivity favourable terms of trade, for man-hour pricing would ensure good prices for their exports and they would pay relatively low prices for the capital-intensive products they import. This was rejected by the more developed partners. Two economists at the Berlin Hochschule für Ökonomie wrote:

> The use of national labour outlays as trade prices between CMEA members as a principle would make more difficult mutual advantage in goods exchange and would hinder the achievement of a rational international division of labour.

Prices, they concluded, must embody all elements contributing to domestic price formation: 'Factors influencing price relationships must also find expression in the autonomous price structure, so that such prices express the economic conditions of all the economies co-operating in the CMEA.'[62]

It would be expected that the Rumanian stand would correspond to the Bulgarian one, although there seems to be no clear statement of its views in this connexion. Comecon's proposals for the prices which underlie specialization agreements are now less favourable for the less-developed, and Rumania may simply wish to be free to seek markets with alternative prices. The Rumanian Party Declaration of April 1964 emphasized that it was

> standing consistently for normal, mutually advantageous economic relations, without ... discrimination; the Rumanian People's Republic, like the other socialist states, develops its economic links with all countries irrespective of their social system.

By deciding, at the end of 1964, to maintain an adapted system of world-market prices for intra-trade until 1970, the Comecon Executive Committee relaxed the pressure of time on its working parties

[61] G. Huber, *Wirts.*, no. 4, 1963, p. 553.
[62] W. Maier and H. Mann, ibid. no. 4, 1964, pp. 601 and 608.

on prime costs and on price formation. The work on prime costs, largely inspired by the chairman of the working party, Bela Csikos-Nagy, Director of the Hungarian State Price Office, is of theoretical as well as of practical interest. In 1962–4 the working party, with the help of national reference groups, eliminated all non-wage items in the prices of 268 goods produced by Comecon members. These wage costs were applied to a standardized production pattern, and exchange rates were derived. The working party completed its report in 1965 and was merged with that for price formation. Until 1965 this latter was under the Chairmanship of the Director of the Price Bureau of the USSR State Planning Commission, Pautin. This Bureau was liquidated (together with the Commission on Prices of the USSR Council of Ministers) and replaced by the State Price Committee of Gosplan already mentioned (p. 188). It is not known whether the Chairman of the new agency, Sitnin, also took over that of the Comecon working party. Under its former head, the working party had received proposals for eighteen variant methods of pricing to relate prime costs to recorded national product (viz. to distribute Marxian 'surplus value'). The working party compressed these variants into four procedures. The first, the Polono-Hungarian, attributes the margin by which prime cost falls short of recorded national product to each branch as a 15 per cent charge on capital inventories. The level of the charge is determined by relative values of the total prime-cost margin ('surplus value') and of the capital stock. The second method, the Rumanian 'two-channel' model, allocates this margin partly by prime costs (i.e. by the wage bill in each industry) and partly by a charge on capital. The rate of the capital charge is that which would yield the value of actual investment. For this reason it is also termed the 'self-financing model'. The third scheme, proposed by Bulgaria, distributes the margin uniquely by prime cost (again the wage-bill of each industry). The fourth system is that of the Soviet 'corrected price', using not prime costs but wholesale prices ruling in each country, corrected to eliminate subsidies.

Penetration of world prices into domestic prices

The opposite approach, which has been advocated in Hungary and Poland, is to use world prices in place of domestic prices. Michal Kalecki proposed as early as 1957 that the internal price structure should be pegged to those of raw materials on the world market 'first to provide a short cut to rationality in the determination of domestic price relationships; and second, to provide a scaffolding for an opportunity cost calculation which would take into account the potentialities of foreign trade'.[63] More recently in Hungary, Liska has suggested that 'prices of all goods which actually or potentially enter foreign trade should oscillate around those prevailing in world markets'.[64]

Although such sweeping changes have not—so far, at least—been adumbrated in official policy, some measures have been introduced to require the direct use of foreign prices in home markets. In Poland in 1962 and in Hungary in 1963, a relationship to foreign-trade prices was introduced at enterprise level by the payment of managerial premia in proportion to the margin between home prices and those paid or realized on foreign markets.[65] This form of premium was payable only in enterprises predominantly manufacturing exports or working up imports, but this by itself covers a large proportion of output—Hungary has the greatest trade dependence in Comecon. The chief architect of the Czechoslovak economic reforms, Ota Sik, attached considerable importance in his original proposals of 1964 to imports at world prices as a protection against domestic inefficiency after devolution of some price-setting authority to enterprise associations. This guard against monopolistic pricing was not, however, formally incorporated into the reforms as enacted for operation by 1967, but the objective appears to have been accepted by the Government. Finally, all eastern European countries have opened retail shops at which consumer goods are available, priced in dollars.[66] Purchases may be made by residents (and, of course, by tourists and other foreigners) against convertible currencies. Such funds may be accrued from remittances, from unspent foreign-exchange allowances while abroad, and in other ways.

Some proponents of world pricing in Comecon trade have been explicit[67] but it is significant that, in laying down rules for its own

[63] A. Zauberman, *Economica*, Feb. 1964 (summarizing M. Kalecki and S. Polaczek, *Gosp. plan.*, no. 9, 1957, and M. Kalecki, *Ek.*, no. 3, 1958).

[64] Ibid. citing an unpublished paper by Liska.

[65] Respectively, W. Rydyger, *Zyc. Part.*, no. 1, 1963, and *Kulk. Ert.*, 20 Feb. 1961.

[66] e.g. PKO (Poland), Tuzex (Czechoslovakia), Vneshposyltorg (USSR).

[67] Vajda, *Tars. Sz.*, no. 12, 1963. See also J. Branik, *Plan. Hosp.*, no. 7, 1966; V. Ivanova, *Ik. misl.*, no. 6, 1966, and M. Savov and N. Velichkov, *Plan. stop.*, no. 7, 1966.

wholesale price reform, the Soviet government required that 'account should also be taken of the aggregated relationship between prices of producers' goods on the world market, so that the new prices help towards a more correct definition of the efficiency of the foreign-trade operations of the USSR'.[68]

[68] Bachurin, *Plan. khoz.*, no. 1, 1962, p. 21. The price reform was then intended to come into effect in 1963; it has since been postponed for a year at a time and its introduction is—as mentioned above—now scheduled for 1967.

X
INTEGRATION

Socialist internationalism

MARX's socialism was internationalist: it would absorb the nation, just as surely as, for Engels, the state would wither away. Stalin rejected the one with 'socialism in one country', and the other with the 'strengthening of the state in the building of communism', but, formally, he maintained the ideological heritage. The tradition of a socialist commonwealth has inspired Soviet policy towards Comecon: in his Leipzig speech of 1959, Khrushchev observed:

> If we want to speak of the future, it seems to me that the further development of the socialist countries will in all probability proceed along lines of reinforcing a single world system of the socialist economy. One after another the economic barriers which separated our countries under capitalism will disappear. . . . Not a single sovereign socialist state is able to shut itself up within its own frontiers and rely exclusively upon its own potential, or its own wealth. If the contrary were true, we would not be communist-internationalists but national-socialists.[1]

The internationalist ideal and the practice of economic integration involve more than Comecon's efforts in trade and technical co-operation, which do not go beyond the normal relationships between states. Comecon's policy on such integration may be examined under three heads—the criteria for integration, the initiative accorded the common agent, and the practical measures attempted.

Comecon has always had a low-income member, once Albania, now Mongolia, and its relations with each has been, and continues to be, one of capital assistance: like OECD, Comecon can concert such aid within national long-term programmes. This, as the Mongolian deputy delegate to the Comecon Executive declared in 1964, 'unquestionably has immense international significance, serving as an example to many sovereign states of Asia and Africa'.[2] Comecon's relationship with a recipient member is of interest in itself, but the

[1] *Pr.*, 27 Mar. 1959.

[2] Tseveen, *Plan. khoz.*, no. 4, 1964. At the Prague conference on Comecon levels of development the Mongolian representative, D. Zagasbaldan, stated that the Mongolian postwar rate of industrial growth had been below the average for socialist countries, and emphasized his country's need for Comecon capital (*Wld Marx. R.*, June 1964, p. 73).

present analysis is confined to the integration involving fuller reciprocity, such as the European members have the opportunity to develop.

The productivity gap for integration

On the world scale, Comecon forms a homogeneous group of moderately developed economies. The United Nations estimates of gross domestic product (GDP) per capita in 1964 run from $50 for the poorest African and Asian states to the $3,000 of the United States. In Comecon, with the exceptions just made (Albania and Mongolia), the 1964 range, according to an American estimate of GNP in terms of west German purchasing power of 1963, was from $680 (Rumania) to $1,470 (Czechoslovakia), a ratio of 1 to 2·2; at official exchange rates the range ($600–$1,280) was from 1 to 2·1. These estimates are for GNP, but in comparisons with eastern Europe its excess over GDP (net factor income from abroad) can be ignored. The spread of Comecon product was rather wider than that in EEC—of 1 to 1·8—but only little more than in EFTA—of 1 to 2·0, if Portugal is excluded. The average for Comecon was $1,020 per head, for EEC $1,465, and for EFTA, $1,583. From the standpoint of aggregate measures of economic activity, the three European groups are in a class together; by contrast, for example, the dispersion of GDP per head in LAFTA was from $130 to $610—of 1 to 3·4 and an average of $370. Comecon's least affluent member, Rumania, was better off than those in the low-income bracket of OECD—Greece, Turkey, Portugal, and Spain.[3]

During the period of Comecon's existence the rate of growth of GNP was, with the exception of the GDR, inversely correlated with present per capita GNP ranking. Thus Bulgaria and Rumania, with almost identical product per head in 1964 ($690 and $680), enjoyed respectively rates of growth of 5·9 and 5·7 per cent during 1950–64; Poland at $890 in 1964 had a 4·9 per cent annual increment; Hungary, with $1,020, had a 4·8 per cent rise; and Czechoslovakia, at $1,470 per head, increased its product annually by 4·0 per cent. The GDR, almost the richest in per capita terms ($1,470), showed a rise of 5·1

[3] GNP estimates for USSR by S. Cohn and for eastern Europe by Ernst, *New Directions*, p. 877; others (GDP) from UN, *Yearbook of National Accounts Statistics 1965* (New York, 1966), pp. 493–6. These aggregates would be significantly smaller on the Janossy or Beckerman estimates (see pp. 134–7).

per cent. Because the GDR population declined during the period 1950–64 (by substantial net emigration until the erection of the Berlin Wall), its high place in aggregate product gave it by far the lead in per capita growth (2·13 times the 1950 level in 1964). Eastern Germany apart, the gap in per capita product has somewhat narrowed over the life of Comecon: if the average for the group other than the USSR (and Albania or Mongolia) was a 72 per cent rise between 1950 and 1964, those for Bulgaria and Rumania were 99 and 87 per cent respectively, for Hungary and Poland 78 and 56 per cent, and for Czechoslovakia, the highest-income member, 53 per cent. A Czechoslovak calculation in terms of net material product (which falls short of GNP by depreciation allowances and the value of 'non-productive' services) shows a similar trend: in 1950 the Bulgarian and Rumanian products per capita had been 35 and 46 per cent of the Czechoslovak, but in 1960 they were, respectively, 47 and 57 per cent of the Czechoslovak. The range in net material product shown in the Czechoslovak estimates is narrower (1 to 2·0) than the American figures just cited, but the other conclusions hold. The poorest Comecon member in terms of NMP is still Rumania (at $423), well above Soviet estimates of NMP per capita in Spain ($369), Greece ($356), Portugal ($222), and Turkey ($169).[4] If grossed up to GNP (as in the text table on p. 135), the average for Comecon is little more than $750 per head, but the spread within the group is smaller (1 to 1·9). The two calculation procedures—typified by the American and Czechoslovak estimates noted here—have already been discussed in Chapter VII.

Unlike EEC and OECD, where the political pre-eminence is held by the highest-product members, the USSR comes third in the income ranking of Comecon. The other members pair off at the top of its scale (Czechoslovakia and the GDR), midway (Hungary and Poland), and at the bottom (Bulgaria and Rumania). As Table 7 (p. 206) shows, rankings within each couple vary according to the method of calculation and the year.

The table also indicates, however, that this relatively compact scale for aggregate product is not valid for industrial output.[5] A Czecho-

[4] GNP from Ernst, *New Directions*, pp. 877, 880, and 882; NMP: growth from Novozamsky, *Vyrovnavani*, p. 168, Comecon levels from Novozamsky, *Pol. Ekon.*, no. 8, 1966, p. 731, and Southern European levels from *Narodnoe khozyaistvo SSSR v 1964 godu* (Moscow, 1965), p. 89.

[5] See esp. Montias, *Wld. Pol.*, July 1966.

slovak calculation, prepared for a major conference in Prague on inter-member mensuration in October 1963,[6] showed the industrial spread as 3·3 or 3·5 in 1958, and a Soviet calculation for 1963 demonstrated one of 3·4.[7] Between the two dates selected (subject to a very serious caveat on the comparability of the measures), the GDR, Hungary, and Bulgaria seem to have raised their position relative to the USSR, while Rumania has apparently lost ground. However that may be, a reliable comparison of industrial growth rates for 1950–64 shows that Bulgaria and Rumania have had annual increments in excess of 9 per cent (outdoing Italy and the German Federal Republic, the leaders in the West), against 5·4 and 7·7 per cent in the GDR and Czechoslovakia respectively.

Agricultural output per head is less dispersed than industrial, but again, Rumania appears to be the least productive, despite more rapid growth since 1950 than any other member. In both years shown on Table 7 its farm output was little more than half the Polish.[8] With Bulgaria, Rumania was at the foot of the rankings for gross capital formation per head in 1958, investing hardly more than one-quarter of the Comecon leader in this sector, the USSR. Yet it has been these three—the smallest and the largest investors in absolute terms—which have devoted the highest percentage of income to gross fixed capital formation.[9] Bulgaria has obtained substantial Soviet loans to finance its investment; for Rumania, low income and high accumulation has kept personal consumption the lowest in eastern Europe. It is noteworthy that a study of 1963 consumption on the Gilbert–Kravis technique by the Research Institute of the USSR Gosplan omitted Rumania from its published results. Four Comecon members were within about 10 per cent of each other (Hungary, Poland, the USSR, and Bulgaria in descending order); the mean of the top two (the GDR and Czechoslovakia) was 40 per cent above them.[10]

Even so, the east German and Czechoslovak levels of personal consumption, very little behind those of western Germany before the

[6] For a detailed analysis of the discussion at this conference see Saltiel, *Cahiers de l'ISEA*, Dec. 1965, pp. 16–34. For official reports see *Wld Marx. R.*, Apr. 1964, pp. 52–63, and June 1964, pp. 71–84, and (in summary), *Plan. khoz.*, no. 1, 1964.

[7] The methods varied radically from each other, viz., respectively a value weighting of global outputs, a physical sample of major products, and a comparison of the Gilbert–Kravis type.

[8] All estimates from Ernst, *New Directions*, pp. 883–4.

[9] For USSR see Cohn, ibid., p. 106; for Rumania the present writer, *Sov. Stud.*, July 1966, p. 88; for other countries Ernst, *New Directions*, p. 890.

[10] Kotovsky and others, p. 229 (see Table 7, n. iii).

war, have fallen to below 60 per cent of that now current in western Germany. Before the war their consumption was something like 15 per cent better than the Austrian: their standards are now about 20 per cent lower. Hungary, too, enjoying better prewar consumption than Austria, is now much worse off than its western neighbour.[11]

From these statistics three main conclusions seem relevant to Comecon's problems of integration. First, the members are not so disparate in overall product that integration is, on this ground, harder than in EEC or EFTA. By taking in only a million of the real poor of the world,[12] Comecon has not had to face the sharp division between the industrialized west and the 'Third World'; the troubles with China have been at the gate, not within the family.

Secondly, that relative homogeneity must nevertheless be qualified by the sharp differential in the degree of industrialization. Bulgaria and Rumania are high savers and, over the life of Comecon, have shown the fastest rates of industrial growth of any member; yet they are still less than one-third as industrially productive as Czechoslovakia and the GDR. But, as a third turn of the problem, Czechoslovakia and eastern Germany have fallen far behind the parity their populations enjoyed in prewar consumption with western Germany. The aspiration of the two poorest members is fixed on the far-ahead lead of the two industrialized members, who themselves take as goal the standards of the west which were once their own.

Comecon's *Basic Principles* echo both these desires—and the organization has suffered from their incompatibility. The criterion of 'efficiency' enshrines the objective of the most-developed, i.e. the 'rational distribution of productive forces throughout the world socialist system, efficient employment of labour and material resources . . . more efficient social production, a higher rate of economic growth'. For the poorest members the *Principles* evoke a group of aims which may be epitomized as 'employment', viz. 'a balanced economy in each country . . . industrialization and gradual removal of historical differences in the economic development levels of the socialist countries'. Together or separately, these can yield the desired

higher living standards for the working people in all the socialist countries

[11] By a quarter (Ernst; Beckerman & Bacon); NMP by nearly half (E. Erlich, *cz. Econ. P.*, no. 7).

[12] Earlier 1·7 m. Albanians, now 1·1 m. Mongolians. Novozamsky (p. 6) estimates Korean and Chinese agricultural output per head at 50–60 per cent of the Soviet, and industrial output per head respectively as one-third and one-tenth.

TABLE 7: *Relative per Capita Outputs in Comecon Countries* (Index numbers GDR = 100)

	Year	*Source*	*Albania*	*Bulgaria*	*Czecho-slovakia*	*Hungary*	*Mon-golia*	*Poland*	*Rumania*	*USSR*	*All Comecon**
95 farm products	1959–63	(i)	68	117	101	136	..	141	97	..	117†
Global output of agriculture	1958	(ii)	37	81	97	99	..	117	63	93	94
	1962	(iii)	..	107	87	107	135	131	75	93	96
	1961–5	(iv)	..	109	89	107	127	130	77	88	93
Sample of 86 industrial products	1958	(ii)	21	28	90	43	..	79	50	74	73
Global output of industry	1958	(ii)	15	31	102	48	..	59	38	78	74
	1960	(v)	..	33	110	55	..	60	36	..	69†
	1960	(vi)	..	31	102	45	..	59	38	77	73
	1961	(vii)	..	30	99	45	..	53	38	70	67
	1963	(iii)	..	44	88	50	15	48	29	65	63
	1965	(iv)	..	47	80	50	13	50	33	67	75
Net output of industry	1961	(viii)	..	30	100	36	..	55	48	..	61†
Gross capital formation	1955	(ix)	..	64	143	..	..	100	57	143	89‡
	1958	(x)	..	30	106	51	..	57	32	111	95
	1960	(ix)	..	80	147	..	..	73	60	133	119‡
	1963	(iii)	..	82	111	77	..	76	72	122	111
	1965	(ix)	..	81	125	..	..	56	69	125	114‡
Personal consumption	1960	(xi)	18	47	118	55	..	58	58	92	86
	1963	(iii)	..	66	92	73	..	71	..	67	..
	1964	(xii)	..	64	96	75	..	66	55	64	68
Net material product	1958	(ii)	23	49	97	81	..	76	51	..	77†
	1960	(xiii)	18	43	101	55	..	69	45	..	70†
	1964	(xiv)	..	56	96	61	..	59	50	75	73
	1965	(xv)	..	62	85	62	..	62	54	77	93
Gross national product	1960	(xvi)	..	47	100	57	..	54	37	64	64
	1964	(xvii)	..	49	105	73	..	64	49	85	81

* Excl. Albania and Mongolia. † Excl. USSR. ‡ Assuming Hungary to be the same level as Poland.

Sources: (i) Gy. Enyedi, Hungarian Inst. of Geography (95 products at FAO-cited prices, corrected for east European variations);

(ii) J. Novozamsky, *Vyrovnavani ekonomicke urovne zemi RVHP* (Prague, 1965), pp. 22–23;

(iii) Ya. Kotkovsky and others, *Sopostavlenie urovnei ekonomicheskogo razvitiya sotsialisticheskikh stran* (Moscow, 1965), pp. 164 and 229 (Gilbert–Kravis methods);

(iv) Kotkovsky, *Vopr. ekon.*, no. 8, 1966, pp. 84–86;

(v) W. Kunz, *Wirts.*, no. 2, 1962, p. 174;

(vi) A. Balek and others, *Zeme socialisticke soustavy* (Prague, 1961);

(vii) 'Rozvoj hospodarstva krajin RVHP', *Plan. Hosp.*, no. 4, 1964, p. 66;

(viii) M. Ernst, in *New Directions*, p. 878 (west German price weights);

(ix) Kotkovsky, *Vopr. ekon.*, p. 89 (physical inputs of capital goods weighted by base-year prices on Gilbert–Kravis method, with national deflators for time series);

(x) Novozamsky, p. 65 (money aggregates at non-commercial exchange-rates);

(xi) W. Beckerman and R. Bacon, *Econ. J.*, Sept. 1966, p. 533 (regression of physical indicators of consumption on Gilbert–Kravis relationships);

(xii) J. Smilek, *Hosp. nov.*, no. 29, 1966, p. 3;

(xiii) A. Karpinski, B. Zielinska, *Gosp. plan.*, no. 6, 1962, p. 4;

(xiv) Novozamsky, *Pol. Ek.*, no. 8, 1966, p. 731, using methods of Janossy (see n. xvi);

(xv) Kotkovsky, *Vopr. ekon.*, p. 88 (consumption on Gilbert–Kravis method applied to share of consumption in NMP at current national prices);

(xvi) Methods of F. Janossy, *A gazdasagi fejlettseg merhetosege es uj meresi modszere* (Budapest, 1963), for Hungary in terms of a sample of market economies and further applied to other Comecon members (regression of physical outputs on GNP at official exchange rates);

(xvii) Ernst, p. 877 (east European quantities weighted at west German values of 1955 and purchasing power of 1963); USSR estimate from S. Cohn, in *New Directions*, p. 108, linked by figures common to both series for west Germany.

. . . and the creation of a material basis for their more-or-less simultaneous transition to communism [i.e. the abundance of consumers' goods] within one and the same historical era.

The design of 'efficiency' is essentially static: the greatest output for the least resources can be got by concentrating production where it is demonstrably more efficient. The 'employment' aim requires that relatively inefficient resources be used rather than be left unexploited, because every country must have some share in the expansion of industry. As a dynamic concept, it can well conform to the purpose of efficiency if the resources chosen for exploitation, though producing with high costs at present, yield planned returns as good—or better—than those at present in use. Both involve a redistribution of income within the frontiers of the integrated group. The profit on concentrating development where it is most efficient must be shared among all, or the loss while the inefficient resources are being improved must be borne by all.[13] Because Comecon set itself simultaneously to pursue both approaches, each form of compensation had to be envisaged.

The first Soviet economist to make these aspects explicit, Oleg Bogomolov, wrote, late in 1963:

> For a variety of reasons, the possible non-coincidence of the economic interests of different socialist countries raises the question how, under such circumstances, to approach the evaluation of economic efficiency and of the worth of the international socialist division of labour, on the one hand from the standpoint of the national economy of the separate countries, and on the other hand from the standpoint of the entire socialist community.

His own solution is a combination of credit, while inefficient resources are developed, with an independent Comecon price-system, which shares the 'overall economic profit arising from the division of labour . . . between countries proportionately to their outlays in developing co-operative production'.[14]

Bogomolov's proposal went to the heart of the problem: a relatively industrialized member which invested on the territory of a less-developed partner should be assured a return in the 'overall economic profit'. Such an arrangement would conform to dynamic cost-advantage and respond to the self-interest both of the investor and the recipient. For him, as for the Comecon *Basic Principles*, efficiency is

[13] See particularly Agoston, pp. 129–31.
[14] O. Bogomolov, *Vopr. ekon.*, no. 11, 1963, pp. 6 and 10.

to be measured within Comecon, but the separate price system would inhibit the direct evaluation of comparative costs in trade with the rest of the world. In a sense this position is a reaffirmation of Stalin's concept of two 'world markets' in his 1952 *Economic Problems of Socialism in the USSR*, based not on political *dicta* but on the argument of different resource endowments. For its next set of plans, as has already been described (p. 185), Comecon has broadly adopted world prices. It is not evident whether the choice of different periods for averaging such prices alters the terms of trade between primary products and manufactures, but any change is unlikely to have been large. Compensation or aid must hence be itemized, not automatically accorded in the routine flow of trade transactions. This specification was to be effected in international sectoral planning which would identify the dynamic-cost equilibrium to be attained. By joint investment in the new capacity each participant would share in the long-term gains.

The form of the conflict

Capital, however, proved to be too scarce for the expected returns to coincide. During the later part of Comecon's crisis and, more clearly, since, it has become evident that the more developed members of the group require a return of 15 per cent on domestic investment. This is the rate eventually announced in the USSR in September 1966 for the review of producer-good prices, but it had been adopted in Hungary and Poland by 1964, and subsequently by Czechoslovakia, for their respective economic reforms. The domestic rate of interest on long-term bank loans in those reforms has emerged at 5 or 6 per cent—in Czechoslovakia, the GDR, Hungary, and Poland.[15] The rate on credits to socialist countries had, however, long been established at 2 per cent (in at least one case—the Soviet loan to China —1 per cent);[16] the Bank for International Economic Co-operation in 1964 set its top rate for short-term lending at 1·5 per cent, but has not yet given long-term credits. In the industrialized capitalist economies the marginal return on long-term capital may be put roughly at 5 or 6 per cent; the World Bank levies 5·75 per cent, and private investors lending abroad may be expected to seek 10 per cent.[17] If the

[15] See Köhler, ch. 4. [16] Ibid. pp. 301–13, and Eckstein, p. 138.

[17] See I. Little and J. Clifford, eds., *International Aid* (London, 1965), p. 63, and J. Pincus, *R. Econ. Statist.*, Nov. 1963, p. 362. Citing these, A. McAuley and D. Matko, *Bulletin of the Oxford University Institute of Economics*, Nov. 1966, pp. 267–9, use 15 per cent as the real dis-

return can be roughly put at double the going rate of interest, Comecon was faced with an 'efficiency' rate of 15 per cent and an 'employment' rate of, say, 5 per cent. It is this gap that must be borne in mind in the polemics between the GDR and Rumania in the course of 1963.

In its March issue of that year, the GDR journal *Wirtschaftswissenschaft* carried an article by Vasile Rausser, editor of the Rumanian *Probleme economice*, entitled 'The Proportional Development of the Economy of the Rumanian People's Republic'. He emphasized

> The greater role of industry in the economy is based upon the achievements of recent years, on the high rate of growth of gross industrial output and on the preferential development of Group A over Group B.... Engineering has been the basis of the rapid rate of growth in 1960–2.[18]

This was answered in the following number by Gerhard Huber, a young research assistant at the Institute of Economics of the German Academy of Sciences, in 'The Determination of the Level of Economic Development of a Socialist Country'.[19] In his opening paragraphs he pointedly inserted a quotation from Khrushchev's speech at the 1960 Congress of the Rumanian Workers' Party. Huber gave prominence to the nine measures of economic levels advanced by a Bulgarian economist, S. Stoilov:[20] gross social product, net national income, industrial and agricultural output, and consumption (all per head); the structure of output (departments I and II in national product, Groups A and B in industry), and of employment; and labour productivity in industry and in social product. He concluded that labour productivity was the desirable measure and that the best index would be national income per person employed in industry and agriculture. From this he drew the significant lesson that, as both industry and agriculture contribute to national income, the priority of heavy industry had lost its force in the present socialist world system, and that more weight should be attributed in development policies to agriculture.

In conclusion it can be said that industrialization is not necessary as a hypothesis for the raising of labour productivity in all sectors and in every

count rate for Soviet lending. J. Thornton (*J. Pol. Econ.*, Dec. 1965) calculates from Soviet data an average rate of return on industrial capital in 1960 of 17·5 per cent gross and 12·9 per cent net.

[18] *Wirts.*, no. 3, 1963, pp. 426–7.

[19] A footnote to Rausser's article stated that it had been completed 'at the end of the second quarter 1962': there was thus ample time for Huber to prepare his comment.

[20] S. Stoilov, *Ik. misl*, no. 10, 1961.

country; on the contrary (for small countries) a partial condition for industrialization can also be achieved through the expansion of agriculture, the already-developed produce of which can be worked up by industry. Perhaps some should undertake an active industrialization, and others a passive industrialization.[21]

This concept of 'passive industrialization' was supported by an analysis of Comecon trade by Gunter Schade, of the Economics Hochschule, in the August issue. He pointed to the advantage which accrued to Rumania by the export of primary products and to the GDR by their imports, but admitted that the greater economic size of the GDR had partly inhibited the expansion of exchanges with Rumania.[22]

Meanwhile, the First Deputy Director of the Rumanian Institute of Economics, Ion Rachmuth, had, in the July number of *Probleme economice*, written on 'The Importance of Rates of Growth for the Equalization of the Economic Level of Socialist Countries'.[23] He argued that efficiency should be a criterion only at a second stage, the first stage being the acceleration of industrial growth in the presently underdeveloped group.

Some compromise having been reached on Comecon's fundamental dispute at its July Session, the editorial board of *Wirtschaftswissenschaft* in November explicitly stated that it did not support its contributors' views: Huber was called a non-Marxist and Schade accused of an erroneous use of statistics. But while allowing that both industry and agriculture should be developed, the board stressed the efficiency principle within each. Specialization should be 'the concentration on those branches of production or types of product which can rationally employ the most modern techniques and mass production and, therewith, the lowest cost per unit of output'.[24]

Rumania has also found occasion to oppose the principle of sovereignty to that of efficiency. This was *à propos* of a paper by E. Valev, Professor of the Economic Geography of the Peoples' Democracies at Moscow University, published in the spring of 1964. Valev concluded that

The analysis of the actual situation and of the development prospects of the economy in the Danubian districts of Rumania, Bulgaria, and the Soviet Union demonstrates the existence of objective premises for the future formation of the inter-state production complex of the lower reaches of the

[21] *Wirts.*, no. 4, 1963, pp. 545–6. [22] Ibid. no. 8, 1963, esp. p. 1243.
[23] *Prob. econ.*, no. 7, 1963. [24] *Wirts.*, no. 11, 1963, p. 1716.

Danube. . . . Hence the necessity arises of a detailed study of the location of the new big industrial projects in the lower Danube region, bearing in mind the interests of the whole of the world socialist economy as well as the most efficient development of the entire territorial production complex of the lower Danube.[25]

An editorial in the Rumanian *Viata economica* of 12 June 1964 criticized the analysis in the severest terms. Valev, it claimed, assigned 'to a still anonymous body' the function of assessing 'the interests of the whole of the world socialist economy'.

Is it necessary again to remind the author that two-thirds of the territory to which he refers is an integral part of the territory of the Rumanian People's Republic, an independent and sovereign socialist state? On this territory nobody has anything to study, neither in detail, nor in lesser detail, without authorization from the Rumanian government, for both the efficient use of resources and the location of objectives, as well as any other problems, big or small, are of the exclusive competence of the Rumanian government and people. The Rumanian regions in the 'district' of the lower Danube are developing within the framework of, and according to, the interests of Rumania's national economy and this is the sole way in which their resources may serve the interests of strengthening socialism as a world system, interests to which schemes of the kind we are now discussing cannot but cause serious prejudice. . . . The more projects of this kind are made in the name of deepening economic co-operation between the member countries of the Council of Mutual Economic Assistance, the less public opinion will understand the relation between these proposals and the basic principles on which CMEA is founded.

This sharp reaction evoked a semi-official disavowal of Valev by Bogomolov in *Izvestia* of 4 July. Meanwhile, economists from the less-developed members argued that cost comparisons would have to be made on a dynamic basis. Tibor Kiss, of the Hungarian State Planning Office, accepted Huber's views on the possibility of specialization on agriculture, provided that in agriculture, as much as in manufacturing, it was the long-run cost advantage that underlay concentration decisions: the expansion which resulted would gradually bring the low-productivity economies up to the level of those at present favourably placed.[26] A similar view was expressed at the same time in Bulgaria by the Deputy Director of the State Planning Commission. He

[25] *Vestnik Moskovskogo universiteta: Seriya geografia*, no. 2, 1964.

[26] T. Kiss, *Koz. Sz.*, no. 4, 1964; his reference to the disavowal of Huber was merely 'See, however, the article of the editorial board in the no. 11, 1963 issue' (p. 402).

accepted the criterion of efficiency, believing that this would ensure the expansion of his own country's mineral exports.[27] In the same issue of the journal, a Professor at the Sofia Economics Institute pointed out that such development would require credit from importers, and that it could only be embraced if the export price of the goods to be supplied by the underdeveloped partner were guaranteed at a higher level than on the world market.[28]

Comecon convened an international conference on the 'equalization of economic levels' in Prague (19–23 May 1964). The Czechoslovak point of view put to the meeting, like that of the GDR, was that the developed countries have no alternative but to intensify their industrial production.[29] Since Czechoslovak industry is already over-diversified, co-operation agreements would be welcome which would both provide bigger production runs for Czechoslovak factories and accelerate the rates of growth in the other partners.

The consequences for Czechoslovakia of the protection of high-cost industries, notably in engineering, are nevertheless serious.[30] Poland too has not gained the benefit for which it hoped. The economies of scale of some engineering goods for which it has entered specialization agreements have not been found large enough to justify the division.[31] Jaroszewicz included in his review of Comecon between 1962 and 1966 the comment that 'many specialization instructions of the past few years are too scattered in their subject matter and not all are justified in technology and economics;' he believed that concentrating specialization in a few key fields was essential.[32] A special conference on some 'highly important questions of the further development of specialization and co-operation in engineering' was held from 22 February to 1 March 1966[33] to discuss the fundamental dilemma that the industrialized members require assurances of markets and materials that other members are unwilling to give.[34] The west offers the latter more technically-advanced equipment, and, by its own integration (EEC and EFTA), is closing its markets against the equipment which Comecon would wish to sell in return.

[27] K. Zarev, *Plan. khoz.*, no. 4, 1964, p. 29. [28] G. Popisakov, ibid. esp. pp. 72–73.
[29] *Prace*, 19 May 1964. [30] See pp. 149–50.
[21] S. Kuzinski, *Zyc. gos.*, 17 Nov. 1963 (cited by Korbonski, p. 33).
[32] *Tryb. Ludu*, 17 May 1966.
[33] Sokolov and Shiryaev, *Int. Aff.*, no. 1, 1966. Its report was discussed at the April 1966 meeting of the Executive Committee.
[34] See G. Aptauer, *Plan. hosp.*, no. 1, 1965.

The problem is now being fairly faced by the USSR, after long reliance on the optimistic superficiality that it was 'evident that co-operation among socialist states facilitates and accelerates the construction of socialism by each nation'.[35] A paper which appeared in Moscow in May 1966 observed:

> It should be realized that the consequences of this situation hitherto ... have been inadequately considered. Development of the international socialist division of labour is directly linked with the problem of a country's balance of trade. The varying foreign-trade efficiency of products prompts countries to optimize their trade pattern by expanding export with the highest level of efficiency and by limiting the import of goods for which relatively inefficient goods are the counter-deliveries. ... These contradictions are chiefly expressed in the difficulty of selling a cargo of manufactures produced under the most favourable conditions, because exporters of raw materials and foodstuffs find it more advantageous to supply their own needs from domestic output (under conditions less favourable than those of the main exporters) than to import manufactures at the expense of exports of raw materials and foodstuffs at relatively unfavourable prices.[36]

The authors recommended, first, 'specific intergovernmental agreements to continue research on possible ways to transfer to a system of foreign-trade prices based on the actual production costs of CMEA members'. Their second proposal was 'the creation by interested countries of a special fund for providing credit for specialization and co-operation': it is this sharing of capital that Comecon has long realized to be essential.

Mobility of capital and labour

The *Basic Principles* require that all countries benefit from the international division of labour, for 'building up in each of them of a rational complex of interrelated and complementary industries'. No country can thus be temporarily held back from development even when the dictates of common efficiency might place priority on the development of other members. This is not of course carried to the absurd extreme that, for example, every country should derive some income growth every year from the division of labour. Indeed, the requirement that the less developed enjoy a 'faster development rate' than the others is phrased 'in the long run'.

[35] Letter of the CPSU to the CPC of 29 Nov. 1963 (*Peking R.*, 8 May 1964, p. 20).
[36] B. Ladygin and Yu. Shiryaev, *Vop. ekon.*, no. 5, 1966, pp. 81–9.

Nevertheless, the 'employment' principle (and many instances of the application of the long-run 'efficiency' criterion) would involve balance-of-payments deficits for the less-developed partners. The *Basic Principles* therefore complements its declaration that 'multilateral co-ordination of plans and the resultant recommendations for specialization and co-operation should ensure that each socialist country has a balanced payments structure' with the provision 'wherever necessary through appropriate forms of co-operation with, and assistance from, the other socialist countries'.

There are two procedures for meeting the requirement of balanced payments: mutual price or exchange-rate adjustments and capital flows. The adjustments could be interpreted as the 'appropriate forms of co-operation' and the capital lending the 'assistance'. An 'independent price basis' was written into the *Principles*, but has been deferred at least until 1970. Adjustments of exchange-rates to give advantage to the country with an impending balance-of-payments disequilibrium is quite possible, for, although nothing is said of it in the *Basic Principles*, consideration of it may be inferred from a recent Hungarian paper by Brody.[37] Neuberger has pointed to the arrangement that could be made in this sphere as follows:

> The specialization assignment in each commodity would be given to the country with the lowest costs [in a common unit of account, e.g. the rouble], and then exchange-rates altered until each country obtained assignments in a sufficient number of commodities to assure it a balance on its international accounts.[38]

A problem he does not raise is that the exchange-rate assuring balance in the intra-Comecon account would by no means necessarily be that balancing its payments with the rest of the world.

Capital lending seems to be more in view: Khrushchev's original integration proposals explicitly envisaged this, and it is the main feature of the new bilateral schemes. The 'movement of resources from country to country', of which he wrote, could of course also be seen as referring to the international mobility of labour. Although some Bulgarian manpower has worked on the 'new lands' in the eastern USSR, there is virtually no flow of manpower from one country to another: the acute labour shortages of Czechoslovakia and the

[37] A. Brody, *Koz. Sz.*, no. 4, 1964.
[38] E. Neuberger, *Amer. Econ. R.*, May 1964, p. 510.

GDR could be mitigated by immigration from some other Comecon states.[39] The possibility of some international mobility seemed to have been gaining currency, to judge by the violence of its condemnation in Rumania. The editorial in *Viata economica* of 12 June 1964 took issue with a paper by P. Alampiev, read to the Fourth Congress of the Geographical Society of the USSR two weeks previously, who

> proclaims the thesis concerning the 'possibility and utility of the seasonal and permanent migration of the population between various socialist countries'. This notion of the international 'migration' of the population is incompatible with socialism. We know only too well that at the time of the bourgeoisie there were situations when the inhabitants of our country had to leave . . . in order to look for jobs even beyond the Atlantic Ocean; we have seen only too well how things develop in the 'Common Market', which has secured the 'free circulation' of the labour force. . . . We have never imagined that a thesis could be voiced concerning the 'possibility and the utility' of a similar process within the framework of the world socialist system.

The special position of agriculture

The inhibition of manpower flows within Comecon particularly affects farming. Seasonal immigration—notably from Bulgaria to Czechoslovakia—was a feature of the prewar economies of the region, and on a longer-term basis could assist the development of Czechoslovak agriculture. The latter, largely by virtue of the expulsion of the Sudeten Germans, has still failed to regain its prewar level and is acutely short of labour. Comecon specialization in farming may also be hindered by the absence of calculations of differential rent. No rent charge appears in price and, in the present interpretation of Marx, this would be ruled out. But within each economy, the concept of differential rent is accepted.

On the general question of agriculture, the view at present exhibited in Comecon discussions coincides with that of de Gaulle with respect to EEC policy, namely that integration is worthless 'if Europe does not feed itself from its own agriculture'.[40] Self-sufficiency in temperate foodstuffs is equally the aim of Comecon, and net imports into the group are regarded as exceptional, although occasionally large (as, after heavy imports in 1963 and 1965, the USSR has con-

[39] See *Econ. Survey Eur. 1957*, ch. VII, and Gy. Fekete, *Koz. Sz.*, no. 5, 1964.
[40] Press conference of 29 July 1963.

tracted for Canadian grain annually to 1968). The rise in real incomes has inevitably shifted consumer demand towards higher-quality foods (notably livestock produce) and has expanded requirements of feed grain, but any substantial increase in agricultural output has been inhibited by the inadequacy of the incentives to produce under collectivized farming. There is, on the other hand, no suggestion that, if comparative-cost calculations were so to indicate, a major, regular, import programme would be envisaged.

Comecon's agricultural programme has, however, been constrained by policies of national self-sufficiency which have run counter to cost-minimization within its area.[41] Czechoslovakia, for example, has not only maintained but diverted manpower into high-cost farming. While certain trade flows arise naturally from climate and geography—notably early vegetables and fruit from Bulgaria—the division of labour has so far been little pressed. Even in April 1964 it was still necessary to insist that Czechoslovakia, the GDR, Hungary, and Poland should be permanent and substantial grain importers, and Bulgaria, Rumania, and the USSR their suppliers.[42] It has been one of the roots of the Rumanian objections to integration that its own role has seemingly been largely cast in terms of grain exports. The big expansion of maize-growing which such targets incorporated was reputedly a minor cause of discontent because Rumanian peasants now despise this crop. Maize flour has until recently been a staple of Rumanian peasant diet: before the war Rumania and Yugoslavia were the only European countries where the deficiency disease pellagra (caused by a lack of vitamin B characterizing a maize-diet) was endemic.

That the alleged consequences of international specialization are perpetuating agrarian export economies became the *leitmotiv* of the attacks on Comecon by Rumania, China, and Cuba. The phrasing of the critique in the key article in *Viata economica* was moderate and general, and focused on the conflict between rising demand for food at home and the export commitments urged by industrialized partners.

> But taking into consideration the insistent proposals that we should export more—of what we have not enough even for ourselves—in order partially to cover the deficit of others who have reached a higher standard than ours, we would like to ask these comrades: how does this fit in with

[41] See J. Liptak, *Mezinarodni delba prace v zemedelstvi RVHP* (Prague, 1966).
[42] L. Makaruk, *Koz. Sz.*, no. 4, 1964, esp. p. 421.

the objective tendency of levelling up economic development? How does this attitude reflect the international character of cooperation between the socialist countries, mutual advantage and assistance?

Chinese criticism was stronger. In a letter to the Central Committee of the Soviet Communist Party, its Central Party Committee alleged: 'You bully those fraternal countries whose economies are less advanced, oppose their policy of industrialization, and try to force them to remain agricultural countries and to serve as your sources of raw materials and as outlets for your goods.'[43]

This contention was amplified after Khrushchev's dismissal to a broader condemnation of his proposals for Comecon.

In the name of 'mutual economic assistance' [Khrushchev] opposed the independent development of the economies of fraternal countries and forced them to become a source of raw materials and an outlet for finished goods, thus reducing their industries to appendages. He bragged that these were all new theories and doctrines of his own invention, but in fact they were the jungle law of the capitalist world, which he applied to relations among socialist countries, taking the Common Market of the monopoly capitalist blocs as his model.[44]

The Cuban intervention was the most vituperative. As has been described in Chapter VI (p. 104), its development aid seems to have been trimmed in late 1963, possibly within Comecon consultation. In January 1964 it had fixed its long-term price for sugar sales to the USSR and in September Fidel Castro had publicly criticized Comecon.[45] In the following February, the then Minister of Industries, Ernesto Guevara, denounced

talk of mutually-beneficial trade based on the prices imposed on underdeveloped countries by the law of value and its by-product, the international relations of unequal exchange. How can 'mutual benefit' mean the sale at world market prices of the raw materials which cost backward countries sweat and boundless suffering and the purchase at those market prices of machinery made in modern, automated factories?[46]

In attempting to achieve an acceptable long-term relationship between prices of food and manufactures, Comecon was facing the

[43] *Peking R.*, 8 May 1964. The letter also claimed that the USSR discriminated against Czechoslovakia and the GDR: 'You bully fraternal countries which are industrially more developed and insist that they stop manufacturing their traditional products and become accessory factories serving your industries.'

[44] Ibid. 27 Nov. 1964, translating an editorial in *Hongqi*, 21 Nov. 1964.

[45] See Tretiak, p. 5. [46] *Hoy*, 26 Feb. 1965, cited ibid. p. 24.

same problems which are bedevilling the UN Trade and Development Board, and which took eight years of negotiation and compromise to solve in EEC. But the latter was declaredly seeking to be supranational; until 1962 Comecon could, institutionally, hardly have been called international. It was, and remains, intergovernmental.

Comecon as an intergovernmental agency

For Comecon as an institution during 1949–60, the closest analogy of the Secretariat is with the European Danube Commission of 1856 and, in legal form, with GATT. The Danube Commission was the first body to have a multinational secretariat. Posts were allotted by nationality—a French secretary-general, a German chief navigation inspector, an Austrian (or after 1918 a Rumanian) port captain at Sulina, and a British technical director.[47] Until 1960 the bulk of Comecon's manpower (the words 'staff' or 'personnel' imply a common employer) was provided by national delegations. These national civil servants did the routine work of Comecon. The Secretary, his deputies and clerical staff were few by comparison. If a precise historical parallel is to be drawn, the Genoa Conference of 1922 provides the precedent—namely, a secretary-general assisted by the secretaries of each participating delegation.[48] A more recent example is provided by the early days of OEEC in 1948, when common duties were performed by the staff of national missions: the international secretariat replaced this *ad hoc* pooling of resources only gradually. When Comecon formed its standing commissions in 1956 it followed the geographical posting of the Danube Commission. Each country was allotted a commission. Albania was then excepted, but Mongolia is now the seat of a commission—that on geology (although the Commission itself has often preferred to meet elsewhere, e.g. in Prague in May 1964 or in Tbilisi in October 1966).[49] It was laid down that the chairman should be from the appointed country,[50] but it has also seemed to be the practice to draw upon the

[47] J. Siotis, *Essai sur le secrétariat international* (Geneva, 1963), pp. 33–38. The pattern was also set by conferences with a multinational secretariat, notably the Congress of Berlin, 1878.

[48] Ibid. p. 29. The previous conferences had officials of selected delegations—e.g. of the Great Powers at the Paris Peace Conference, 1919—not of all.

[49] The Standing Commission on Currency and Finance Questions met in Ulan-Bator in October 1966: as Cuba and Vietnam were represented, Mongolia was something of a mid-point for travel.

[50] Shurshalov, p. 291.

same state for the chief of the headquarters department concerned with the branch.[51] As Appendix VII shows, this is strictly so for the chairmen; on the staff it is apparently the case, for the Chief of the Agricultural Division, whose Commission is located in Sofia, is a Bulgarian, N. Darnatov, and the Chief of the Statistics Division is a Soviet citizen, I. Ryzhov, the Commission being in Moscow. This branch and nationality rule seems to apply only to heads of divisions; the secretariat is recruited from all member states, and, as the Charter lays down, 'in carrying out their duties the Secretary of the Council, his deputies and the Secretariat staff shall act as international officials'. As with some intergovernmental, as distinct from international, organizations, the head of the secretariat is a national of the country housing the headquarters. Comecon has always had a Soviet national as Secretary and now has Deputy Secretaries from each of the European members. As an institution without a statute during its first eleven years the closest analogy is probably with GATT. Created a year before Comecon, it still lacks a charter, and derives its status from the collective will of the Contracting Parties. The Charter of 1960 endowed Comecon with an international form, but the national delegations continued to play a major part in its manpower. The numerical predominance of the secretariat over the national mission-staff probably dates only from the large increase in recruitment authorized in June 1962.[52]

The line between an intergovernmental and an international organization was drawn at the inception of the League of Nations. Arthur Balfour, in his report to the League in 1920, wrote

> Evidently, no one nation or group of nations ought to have a monopoly in providing the material for this international institution. I emphasize the word 'international' because the members of the Secretariat, once appointed, are no longer the servants of the country of which they are citizens, but become for the time being the servants only of the League of Nations.[53]

The late Secretary-General of the United Nations, Hammarskjöld, took over a Secretariat already moulded in this tradition. For him, Article 99 of the United Nations Charter 'transformed the Secretary-

[51] The departments were set up for the first time in the second half of 1962 (Miroshnichenko, *Vopr. ekon.*, no. 9, 1963).
[52] J. Kaplar, *Tars. Sz.*, nos. 8–9, 1963; see also Miroshnichenko, *Vopr. ekon.*, no. 9, 1963.
[53] *League of Nations Official Journal*, i. 137.

General of the United Nations from a purely administrative official to one with an explicit political responsibility', and his own interpretation of the Secretariat of the Organization went

> beyond the concept of a non-political civil service into an area where the official, in the exercise of his functions, may be forced to take stands of a politically controversial nature [but] on an international basis and, thus, without departing from the basic concept of 'neutrality'.

He contrasted this with 'an intergovernmental secretariat, the members of which obviously would not be supposed to work in the direction of an internationalism considered unpalatable to their governments'.[54]

The Secretary of Comecon (according to Art. IX (1) of the Charter) is 'the chief official of the Council' and by the list of his activities has essentially administrative functions. The Comecon secretariat is 'intergovernmental' in Hammarskjöld's sense, but the conformity with the views of member governments is vested in ideological unity. For the member states and for the secretariat of Comecon, 'socialist internationalism and comradely help permeates all the work of CMEA'.[55]

> Proletarian internationalism is the ideology of brotherhood and friendship of the workers of all countries. It is also the ideology of the friendship of nations. Proletarian internationalism reflects not only the interests of the working class but the interests of all who labour.[56]

The ideology rejects the possibility of contradictions within socialist internationalism and thus also between a socialist secretariat and its authorities. Just as, for Khrushchev, 'there can be no such thing as an impartial civil servant in this deeply divided world',[57] so there can be only partial civil servants in each segment. The identical *Weltanschauung* postulated for Comecon members should conduce to the 'internationalization of production and exchange',[58] and of its executant, but as Khrushchev observed in June 1964: 'Many of us communists at first thought that in relations between socialist countries there ought not, in principle, to be a single hitch. But life has proved to be more complicated and contradictory than ideological conjectures.'[59]

[54] D. Hammarskjöld, *The International Civil Servant in Law and in Fact* (Oxford, 1961), pp. 10, 14, and 28.
[55] Shurshalov, p. 276. [56] Tunkin, *Sov. gos. pravo*, no. 1, 1959, p. 83.
[57] Walter Lippmann's interpretation of Khrushchev's view, *NY Herald Tribune*, 17 Apr. 1961.
[58] Tunkin, p. 82. [59] *Pr.*, 13 June 1964.

In 1966 two Soviet authors crystallized the principles of intergovernmental operation into four rules. The main principle was of intergovernmentalism itself, as a guarantee against any supranational decision that could 'run counter to national interests'. States should, secondly, participate voluntarily and under 'strict equality'. Any joint undertaking should, thirdly, be of 'mutual benefit' and, finally, should not aim at 'erecting economic barriers to divide countries'. This last criterion was held to require that no restrictions be posed to new entrants, save in 'some bilateral or essentially regional bodies.'[60]

It would be wrong to infer from this last rule that Comecon is open to governments with political systems significantly different from those of the present membership. It is, according to its Secretary in a volume commemorating the fifteenth anniversary, 'the embodiment of a new type of intergovernmental relations between countries having a uniform social and economic system, a common ideology and a single aim, the building of communism'.[61]

The future of integration

The hopes to transform Comecon went astray because domestic political similarities were no longer enough. When the organization was founded, such a form of supranational integration would have been feasible because there was general conformity not only to Soviet leadership but also to the Soviet economic system. In 1963 Comecon was obliged to recognize that the long-standing political and economic formulae within which it had functioned were changing. The Rumanian declarations on sovereignty expressed the one; the opening-up of a new level of bilateral planning epitomized the other. The exchange of production between members—whether implicit in co-ordinating long-run investment programmes or explicit in short-run trade agreements—was to be increasingly in the hands of specialized departmental officials.[62] If the problems of the comparability of prices and costs are successfully solved, this decentralization brings an optimal programme within easier reach than by the grand decision of a supranational authority. How far the domestic devolution can go towards the enterprise—the producers, consumers, and distributors of goods and services—is now the crucial debate in

[60] Sokolov and Shiryaev, *Int. Aff.*, no. 1, 1966, pp. 40–41. [61] Faddeev, p. 167.

[62] A conference of economists from Comecon states discussed this decentralization in Hrazany (Czechoslovakia), 13–17 Dec. 1966 (*RP*, 14 Dec. 1966).

eastern Europe. To spread authority is not, of course, necessarily to transmute a planned economy into a competitive market. Electronic computers and mathematical logic are at hand to simulate economic interrelations. An optimal programme so demonstrated can serve a nationalized industry as well as a capitalist corporation, and there are many permutations of programming with incentives at the level of actual production and distribution. The more initiative that is accorded to each enterprise, the more the Comecon framework will approach that of a Common Market. Symmetrically, the further Comecon evolves as a Common Market, the greater the pressure to increase the autonomy of the enterprise.

When the organization was founded, its structure and functions were dictated by the economic system of its members—that is, centralized physical planning created by the USSR in the 1930s. Kosygin, the present Chairman of the Soviet Council of Ministers, has taken the lead in promoting the new fashion of economic management; his career has brought him close to Comecon both when it was founded and when it was endowed with a Charter (see p. 23). During his visit to Britain in February 1967 he proposed for Anglo-Soviet trade much the same technique as Comecon is now using—namely, that the two countries should guarantee to take adequate quantities of goods from each other over a long enough term to recoup the investments specific to meeting such orders. He proposed joint programmes to 1975 (the period on which Comecon is to negotiate in 1968). The scheme is of a different order to existing arrangements for current sales or the supply of capital goods, and would assure British participants a place in Comecon's 'material balances'. The new inter-corporation pattern of foreign trade emerging within the agency seems to make decisive this entry at the planning level, for Comecon has much attenuated the divergence and rigidity of prices which, until 1965, markedly separated inter-member contracts from the world of business. The earlier British negotiations to join the Common Market impelled Khrushchev's attempt to turn Comecon in upon itself: now that Britain is again approaching EEC, Kosygin has half opened the door to Comecon.

Appendix I

SESSIONS OF THE COUNCIL

(with summaries compiled from official or semi-official sources)

Session	Date	Place	Summary
1949			
	Jan.	Moscow[1]	Constituent conference.
	Feb.	[2]	Albanian application for membership accepted.
1st	26–28 Apr.	Moscow	Establishment of the organization.
2nd	25–27 Aug.	Sofia	Arrangements for scientific and technical co-operation; consideration of long-term plan co-ordination.
1950			
	29 Sept.	[2]	GDR application for membership accepted.
3rd	24–25 Nov.	Moscow[3]	Inter-regional trade.
1954			
4th	26–27 Mar.	Moscow	Co-operation in drawing up 1956–60 trade targets; specialization by bilateral agreement ('Industrial Treaties').
5th	24–25 June	Moscow	Discussion of the distribution of national investment; preliminary talks on unified grid; industrial and agricultural development; foreign trade.
1955			
6th	7–11 Dec.	Budapest	Co-ordination of production plans to 1960; discussion of long-term trade agreements; specialization in engineering.
1956			
7th	18–25 May	Berlin	Transformation of temporary committees into 12 Standing Commissions (see App. VIII); creation of Danube subcommittee; specialization in engineering, raw materials, fuel and foodstuffs; preliminary recommendations on clearing agreement; grain and fertilizer requirements; grid exchanges prepared.

[1] Also at Matrahaza (Hungary); see p. 22.
[2] Submission and approval apparently by correspondence.
[3] Substantive discussions took place at Hollohaza (Hungary); see p. 49.

1957			
8th	18–22 June	Warsaw	Swing-credit clearing scheme agreed (sgd 20 June); inter-member rail and water transport improvement; revision of trade plans for 1957–60; principle of 10–15 year planning adopted; recommendations on Polish coal and sulphur mining; warning on hindrance to trade expansion represented by Common Market proposals.
1958			
9th	26–30 June	Bucharest	Implementation of decisions of May meeting of Communist and Workers' Party representatives; 3 Standing Commissions set up (see App. VIII); recommendation on principles for establishing prices in intra-trade; exchanges to 1965; expansion of coking coal output.
10th	11–13 Dec.	Prague	Specialization in chemicals and engineering; joint construction of oil pipeline (sgd 19 Dec. 1959); balances of fuel and power and of rolling-mill and tube-mill output to 1965; commission set up on light and food industries; recommendations on draft Charter.
1959			
11th	13–16 May	Tirana	Project for 220-KV electricity grid; specialization in rolled products, mining machinery, civil engineering, oil refining, bearings, and rolling-mill equipment, chemical engineering and chemicals; 1965 balances and trade in coking coal, ferrous and non-ferrous metals and flat steel; trade with Asian socialist states.
12th	10–14 Dec.	Sofia	Charter and Convention on Immunities; multilateral veterinary, quarantine, and plant-protection agreement; specialization in equipment for chemicals, sugar, meat-processing, and paper industries; co-ordinated expansion of ferrous metals; aid for Albanian and Bulgarian exploitation of iron ore; joint efforts to develop non-ferrous extraction; wool, fruit, and vegetable targets for 1965; discussion of transport costs; exchange of views on post-1965 plans.

1960			
13th	26–29 July	Budapest	Specialization in agriculture (espec. feed grains), agricultural engineering, and farm chemicals; expansion of consumers' goods; specialization in finishing mills, wire-drawing tools and roller-bearing, oil-refinery, building-materials, milk-processing and canning equipment; measures for improving quality of engineering goods; unification of long-term plan period with 1980 horizon; commission set up on use of nuclear energy for peaceful purposes; Rules of Procedure for Session, Conference of Representatives, and Standing Commissions.
1961			
14th	28 Feb.–3 Mar.	Berlin	Specialization in chemicals (espec. plastics, synthetic rubber, fibres, and petrochemicals); trade agreements for 1961–5 concluded; review of work in co-ordination of plans to 1980; maritime transport.
15th	12–15 Dec.	Warsaw	*Basic Principles* adopted (ratified by Meeting of Party Secretaries, Moscow, 6–7 June 1962); 1965 trade and output balances of fertilizers; joint exploitation of raw materials and fuels; specialization in fertilizers, pesticides, livestock-breeding equipment, and shipbuilding; development of inter-member water and road transport; set up Control Office for Power System; Agreement on Technical Surveillance of Shipping and Classification of Vessels (sgd 15 Dec.).
1962			
16th	7 June	Moscow	'Extraordinary Session' implementing recommendations of Party Meeting, 6–7 June. Set up Executive Committee, 3 Standing Commissions (see App. VIII), Bureau for Integrated Planning Problems, and Inst. of Standardization; amended Charter to admit non-European countries; admitted Mongolia; protocols on supplementary deliveries 1962–5; recommended standardization of statistics and planning indicators.

1962 cont.			
17th	14–20 Dec.	Bucharest	Co-ordination of investment plans beyond 1965; model of 1980 fuel and energy balance to indicate problems requiring decision; recommendations on eliminating duplication in engineering and on specialization in metal-cutting tools, forging-pressing equipment, sugar refinery plant &c.; 1963–5 intra-trade exchanges; expansion of trade with underdeveloped areas; set up Standing Commission on Currency and Finance; proposed creation of international bank; recommendations on sea and railway transport between members and on port and frontier-station facilities; expansion of agriculture and specialization in tractors, self-propelled chassis and major farming machines, and land melioration equipment.
1963			
18th	25–26 July	Moscow	Created separate Standing Commissions for light and for food industries; set up Commission for Radio-Technical and Electronic Industry; re-established Commission for Geology; draft agreement on International Bank for Economic Co-operation.
1965			
19th	28 Jan.– 2 Feb.	Prague	Report on bilateral agreements on basis of CMEA material balances for 1966–70; specialization in radio-electronics, free-play bearings, chemical engineering, oil refinery equipment (catalytic reforming and hydro-purification of diesel-fuel), timber, and textile machinery. Co-ordination of research. Ratification of Yugoslavia as observer.
1966			
20th	8–10 Dec.	Sofia	Co-ordination of research and discussion of convertibility; joint investments in non-ferrous metals; plan co-ordination for 1971–5 to begin by 1968.

Appendix II

MEETINGS OF THE EXECUTIVE COMMITTEE[1]

(Deputy Chairmen of Councils of Ministers)

Note: All meetings were held in Moscow except where otherwise stated; the summaries are taken from official reports.

1962		
1st	10–12 July	Plan of work adopted for expanding operations of Comecon; draft of 'Principles of International Specialization in Engineering', elaborated by Engineering Commission, approved.
2nd	25–28 Sept.	Charters of Commissions on Scientific and Technical Research, on Standardization, and on Statistics; discussed currency and finance co-operation; agreement on outline indicators for five-year-plan co-ordination, incl. arrangements for investment co-ordination; recommendations on farm machinery, seed potatoes, and railway waggons.
3rd	16–20 Dec. (Bucharest)	Proposals for currency transferability, for Internat. Bank for Economic Co-operation, for Common Waggon Pool, and for lorry and shipping co-operation; Charter of Inst. of Standardization; deliveries of equipment to 1965 under specialization agreements; revision of intra-trade prices on basis of 1957–62 world average (but see n. 18, p. 184).
1963		
4th	15–21 Feb.	Fuel balance of 1962 and for long-term plan; work of conference of geological organizations of Comecon countries; convocation of conference of water-resources agencies of Comecon countries and approval of methodology for planning work on water pollution.
5th	17–25 Apr.	Co-ordination of 1966–70 plans (with participation of chairmen of national planning commissions); ratification of Agriculture Commission's 1970 plan for clover and lucerne (alfalfa); drafts on clearing and international bank; Charter of Currency and Finance

[1] Set up by Decision of 16th Session.

1963 cont.		Commission; specialization of machine-tool production for ball-bearing industry (with provisional commission for latter); 1964–5 investment plans.
6th	10–13 May (Warsaw)	Scientific co-operation; agriculture; foreign trade; currency and finance problems.
7th	3–6 July	Agreement on opening of bilateral talks with Mongolia; specialization in equipment for oil refining, textiles, building and civil engineering, cable-making, electronics, and chemicals; standardization of chemical equipment; recommendations on oil and gas prospecting; development of the coal industry.
8th	26 July	Implementation of decisions of 18th Session.
9th	15–22 Oct.	Report of Bureau of the Executive on a list of industrial investment projects planned for 1964–5; basic directions of 1966–70 investment plans; production and deliveries of farm machinery in 1964–5; expansion of rolled steel. [Creation of International Bank of Economic Co-operation, and agreement on multilateral clearing in separate session on 22 Oct.]
10th	17–21 Dec. (Bucharest)	Charters of Commissions on Light Industry, on Food Industry, on Geology, and on Radio-Technical and Electronic Industry; specialization in measuring instruments and chemical, oil-refining, and food-processing equipment; abolition of provisional commission on ball-bearings. [Creation of Common Waggon Pool in separate session on 21 Dec.]
1964		
11th	25–28 Feb.	Technology research plan for 1964–5; discussion on standardization; appointment of delegation to UN Trade and Development Conference (Mar.–June 1964); reports on Water-Resource Conference and on 1966–70 plan co-ordination.
12th	21–25 Apr.	Report by Secretary on Fifteenth Anniversary of Comecon; declaration on development aid to less-industrialized members and to developing countries elsewhere; Bureau report on progress of 1966–70 plan co-ordination; proposals for intensification of agriculture, expansion of fodder amino-acids and vitamins; balances of food, textiles, pharmaceuticals, radio-engineering, and shipbuilding 1964–70; aid to Mongolia for agricultural research and geological survey.

1964 cont.		
13th	14–16 July	Report by Bureau on studies of standing commissions, bilateral consultations between plan offices, and Secretariat aggregation of summary industrial balances of output and trade 1966–70; co-operation of interested countries in investment in coal mining; expansion of output of low-viscosity oils in 1966–70 and of trade in consumers' goods. [Creation of Intermetall in separate Session on 15 July.]
	17 Sept.	Agreement signed by Yugoslav Ambassador to USSR and Secretary of Comecon 'on behalf of Executive Committee and Secretariat' to admit Yugoslavia to seven Standing Commissions (Foreign Trade, Currency and Finance Questions, Ferrous Metals, Non-Ferrous Metals, Chemicals Industry, Engineering, and Co-ordination of Scientific and Technical Research).
14th	13–16 Oct.	Agenda for 19th Session of Council; Draft report of Executive Committee to Session discussed. Recommendations for transport co-ordination, for specialization in non-ferrous metals, for patent protection among members, for co-operation in water conservation, and on standardization of statistical indicators for engineering specialization.
15th	2–3 Dec.	Discussion of prices for long-term trade agreements among members; transport co-ordination.
1965		
16th	29 Jan.–2 Feb.	Co-operation in oil and gas industries (esp. on use of 'Friendship' pipeline); specialization in chemicals engineering, electro-technical, metal-working, and consumer-good equipment; internationally standardized statistics of level and growth of production and uniform list for industrial and agricultural production.
17th	7–9 Apr.	Preliminary report of Commission for Scientific Research on 1966–70 co-ordination; implementation of 19th Session recommendations on specialization in engineering and radio-electronics (conference thereon to be convened in second half of 1965); recommendations to open bottlenecks in certain engineering products; draft agreement between CMEA and Organization of Socialist Countries for Posts and Telecommunications.

1965 cont.

18th	25–29 June (Leningrad)	Report of Bureau on 1966–70 Plan co-ordination and on bilateral consultations; report of Finance Commission on International Bank for Economic Co-operation in 1964, of Engineering Commission on mutual deliveries during 1966–70 of over 200 types of textile equipment and over 30 types of timber machinery. Standard list of types of sea-going ships to be built by members in 1966–70.
19th	21–23 Sept.	Report of Bureau on problems raised by 1966–70 energy balance with objective of CMEA self-sufficiency; specialization in equipment for opencast mining, pumps, compressors, equipment for sheet-glassmaking; procedure for 1966 trade agreements within multilateral clearing scheme; report of water resources conference.
20th	30 Nov.–3 Dec.	Agricultural development plan 1966–70; unified plan for scientific and technological co-ordination 1966–70 (including Yugoslavia). Progress report on trade negotiations for 1966–70 between members. Discussions on payments and standardization problems. 1966 Budget approved.

1966

21st	8–11 Feb.	Recommendations on reports of Commissions for Ferrous Metals, Chemicals Industry, Radio-Technical and Electronic Industry, Light Industry, and Transport on Plan co-ordination beyond 1970. Revision of previous specialization agreements on chemicals and oil-refinery equipment; recommendations on specialization of radio-electronic components, of freight and fishing vessels, and of equipment for protective covering and finishing of rolled steel, for geological survey of deep strata and for complete processes in oil-refining. Approved 'General Principles for the Assurance of Spare Parts for Equipment traded between CMEA members and Yugoslavia'.
22nd	19–22 Apr.	Reports by Bureau on conclusion of bilateral and multilateral negotiations on 1966–70 Plan co-ordinating and by Commission for Engineering on 'Basic problems arising from the co-ordination of engineering plans for 1966–70'. Report of Conference on Specialization on Co-operation attended by experts from CMEA members and Yugoslavia. Recommendations on specialization of equipment for

1966 cont.		building-materials industry, for geological survey of usable minerals, for hydro-geology and for engineering geology, of complete plant in chemical manufacture and of mineral fertilizers (and their raw materials and semi-manufactures).
23rd	7–11 June	Report drafted for presentation to Twentieth Session on activities of CMEA and future tasks of economic co-operation.
24th		No communiqué; presumably held in conjunction with Bucharest meeting of Party leaders and Heads of Government, 7 July 1966.
25th	4–7 Oct.	Report of conclusion of long-term trade agreements among members and with Yugoslavia, 1966–70. Specialization for 1967–70 in marine diesel-engines. Convocation of Twentieth Session for December 1966.
26th	1–2 Nov.	Approval of documents for Twentieth Session.
27th	10–13 Dec. (Sofia)	Review of recommendations on specialization plans to 1970 for rolled metal, pipe, alloys, and machinery for building and civil engineering industries, and for manufacture of plastic goods. Approval of budget and work programme for 1967.
1967		
28th	21–24 Feb.	Specialization in chemicals and agricultural equipment. Accepted reports on co-operation by Engineering and Radio-technical and Electronic Industry Commissions.

Appendix III

MEETINGS OF REPRESENTATIVES OF COMMUNIST PARTIES OF COMECON MEMBER COUNTRIES

(Held in Moscow except where otherwise stated.)

1951	November (Hollohaza)	Meeting of political leaders (no communiqué issued).
1958	20–23 May	Representatives of the Communist and Workers' Parties of member countries.
1960	2–3 Feb.	Representatives of Communist and Workers' Parties in European socialist countries, on agricultural development.
1962	6–7 June	Communist and Workers' Party Representatives of member countries.
1963	24–26 July	First Secretaries of Communist and Workers' Parties and of Heads of Governments of member countries.
1966	7 July (Bucharest)	Leaders of Communist and Workers' Parties and Heads of Government of member countries.

Appendix IV

THE COMECON CHARTER, 1960[1]

With amendments adopted by the Sixteenth and Seventeenth Sessions but still requiring ratification (in italics).[2]

STATUTES OF THE COUNCIL FOR MUTUAL ECONOMIC ASSISTANCE

The Governments of the People's Republic of Albania, the People's Republic of Bulgaria, the Hungarian People's Republic, the German Democratic Republic, the Polish People's Republic, the Rumanian People's Republic, the Union of Soviet Socialist Republics and the Czechoslovak Republic,

Considering that the economic co-operation which is being successfully carried out between their countries is conducive to the most rational development of the national economy, to raising the standard of living of the population and to strengthening the unity and solidarity of these countries;

Being fully determined henceforward to develop all-round economic co-operation on the basis of consistently bringing about the international socialist division of labour in the interests of the building of socialism and communism in their countries, and in the interests of ensuring lasting peace throughout the world;

Being convinced that the developments of economic co-operation between their countries promotes the achievement of the purposes defined in the Charter of the United Nations;

Confirming their readiness to develop economic relations with all countries irrespective of their social and political structure on the basis of equality, mutual advantage and non-interference in each other's internal affairs;

Recognizing the constantly increasing role of the Council for Mutual Economic Assistance in the organization of economic co-operation between their countries;

Have agreed for these ends to adopt the present Statutes.

[1] Trans. by R. Nötel (Professor, Graduate Institute of International Studies, Geneva) from the Russian, German, and Hungarian texts in *Vedomosti verkhovnogo soveta SSSR*, no. 15, 1960, *Gesetzblatt der DDR*, 10 May 1960, pp. 284–92, and *Magyar Kozlony a Magyar Nepkoztarsasag hivatalos lapja*, no. 49, 10 June 1960, pp. 337–44; use was also made of the English translation published by the Comecon Secretariat.

[2] Trans. by author with advice of R. Szporluk (Professor at the University of Michigan) from *Rada Wzajemnej Pomocy Gospodarczej: Wybor Materialow i Dokumentow* (Warsaw, 1964), pp. 191–202, which provides the official Polish text of the original Charter (*Dzennik Ustaw*, 23 July 1960) with amendments.

ARTICLE I

PURPOSES AND PRINCIPLES

1. The purpose of the Council for Mutual Economic Assistance is to promote, by uniting and co-ordinating the efforts of the member countries of the Council, the planned development of the national economy, the acceleration of economic and technical progress in these countries, the raising of the level of industrialization in the industrially less-developed countries, a steady increase in the productivity of labour and a constant improvement in the welfare of the peoples of the member countries of the Council.

2. The Council for Mutual Economic Assistance is established on the basis of the principle of the sovereign equality of all the member countries of the Council.

Economic, scientific, and technical co-operation between the member countries of the Council shall be carried out in accordance with the principles of full equality of rights, respect for each other's sovereignty and national interests, mutual advantage and friendly mutual assistance.

ARTICLE II

MEMBERSHIP

1. The original members of the Council for Mutual Economic Assistance are the countries which have signed and ratified the present Statutes.

2. Admission to membership of the Council shall be open to other countries which share the purposes and principles of the Council and have expressed their readiness to accept the obligations contained in the present Statutes.

3. Any member country of the Council may withdraw from the Council upon giving notice to the depositary of the present Charter to this effect. This notice shall come into force six months after its receipt by the depositary. The depositary shall inform the member countries of the Council of such notice upon receipt.

4. Member countries of the Council shall agree:

(*a*) to ensure the fulfilment of the recommendations of the Council organs adopted by them;

(*b*) to render the Council and its officials the necessary co-operation in the discharge by them of the functions stipulated in the present Charter;

(*c*) to submit to the Council the materials and information necessary for carrying out the tasks entrusted to it;

(*d*) to inform the Council about progress in fulfilling the recommendations adopted in the Council.

ARTICLE III

FUNCTIONS AND POWERS

1. In accordance with the purposes and principles laid down in Article I of these Statutes, the Council for Mutual Economic Assistance:

(*a*) shall organize all-round economic, scientific and technical co-operation betweeen the member countries of the Council with a view to making the most rational use of their natural resources and to accelerating the development of their productive capacities;

(b) *shall co-operate in the improvement of the international socialist division of labour by means of the co-ordination of national economic plans, and of the specialization and co-operation of production of member countries of the Council;*

(c) *shall adopt measures in order to study the economic and scientific-technical problems of member countries of the Council;*

(d) *shall co-operate with member countries of the Council in elaborating and implementing common undertakings in the fields of:*

the development of industry and agriculture of member countries of the Council;

the development of transport so as primarily to satisfy the ever-increasing freight traffic in the imports, exports and transit of member countries of the Council;

the most effective utilization of investment funds *allocated by member countries of the Council for the expansion of the extractive and manufacturing branches of industry and for the construction of major projects of interest to two or more countries;*

the development of the exchange of goods and services between the member countries of the Council and with other countries;

the exchange of scientific and technical knowledge and advanced production experience.

(*e*) shall undertake other activities necessary for the achievement of the objectives of the Council.

2. The Council for Mutual Economic Assistance, as represented by its organs, acting within the bounds of their competence, is empowered to make recommendations and decisions in conformity with the present Charter.

ARTICLE IV

RECOMMENDATIONS AND DECISIONS

1. Recommendations shall be adopted on matters of economic, scientific and technical co-operation. Recommendations shall be communicated to the member countries of the Council for consideration.

The recommendations adopted by the member countries of the Council shall be implemented by decisions of their governments or competent authorities in accordance with their national legislation.

2. Decisions shall be made on organizational and procedural matters.

3. All recommendations and decisions by the Council shall be adopted only with the consent of the interested member countries of the Council, and each country shall be entitled to declare its interest in any matter considered by the Council.

The effects of recommendations and decisions shall not extend to countries which have declared their lack of interest in the question concerned. Each such country may, however, accede subsequently to recommendations and decisions adopted by the other member countries of the Council.

ARTICLE V

ORGANS

1. The Council for Mutual Economic Assistance shall have the following principal organs for discharging the functions and powers referred to in Article III of these Statutes:

the Council Session,
the *Executive Committee*,
the Standing Commissions,
the Secretariat.

2. Such other organs as may prove to be necessary shall be established in accordance with the present Statutes.

ARTICLE VI

THE COUNCIL SESSION

1. The Council Session is the supreme organ of the Council for Mutual Economic Assistance. It shall be empowered to discuss all matters coming within the competence of the Council, and to adopt recommendations and decisions in accordance with the present Statutes.

2. The Council Session shall consist of delegations from all the member countries of the Council. The composition of each country's delegation shall be determined by the government of the country concerned.

3. A regular Session of the Council shall be held *once* a year in the capital of each of the member countries of the Council in turn, and shall be presided over by the head of the delegation of the country in which the Session is held.

4. An Extraordinary Session of the Council may be held at the request or with the consent of not less than one-third of the member countries of the Council.

5. The Session of the Council

(a) *shall consider basic problems of economic and scientific-technical co-operation, the definition of the main directions of the activity of the Council, and the report of the Executive Committee on the activity of the Council;*

(b) *shall exercise other functions necessary for the achievement of the purposes of the Council.*

6. The Session of the Council is empowered to set up such organs it may deem necessary for discharging the functions entrusted to the Council.

7. The Session of the Council shall establish its own rules of procedure.

ARTICLE VII

EXECUTIVE COMMITTEE

The *Executive Committee* of the Council shall consist of the representatives of all the member countries of the Council, on the basis of one from each country.

1. *The Executive Committee is the chief executive organ of the Council.*

The Executive Committee has a Bureau for Integrated Planning Problems in which each country is represented by a deputy chairman of the state planning organ.

2. *The Executive Committee holds its meetings not less frequently than once every two months.*

3. *The Executive Committee within the sphere of its competence has the right to adopt recommendations and decisions in accordance with this Charter. The Executive Committee may submit proposals to be considered by the Council Session.*

4. *The Executive Committee:*

(a) *shall direct the totality of work connected with the execution of tasks posed before the Council in accordance with the resolutions of the Council Sessions, and shall systematically supervise the execution by member countries of the duties which follow from recommendations adopted by organs of the Council;*

(b) *shall direct the work of co-ordinating plans of national economic development, specialization and co-operation of the production of member countries of the Council, and shall organize the elaboration of the basic direction of the national division of labour in the major production branches of those countries;*

(c) *shall consider proposals of member countries of the Council, Standing Commissions, the Bureau of the Executive Committee for Integrated Planning Problems, the Secretariat of the Council, and other organs of the Council concerning questions of economic and scientific-technical co-operation, shall analyse the state of that co-operation and shall elaborate undertakings for its further development;*

(d) *shall elaborate basic directions and measures for the development of the exchange of goods and services between the member countries of the Council, and of scientific-technical co-operation between member countries of the Council;*

(e) *directs the work of the Secretariat of the Council and of the Standing Commissions of the Council, and determines the basic lines of activity of those Commissions;*

(f) *shall approve:*

the staffs and budget of the Council Secretariat and also the report of the Council Secretariat on the fulfilment of the budget; the regulations governing the Standing Commissions, the Bureau of the Executive Committee for Integrated Planning Problems, and the Secretariat of the Council;

(g) *shall establish control agencies for checking the financial activity of the Council Secretariat;*

(h) *shall discharge other functions which follow from the present Charter and also from the recommendations and decisions of the Session of the Council.*

5. *The Executive Committee may set up such organs as are needed for the execution of its functions.*

6. The *Committee* shall establish its own rules of procedure.

ARTICLE VIII

STANDING COMMISSIONS

1. Standing Commissions of the Council for Mutual Economic Assistance shall be established by the Council Session for the purpose of promoting the further development of economic relations between the member countries of the Council and the organization of multilateral economic, scientific, and technical co-operation in individual sectors of the economy in these countries.

Regulations governing the Standing Commissions shall be approved by the Executive Committee of the Council.

2. *Each member country of the Council shall appoint its representatives to the Standing Commissions.*

3. *The Standing Commissions, within the limits of their competence, have the right to adopt recommendations and decisions in conformity with the present Charter. The Commissions may also submit proposals for the consideration of the Session of the Council and the Executive Committee of the Council.*

4. The Standing Commissions shall work out measures and prepare proposals for the achievement of the economic, scientific, and technical co-operation referred to in paragraph 1 of this Article, and also discharge such functions as arise from the present Statutes, and from the recommendations and decisions adopted by the Council Session and the *Executive Committee of* the Council.

The Standing Commissions shall submit to the Council annual reports on the work they have accomplished and on their future activities.

5. The meetings of the Standing Commissions shall, as a rule, be held at the place where they are permanently located, which shall be determined by the Council Session.

6. The Standing Commissions may, *in order to fulfil their functions and in accordance with their plans of work, establish auxiliary organs to prepare for the consideration of the Commissions and to discuss questions within the competence of the Commissions, and may convene scientific-technical conferences and other meetings.*

The composition and competence of such organs, conferences, and meetings and also the place and date of their convocation shall be established by the Commissions.

7. *The function of the secretariat of the Standing Commissions shall be fulfilled by the appropriate departments of the Secretariat of the Council.*

8. The Standing Commissions shall draw up their own rules of procedure.

ARTICLE IX

THE SECRETARIAT

1. The Secretariat of the Council for Mutual Economic Assistance shall consist of the Secretary of the Council, his deputies, and such staff as may be required for the performance of the Secretariat's functions.

The Secretary of the Council shall be appointed by the Session of the Council *and his deputies by the Executive Committee.*

The Secretary and his deputies shall direct the work of the Council Secretariat. The staff of the Secretariat shall be recruited from citizens of the member countries of the Council in accordance with the rules and regulations of the Secretariat of the Council.

The Secretary of the Council shall be the chief official of the Council. He shall represent the Council before officials and organizations of the Council member countries and other countries, and also before international organizations. The Secretary of the Council may empower his deputies and also Secretariat officials to act on his behalf.

The Secretary and his deputies may take part in all meetings of the organs of the Council.

2. The Secretariat of the Council:

(a) *shall organize the preparation, and shall collaborate in the conduct of, the meetings conducted within the framework of the Council, and shall prepare materials for the meetings of the organs of the Council in accordance with the work plans of those organs;*

(b) *shall prepare economic surveys and analyses on the basis of materials of the member countries of the Council, shall prepare and publish information, reference and other material related to problems of economic, scientific and technical collabora-*

tion among members of the Council, and shall prepare other surveys and analyses;

(c) *shall prepare proposals on scientific problems of the work of the Council for the consideration of the appropriate organs of the Council;*

(d) *shall organize, jointly with the Standing Commissions of the Council, the drafting of multilateral agreements on questions of economic and scientific and technical co-operation on the basis of recommendations and decisions of the organs of the Council;*

(e) *shall organize and maintain records of the execution of the recommendations and decisions of the organs of the Council and shall draw up suitable proposals for consideration by the Executive Committee and Standing Commissions of the Council;*

(f) *shall take other actions which follow from the present Charter, from the recommendations and decisions adopted in the Council, and also from the Regulations Governing the Secretariat of the Council.*

3. In carrying out their duties, the Secretary of the Council, his deputies and the Secretariat staff shall act as international officials.

4. The seat of the Council Secretariat shall be in Moscow.

ARTICLE X

PARTICIPATION OF OTHER COUNTRIES IN THE COUNCIL'S WORK

The Council for Mutual Economic Assistance may invite countries which are not members of the Council to take part in the work of the Council's organs.

The terms on which the representatives of these countries may participate in the work of the Council organs shall be determined by the Council by understanding with the countries concerned.

ARTICLE XI

RELATIONS WITH INTERNATIONAL ORGANIZATIONS

The Council for Mutual Economic Assistance may establish and maintain relations with the economic organs of the United Nations and with other international organizations.

The nature and form of these relations shall be determined by the Council by understanding with the corresponding international organizations.

ARTICLE XII

FINANCIAL MATTERS

1. The member countries of the Council for Mutual Economic Assistance shall bear the cost of maintaining the Secretariat and financing its work. The proportion of the cost to be borne by each member country shall be

determined by the Council Session, and other financial matters shall be settled by the *Executive Committee of* the Council.

2. The Secretariat of the Council shall submit to the Executive Committee of the Council a report on the fulfilment of the budget for each calendar year.

3. The expenditure for the maintenance of the participants in the Session of the Council, the Executive Committee of the Council, and meetings of the Council's Standing Commissions and also in conferences held within the framework of the Council shall be borne by the country which sends its representatives to these meetings and conferences.

4. The expenditure involved in making available accommodation and technical equipment for the meetings and conferences indicated in Paragraph 3 of the present Article shall be borne by the country in which these meetings and conferences are held, except when such meetings or conferences take place on the premises of the Secretariat of the Council.

ARTICLE XIII

MISCELLANEOUS PROVISIONS

1. The Council for Mutual Economic Assistance shall enjoy, in the territory of each member country of the Council, the legal capacity necessary for the discharge of its functions and the achievement of its purposes.

2. The Council and also representatives of the Council member countries and Council officials shall enjoy on the territory of each of these countries the privileges and immunities needed to discharge the functions and achieve the purposes envisaged in the present Charter.

3. The competence, privileges and immunities indicated in the present Article shall be determined by a special Convention.

4. The provisions of these Statutes shall not affect the rights and obligations of the member countries of the Council arising from their membership in other international organizations, or from international agreements concluded by them.

5. *Representatives of countries in the Executive Committee of the Council are simultaneously permanent representatives of their countries in the Council. A Permanent Representative of a country to the Council has, at the seat of the Secretariat of the Council, a deputy, the necessary number of advisers and other employees.*

ARTICLE XIV

LANGUAGES

The official languages of the Council for Mutual Economic Assistance shall be the languages of all the member countries of the Council.

The working language of the Council shall be Russian.

ARTICLE XV

RATIFICATION AND ENTRY INTO FORCE OF THE STATUTES

1. The present Statutes are subject to ratification by the signatory countries in accordance with their constitutional procedures.

2. The instruments of ratification shall be deposited with the depositary of the present Charter.

3. The Charter shall enter into force immediately upon the deposit of the ratification instruments by all the countries which signed the present Charter, of which the depositary shall inform these countries.

4. The admission of any country which, in accordance with Paragraph 2 Article II of the present Charter, enters the Council for Mutual Economic Assistance and ratifies this Charter, shall enter into force on the day of deposit of the instrument of ratification by that country, of which the depositary shall inform the other member countries of the Council.

ARTICLE XVI

PROCEDURE FOR AMENDING THE STATUTES

Each member country of the Council for Mutual Economic Assistance may submit proposals for the amendment of the present Statutes.

Amendments to these Statutes approved by the Council Assembly shall enter into force as soon as all the member countries of the Council have deposited with the depositary their instruments of ratification of the amendment.

ARTICLE XVII

FINAL PROVISIONS

The present Charter is done in one copy in the Russian language. The Charter shall be deposited with the Government of the Union of Soviet Socialist Republics, which shall send certified copies of the Charter to the Governments of all the other member countries of the Council, and shall also inform these Governments and the Secretary of the Council on the deposit of the ratification instruments with the Government of the USSR.

In witness whereof the representatives of the Governments of the member countries of the Council for Mutual Economic Assistance have signed the present Charter.

Done in Sofia on 14 December 1959.

For the Government of the People's Republic of Albania

A. KELEZI

For the Government of the People's Republic of Bulgaria

R. DAMIANOV

For the Government of the Czechoslovak Republic

O. SIMUNEK

For the Government of the German Democratic Republic

B. LEUISCHNER

For the Government of the Hungarian People's Republic

A. APRO

For the Government of the Polish People's Republic

P. JAROSZEWICZ

For the Government of the Rumanian People's Republic

A. BIRLADEANU

For the Government of the Union of Soviet Socialist Republics

A. KOSYGIN

NOTE: Comecon's own English text of the Charter states that 'the Seventeenth Session . . . examined some other amendments to the Charter of the Council'. On the other hand the Polish compendium of 1964 cited above, which gives apparently the only published text of the 1962 Amendments, observes that they were adopted but awaited ratification; this implies that all attending voted in favour, since neither the Charter nor the Rules of Procedure allow majority decisions. Ratification, according to Article XVI, must be unanimous. Thus, if Rumania voted for the amendments at the Seventeenth Session, it could have insisted that Albania's ratification be awaited, rather than withhold its own ratification. Article 20 of the Session's Rules of Procedure (published in *Rada Wzajemneh Pomocy Gospodarcze: Wybor materialow i dokumentow*, pp. 208–15) lays down that: 'The Session of the Council is legitimate (*prawomoczna*) if all delegations of every member country are present at it.' If the Session was incapable of suspending this (see below), Albania's absence from the Sixteenth and Seventeenth Session would have frustrated action. It did not declare its lack of interest in accordance with Article IV of the Charter or in the corresponding provisions of the Rules of Procedure—Article 20 of which reiterates that decisions may be taken

> only with the consent of the interested countries which are members of the Council, and any country has the right to declare its interest. . . . [They] do not apply to those countries which have declared that they are not interested in a given matter. However, any of those countries may accede to recommendations and decisions made by the remaining members of the Council.

It seems that the amendments made by the Sixteenth and Seventeenth Sessions are invalid. This was the conclusion of R. Szawlowski, who was the first to remark the Polish source for the changes in a western journal (*Sov. Stud.*, Oct. 1965, p. 263). He had earlier (ibid. Apr. 1965, p. 463) pointed out that Albania must have legally blocked the amendments by non-ratification. He ignored, however, the explicit failure to ratify when denying the qualification 'extra-statutory' to the bodies thus provisionally created.

But, while such agencies are patently unconstitutional, the legality of the admission of Mongolia is affected on rather different grounds. Admission of new members according to Article II of the Charter is 'by decision of the Session'; Article 30 of the Rules of Procedure of the Session does not, however, require unanimity among members for admission. Szawlowski (p. 462) contends that Mongolia could not have been legally admitted so long as Article II stated that membership 'shall be open to all countries of Europe'. The excision of 'of Europe' by the Sixteenth Session has not been ratified, but it might be argued that the original Charter did not specify 'only to countries of Europe'. Furthermore, because the Session has the right to lay down its own Rules of Procedure (Art. VI), it could probably lift the embargo requiring all members to be present (Art. 20, cited above). Articles 30 and 34 of the Rules of Procedure respectively do not require unanimity on the admission of new members or on changes in the Rules themselves.

Appendix V

CONVENTION ON IMMUNITIES
(Extracts)

CONVENTION ON THE LEGAL CAPACITY, PRIVILEGES, AND IMMUNITIES OF THE COUNCIL FOR MUTUAL ECONOMIC ASSISTANCE[1]

Article I
Legal capacity

The Council for Mutual Economic Assistance shall possess juridical personality. It shall have the capacity: (*a*) to conclude agreements; (*b*) to acquire, lease and dispose of property; (*c*) to engage in legal proceedings.

Article II
Property, assets, and documents

1. The premises of the Council for Mutual Economic Assistance shall be inviolable. The property, assets, and documents of the Council, wherever situated, shall enjoy immunity from every form of administrative and judicial interference, except when the Council itself waives immunity in any particular case. . . .

Article III
Privileges in respect of communications

The Council for Mutual Economic Assistance shall enjoy in the territory of each member country of the Council treatment not less favourable than that accorded in that country to diplomatic missions in the matter of priorities, rates and taxes on mails, telegrams and telephone communications.

Article IV
Representatives of the member countries of the Council

1. Representatives of member countries to the organs of the Council for Mutual Economic Assistance, and to meetings held under the Council's auspices, shall, while exercising their functions, enjoy the following privileges and immunities:

[1] *Gesetzblatt der DDR*, 10 May 1960, pp. 293–6 ff. (trans. as App. IV).

(*a*) immunity from personal arrest or detention, and from the jurisdiction of judicial institutions, in respect of any act performed by them in their capacity as representatives;

(*b*) inviolability for all papers and documents;

(*c*) the same customs privileges in respect of their personal baggage as are accorded in the country concerned to members of diplomatic missions of equivalent rank;

(*d*) exemption from personal service and from payment of direct taxes and levies on the salary paid to representatives by the appointing country. . . .

3. The privileges and immunities provided for in this article shall be accorded to the persons mentioned therein only for official purposes. It shall be the right and duty of each member country of the Council to waive its representative's immunity in all cases in which, in the view of that country, the immunity would hamper the administration of justice and the renunciation of immunity would not be detrimental to the purposes for which the immunity is granted.

4. The provisions of paragraphs 1 and 2 of this article shall not apply to relations between a representative and the organs of the country of which he is a citizen. . . .

Article V

[As Article IV but with respect to members of the Secretariat.]

Appendix VI

BASIC PRINCIPLES OF INTERNATIONAL SOCIALIST DIVISION OF LABOUR[1]

(Extracts)

1. COMMUNITY OF SOCIALIST COUNTRIES AND INTERNATIONAL SOCIALIST DIVISION OF LABOUR

The world socialist system is a social, economic and political community of free, sovereign nations following the path of socialism and communism, united by common interests and goals and by indestructible ties of international socialist solidarity.

The close union of the socialist countries within a single system is necessitated by the objective laws of economic and political development. . . .

The community of socialist countries achieves its aims through all-round political, economic and cultural co-operation, with all the socialist countries guided by the principles of full equality, mutual respect for each other's independence and sovereignty, fraternal assistance and mutual benefit. No member of the socialist camp has, or can have, any special rights or privileges. Adherence to the principles of Marxism–Leninism and socialist internationalism is an indispensable condition for the successful development of the world socialist system. . . .

Each socialist country maps out its own economic development plans based on the concrete conditions in the given country, the political and economic goals set by the Communist and Workers' Parties, and the needs and potentialities of all the socialist countries. The new social system makes it possible organically to combine the development of each national economy with the development and consolidation of the world economic system of socialism as a whole. The progress of the entire world socialist system depends on the contribution of each country.

The socialist countries consider it their internationalist duty to direct their efforts to securing a high rate of development in the industry and agriculture of each country commensurate with available potentialities, progressively equalizing economic development levels, and successfully solving the problem of exceeding the world capitalist system in absolute volume

[1] *New Times* (Moscow), no. 27, 1962, pp. 33–40 (trans. slightly clarified).

of industrial and agricultural production and subsequently surpassing the economically most developed capitalist countries in per capita production and in living standards of the working people. . . .

In contrast to international capitalist division of labour, which reflects the exploitation of the weak by the strong and is formed spontaneously, through sharp monopoly rivalry and expansion, accentuating unequal economic development levels and producing an ugly, one-sided economic structure in underdeveloped countries, international socialist division of labour is carried out consciously, according to plan, in conformity with the vital interests of the peoples and with the aim of ensuring harmonious and all-round development of all the socialist countries, and adding strength to their unity.

Planned international socialist division of labour makes for maximum utilization of the advantages of the world socialist system, for a balanced economy in each country, rational distribution of the productive forces throughout the world socialist system, efficient employment of labour and material resources, and enhancement of the defence potential of the socialist camp. Division of labour must guarantee each country the possibility to market its specialized products and to buy the necessary raw materials, equipment and other goods.

The objectives of international socialist division of labour are more efficient social production, a higher rate of economic growth, higher living standards for the working people in all the socialist countries, industrialization and gradual removal of historical differences in the economic development levels of the socialist countries, and the creation of a material basis for their more-or-less simultaneous transition to communism, within one and the same historical era.

At the same time, international socialist division of labour helps to accomplish the basic tasks facing each socialist country and the whole of the world socialist system at each historical stage.

International socialist division of labour takes into account the world division of labour. By expanding their economic ties with all countries of the world, the socialist countries thus strengthen the material basis for peaceful co-existence of the two world socio-economic systems. . . .

2. CO-ORDINATION OF ECONOMIC PLANS—THE PRINCIPAL MEANS OF SUCCESSFULLY DEVELOPING AND EXTENDING INTERNATIONAL SOCIALIST DIVISION OF LABOUR

. . . CMEA experience in economic co-operation has shown that co-ordination of plans should seek to implement the following inter-related objective principles of international socialist division of labour:

—adequate assessment of the objectively required proportions in the economic development of each country and the world socialist system as a whole, so as to attain a balanced economy in each country;

—high economic efficiency of international socialist division of labour, i.e. a high rate of growth in production and maximum satisfaction of the needs of the population in each country with minimum expenditure of social labour;

—combination of international specialization in production with all-round, comprehensive development of the economies of the individual socialist countries with a view to the fullest and most rational utilization in all the countries of natural and economic resources, including man-power;

—steady elimination of historical differences in the economic development levels of the individual countries, primarily through industrialization of countries with relatively low economic levels, and through maximum utilization of the internal potentialities of each country and of the advantages inherent in the world socialist system. . . .

The interconnection between the economies of the individual countries, stemming from division of labour, should be strong and stable, for any deviation, even by a single country, would inevitably lead to disturbances in the economic cycle in the other socialist countries.

Co-ordination of economic plans should take the fullest account of the necessity to produce, within the framework of the world socialist system, staple goods in quantities sufficient to meet the needs of the socialist countries with due allowances for their ever-expanding trade with other countries. . . .

3. BASIC DIRECTIONS IN RATIONAL DIVISION OF LABOUR IN KEY BRANCHES OF THE ECONOMY

. . . Interstate specialization implies concentrating production of similar products in one or several socialist countries so as to meet the needs of all interested countries, thus improving industrial techniques and management, and establishing stable economic ties and co-operation. International specialization should serve to expand production, reduce costs, raise productivity and improve quality and technical standards.

As a stimulating factor of technical progress, international specialization and co-operation in production help the rapid industrialization of all the socialist countries.

International specialization and co-operation are potent economic factors in the development of all industries, especially engineering, chemicals, ferrous and nonferrous metallurgy. Specialization permits a rapid changeover to new types of goods, the manufacture of which is made possible by technical progress. . . .

Every encouragement [must] be given to the production in all the countries of the materials scarce in the socialist camp, taking into account natural and economic conditions. . . .

International socialist division of labour in metallurgy should stimulate rapid expansion of ferrous and non-ferrous metal production in amounts and grades that meet the growing requirements of the socialist countries and reduce production costs.

Division of labour in metallurgy is determined by the need to develop this industry in all socialist countries depending on available supplies of raw materials, processed fuels and power, or on the possibility of importing raw materials at reasonable cost from other countries. Integrated iron and steel centres should preferably be set up in countries that are fully, or nearly fully, provided with ore and processed fuel, or at least possess one of the two. . . .

Specialization in the engineering industries of the socialist countries should not be limited to individual products, types or sizes. Main emphasis in long-range planning should be on specialization in basic groups and types of engineering goods. . . .

The socialist countries differ in per capita farm land and in soil and climatic conditions: the exchange of farm produce between them will therefore continue and will increase. This makes it necessary to co-ordinate plans and explore possibilities for further specialization in agricultural production in accordance with their needs and potentialities. In tackling the problem of specialization, emphasis should be on maximum increase in grain and livestock production in each socialist country. . . .

4. ATTAINMENT OF HIGH ECONOMIC EFFECT OF INTERNATIONAL SOCIALIST DIVISION OF LABOUR

. . . The principal criterion of economic effect in international socialist division of labour is the growth of productivity of social labour, i.e., minimum production and transport costs in terms of materials and labour. . . .

Higher efficiency in social production through perfection of international socialist division of labour fully meets both the national and common interests of the socialist countries. The desire of any socialist country for further international division of labour, beneficial to the world socialist system as a whole, will be met, whenever necessary, through appropriate forms of co-operation with, and assistance from, the other socialist countries.

In co-ordination of plans, the relative economic effect of investments and production in the socialist countries, as well as the economic effect of foreign trade, are an important, though not the only, criterion in defining the best ways of extending international socialist division of labour. . . .

5. INTERNATIONAL SPECIALIZATION AND COMPREHENSIVE ECONOMIC DEVELOPMENT IN INDIVIDUAL SOCIALIST COUNTRIES

The world socialist economic system provides favourable conditions not only for the consistent and planned extension of division of labour between countries, but also for building up in each of them a rational complex of inter-related and complementary industries. . . .

The economic complex in each country should be developed in a way that will continuously raise the country's economic level. This presupposes above all maximum development of each country's socialist industry as the leading branch of the national economy, with priority given to the output of the means of production. . . .

As to industries which exist in all or in the majority of the socialist countries, it is advisable to extend inter-state specialization by product. In furthering specialization, account should be taken not only of the requirements of the socialist countries, but also of possibilities for export outside the world socialist system. . . .

6. ELIMINATION OF HISTORICAL DIFFERENCES IN ECONOMIC DEVELOPMENT LEVELS OF THE SOCIALIST COUNTRIES

When they set out to build a socialist society, the countries of the world socialist system differed in level of development of their productive forces. The very nature of socialism dictates equalization of these levels. . . .

In the course of building socialism and communism there will be eliminated the substantial differences in the level of development of national productive forces, differences that stem from the historical conditions of capitalist development. . . .

To enhance the effect of these countries' efforts in accelerated economic expansion, the other socialist countries:

—share their advanced knowledge in science and technology;

—help in designing modern plants, prospecting and exploration, and in the training of skilled personnel;

—supply industrial equipment, notably complete plant, and assist with its installation and adjustment;

—grant credits and other forms of aid. . . .

7. DIVISION OF LABOUR AND TRADE BETWEEN SOCIALIST COUNTRIES

International socialist division of labour is the basis for trade between the socialist countries, which is carried out on the principle of equivalent exchange. . . .

Multilateral co-ordination of plans and the resultant recommendations for specialization and co-operation should ensure that each socialist country has a balanced payments structure, notably through wider use of multilateral settlements. . . .

It is necessary continually to perfect the system of price formation on the world socialist market in keeping with the requirements of the planned extension of the international socialist division of labour, steady expansion of trade, and accelerated development of the world socialist economy, while creating conditions for the gradual change-over to an independent price basis. . . .

As economic co-operation between the socialist countries grows in strength and scope and more experience is gained in international specialization and co-operation of production, the principles of international socialist division of labour formulated here will be perfected, elaborated and enlarged.

Appendix VII

SENIOR OFFICERS OF COMECON, 1966

EXECUTIVE COMMITTEE

(all Deputy Premiers)

A. Apro, Hungary; J. Balkow, GDR; D. Gombozhav, Mongolia; P. Jaroszewicz, Poland; M. A. Lesechko, USSR; G. Radulescu, Rumania; O. Simunek, Czechoslovakia; S. Todorov, Bulgaria

CHAIRMEN OF STANDING COMMISSIONS

Commissions in Moscow

Statistics: V. N. Starovsky, Director of the Central Statistical Administration of the USSR.

Economic Questions: A. V. Korobov, Deputy Chairman of the USSR State Planning Commission.

Foreign Trade: N. S. Patolichev, Minister of Foreign Trade of the USSR.

Currency and Finance Questions: V. F. Garbuzov, Minister of Finance of the USSR.

Co-ordination of Scientific and Technical Research: D. M. Gvishiani, Deputy Chairman of the USSR State Committee for Co-ordination of Scientific and Technical Research.

Electric Power: N. S. Neporozhny, Minister for Energy and Electrification of the USSR.

Use of Atomic Energy for Peaceful Purposes: A. M. Petrosyants, Chairman of the USSR State Committee for the Use of Atomic Energy.

Ferrous Metals: V. E. Boiko, Minister of Ferrous Metallurgy of the USSR.

Berlin

Chemicals: G. Wyschofsky, Minister of Chemical Industry.

Construction: G. Kosel, President of the Construction Academy.

Standardization: R. Görbing, Director of the Standardization Office.

Bucharest

Oil and Gas: A. Boaba, Minister of the Oil and Chemicals Industry.

Budapest

Non-ferrous Metals: F. Levardi, Minister of Heavy Industry.

Radio-technical and Electronic Industry: Gy. Horgos, Minister of Metallurgy and the Machine Industry.

Prague

Engineering: K. Polacek, Minister without Portfolio.

Light Industry: B. Machacova-Dostalova, Minister of Consumers' Goods Industry.

Sofia

Agriculture: N. Palagchev, Minister of Agricultural Production.

Food Industry: A. Dimitrov, Minister of Food and Light Industry.

Ulan-Bator

Geology: M. Pelzhee, Minister of Geology.

Warsaw

Coal: J. Mitrega, Minister of Coal Mining and Power.

Transport: P. Lewinski, Minister of Transport.

SECRETARIAT

Secretary: N. V. Faddeev (USSR).

Deputy Secretaries: K. Gregor (GDR); K. Martinka (Czechoslovakia); N. Tabacopol (Rumania); I. Vincze (Hungary); G. Zhelev (Bulgaria); Z. Zborowski (Poland).

Director of Department of Economic and Scientific-Technical Information: K. Laur.

INTERNATIONAL BANK OF ECONOMIC CO-OPERATION, 1965

COUNCIL

K. Nestorov, D. Bazhdarov, V. Todorov (Bulgaria); O. Pohl, M. Dluhos, M. Honusek (Czechoslovakia); H. Dietrich, R. Mager, F. Linder (GDR); B. Sulyok, A. Laszlo, I. Baczoni (Hungary); L. Lkhamsuren, E. Ochir (Mongolia); S. Majewski, H. Kotlicki, M. Dmochowski (Poland); R. Manescu, C. Maioreanu, V. Rauta (Rumania); A. Poskonov, P. Maletin, L. Zorin (Soviet Union).

BOARD

K. Nazarkin (Chairman), N. Anghel, A. Fodor, G. Kulessa, J. Malat, R. Malesa, Ts. Molom, G. Terziev.

Appendix VIII

COMECON PERMANENT AGENCIES

Note: The list of subcommittees and working parties is incomplete.[1]

Title	*Date of authorization*	*Amendments*	*HQ*	S: *Subcommittee* (*sektsiya*) WP: *Working Party* (*rabochaya gruppa*)
Standing Commissions				
1. Agriculture	May 1956	After June 1958 included forestry (separate Commission 1956–8)	Sofia	S: (*a*) fruit and vegetables, (*b*) agricultural fairs, (*c*) veterinary problems, (*d*) agricultural co-operatives, (*e*) packaging, (*f*) grain, (*g*) irrigation and melioration, (*h*) forestry.
				WP: (*a*) agricultural research, (*b*) maize, (*c*) pests (formerly on Colorado beetle), (*d*) mechanization, (*e*) livestock, (*f*) seeds.
				S: petrochemicals.

[1] The list of subcommittees and working parties has been revised in the light of the chronology of meetings in Agoston, pp. 280–309. This has, for example, permitted the identification of subcommittees of the Engineering Committee (reported as 13 by *N. Deutsch*, 3 May 1964). In some cases Agoston has a different classification (S for WP or WP for S as the case may be) and the precise position is by no means clear. Thus he lists a meeting on coke chemicals (Prague, October 1958) both as an 'expert group' of the Ferrous Metals Commission and as a Subcommittee of the Coal Commission; this dual classification is included in the above list.

Title	*Date of authorization*	*Amendments*	*HQ*	S: *Subcommittee* (*sektsiya*) WP: *Working Party* (*rabochaya gruppa*)
Standing Commissions cont.				
2. Chemicals Industry	May 1956		Berlin	WP: (*a*) mineral fertilizers, (*b*) pesticides, (*c*) plastics, (*d*) chemical fibres, (*e*) synthetic rubber, (*f*) rubber & tyre industry, (*g*) textile auxiliaries & detergents, (*h*) inorganic products, (*i*) photographic chemicals, (*j*) cellulose & paper, (*k*) varnishes & paints, (*l*) dyestuffs, (*m*) pharmaceuticals, (*n*) complete projects, (*o*) long-term planning.
3. Coal	May 1956		Warsaw	S: coke chemicals. WP: (*a*) mechanization of extraction, (*b*) prospecting, (*c*) pressure gasification of brown coal.
4. Electric Power	May 1956		Moscow	S: (*a*) international grid and general power problems, (*b*) hydro-electric power, (*c*) thermal power, (*d*) research, (*e*) Danube development.
5. Engineering	May 1956		Prague	S: (*a*) roller-friction bearings, (*b*) instrument-making & automation, (*c*) machine tools, (*d*) motor vehicles, (*e*) tractors & agricul-

				tural engineering, (*f*) telecommunications, (*g*) heavy engineering, (*h*) general engineering, (*i*) electrical engineering, (*j*) shipbuilding, (*k*) ball bearings, (*l*) mining equipment, (*m*) electronics.
6. Ferrous Metals	May 1956		Moscow	S: (*a*) coke chemicals, (*b*) rolled steel, (*c*) pig-iron smelting & ore processing.
7. Non-Ferrous Metals	May 1956		Budapest	S: (*a*) non-ferrous metals processing; (*b*) analysis of rare metals. WP: enrichment.
8. Foreign Trade	May 1956		Moscow	S: arbitration.
9. Oil and Gas	May 1956		Bucharest	WP: (*a*) pipelines, (*b*) lubricants.
10. Timber and Cellulose	May 1956	Abolished June 1958[2]	Budapest	
11. Geology	May 1956	Abolished June 1958, revived July 1963[3]	Moscow 1956–58; Ulan-Bator 1963	
12. Construction	June 1958		Berlin	S: (*a*) town planning, (*b*) building specification, (*c*) refractories, (*d*) building materials, (*e*) planning, (*f*) economics.

[2] Became WP of Chemicals Commission (1st meeting Budapest, Nov. 1958).
[3] A conference of heads of Central Geological Agencies of Comecon countries was held in Moscow in June 1963.

Title	Date of authorization	Amendments	HQ	S: *Subcommittee* (*sektsiya*) WP: *Working Party* (*rabochaya gruppa*)
Standing Commissions cont.				WP: (*a*) building equipment, (*b*) glass and ceramics, (*c*) standardized buildings, (*d*) rural construction.
13. Economic Questions	June 1958		Moscow	WP: (*a*) national income, (*b*) accounting (real-income comparison), (*c*) industrial classification [(*a*)–(*c*) transferred to Statistics Commission, 1963], (*d*) investment efficiency, (*e*) prime costs (combined with (*f*), 1965), (*f*) price formation.
14. Transport[4]	June 1958		Warsaw	S: air transport.
				WP: (*a*) railway electrification, (*b*) air transport, (*c*) road feeders to rail transport, (*d*) long-distance road haulage, (*e*) maritime transport, (*f*) inland waterways.
15. Light [and Food] Industries	Dec. 1958	Food industry separated in July 1963	Prague	S: (*a*) co-ordination of research in textiles, leather, footwear, & food processing, (*b*) cotton.
				WP: (*a*) footwear, (*b*) textiles, (*c*) edible oils.
16. Use of Atomic Energy for Peaceful Purposes	July 1960		Moscow	S: (*a*) nuclear power, (*b*) nuclear engineering. WP: radio-active isotopes.

17. Co-ordination of Scientific and Technical Research	June 1962	Moscow	
18. Statistics[5]	June 1962	Moscow	WP: (*a*) classification of divisions of the national economy, (*b*) indicators of the level of economic development, (*c*) industrial statistics, (*d*) agricultural statistics, (*e*) foreign trade statistics,[6] (*f*) basic labour statistics, (*g*) family budgets, (*h*) mechanization of records & statistical systems.
19. Standardization	June 1962	Berlin	
20. Currency and Finance Questions	Dec. 1962	Moscow	
21. Food Industry	July 1963	Sofia	WP: food preserves.
22. Radio-Technical and Electronic Industry	July 1963	Budapest	
Comecon Institutes			
23. Institute of Standardization	June 1962	Moscow	
24. Central Control Office for Interconnected Power System	July 1962	Prague	

[4] Previously an Operational Group (*Operativnaya gruppa*) (1st meeting Warsaw, Aug. 1957). Air agreement signed in Berlin, Oct. 1965.

[5] A Conference of Directors of Central Statistical Offices of Comecon countries was held in Moscow in March 1962.

[6] A Conference of Foreign-Trade Statisticians of Comecon countries was held in Moscow in March 1959.

Title	Date of authorization	Amendments	HQ	S: *Subcommittee* (*sektsiya*) WP: *Working Party* (*rabochaya gruppa*)
Comecon Institutes cont.				
25. Bureau for the Co-ordination of Ship Charters	Dec. 1963		Moscow	
26. Bureau of Executive Committee for Integrated Planning Problems	1963[7]		Moscow	
27. International Bank of Economic Co-operation	Oct. 1963		Moscow	
Agencies within the Framework of Comecon but not Embracing All Members				
28. Common Waggon Pool (OPW)	Dec. 1963		Prague	
29. Intermetall	July 1964		Budapest	
30. Organization for Co-operation in the Ball-bearing Industries	April 1964[8]		Warsaw	

[7] Probably authorized in July 1963.

[8] Committee for Ball Bearings created as 'provisional commission' in Apr. 1963, abolished Dec. 1963, reverting to subcommittee of Engineering Commission.

Appendix IX

NON-COMECON AGENCIES OF SOCIALIST COUNTRIES

Note: For fuller details see A. Alekseev and Yu. Shiryaev, eds., *Mezhdunarodnye ekonomicheskie i nauchnotekhnicheskie organizatsii sotsialisticheskykh stran* (Moscow, 1966).

Title	*Place & date of creation*	*HQ*
1. Danube Commission	In present form Belgrade, July 1948	Galatz to 1954; subsequently Budapest
2. Warsaw Treaty Organization	Warsaw, May 1955	Moscow
2a. Economic Commission of WTO[1]	Melnik (Czechoslovakia) Dec. 1957	Moscow
3. United Institute for Nuclear Research	Moscow, Mar. 1956	Dubna (USSR)
4. Organization for International Railway Co-operation	Sofia, June 1956	Warsaw[2]
4a. Control-Regulation (Exploitation) Office	Prague, 1959	Prague
5. Organization for the Co-operation of Socialist Countries in Telecommunications and Posts	Moscow, Dec. 1957	[3]
6. Mixed Commission for the Application of Agreements on the Regulation of Fisheries in Danubian Waters	Bucharest, Jan. 1958	Bucharest
7. Conference of Central Banks of Socialist Countries	Prague, May–June 1958	[4]

[1] May form a Defence Industry Commission of Comecon, the activities of which are not reported.

[2] By decision of 2nd sess. (Peking, May–June 1957) the headquarters should move every five years; it has, however, remained in Warsaw.

[3] The postal administration of the country in which the next ordinary annual meeting is to be held.

[4] No permanent secretariat.

Title	*Place & date of creation*	*HQ*
8. Conference of Directors of Danube Shipping Lines of Member-Countries of CMEA	Bratislava, Sept. 1955	[4]
9. Kubalko (Joint Shipping Conference of Cuba, GDR, Poland, and Czechoslovakia)	Nov. 1962	Gdynia
10. International Organization for Radio and Television	Prague July 1946	Prague
10a. Intervisia	Budapest Jan. 1960	Prague

[4] No permanent secretariat.

Bibliographical Abbreviations

Auss.:	*Der Aussenhandel* (GDR)
BSE:	*Bolshaya Sovetskaya Entsiklopediya* (USSR)
Chim. Tech.:	*Chimische Technik* (GDR)
Cz. Econ. P.:	*Czechoslovak Economic Papers* (Czechoslovakia)
Den. i Kr.:	*Dengi i Kredit* (USSR)
Econ. B. Eur.:	*Economic Bulletin for Europe* (UN)
Econ. Survey Eur.:	*Economic Survey of Europe* (UN)
Econ. J.:	*Economic Journal* (UK)
Econ. Plan.:	*Economics of Planning* (Norway)
Ek.:	*Ekonomista* (Poland)
Ek. gaz.:	*Ekonomicheskaya gazeta* (USSR)
Ek. pop.:	*Ekonomia popullore* (Albania)
Fin. SSSR:	*Finansy SSSR* (to 1954 *Finansy i Kredit*) (USSR)
Gosp. plan.:	*Gospodarka planowa* (Poland)
Hand. zag.:	*Handel zagraniczny* (Poland)
Hosp. nov.:	*Hospodarske noviny* (Czechoslovakia)
Ik. misl:	*Ikonomicheska misl* (Bulgaria)
Information on Economic Co-operation:	*Information on Economic Co-operation between the countries of the CMEA* (Comecon, 1963)
Int. Aff.:	*International Affairs* (USSR)
Int. Con.:	*International Conciliation* (USA)
Inwest. bud.:	*Inwestycje i budownictwo* (Poland)
Iz.:	*Izvestia* (USSR)
J. Int. Aff.:	*Journal of International Affairs* (USA)
J. Pol. Econ.:	*Journal of Political Economy* (USA)
Komm.:	*Kommunist* (USSR)
Koz. Sz.:	*Kozgazdasagi Szemle* (Hungary)
Kulk. Ert.:	*Kulkereskelmi Ertesito* (Hungary)
Mezh. sels. zhur.:	*Mezhdunarodny selskokhozyaistvenny zhurnal* (Comecon)
Mir. ekon.:	*Mirovaya ekonomica i mezhdunarodnye otnoshenie* (USSR)
Monthly B. Statist.:	*Monthly Bulletin of Statistics* (UN)
N. Deutsch.:	*Neues Deutschland* (GDR)
N. drogi:	*Nowe drogi* (Poland)

Nep.: *Nepszabadsag* (Hungary)
Peking R.: *Peking Review* (China)
Plan. Hosp.: *Planovane Hospodarstvi* (Czechoslovakia)
Plan. khoz.: *Planovoe khozyaistvo* (USSR)
Plan. stop.: *Planovo stopanstvo i statistika* (Bulgaria)
Pol. Ek.: *Politicka Ekonomie* (Czechoslovakia)
Pr.: *Pravda* (USSR)
Prob. econ.: *Probleme economice* (Rumania)
R. éc. et soc.: *Revue économique et sociale* (Switzerland)
R. Econ. Statist.: *Review of Economics and Statistics* (USA)
RP: *Rude Pravo* (Czechoslovakia)
R. pol. int.: *Revue de la politique internationale* (Yugoslavia)
Rab. delo: *Rabotnichesko delo* (Bulgaria)
Sc.: *Scinteia* (Rumania)
Slav. R.: *Slavic Review* (USA)
Sov. gos. pravo: *Sovetskoe gosudarstvo i pravo* (prewar *Sovetskoe gosudarstvo*) (USSR)
Sov. Stud.: *Soviet Studies* (UK)
Statist. Bs: *Statistical Bulletins* (OECD)
Statist. Yb.: *Statistical Yearbook* (UN)
Stats. Tid.: *Statsokonomisk Tideskrift* (Norway)
Sz. Nep: *Szabad Nep* (Hungary)
Tars. Sz.: *Tarsadalmi Szemle* (Hungary)
Tryb. Lud.: *Trybuna Ludu* (Poland)
Ved. Verkh. Sov. SSSR: *Vedomosti verkhovnogo Soveta SSSR* (USSR)
Vest. stat.: *Vestnik statistiki* (USSR)
Vnesh. pol. SS: *Vneshnyaya politika Sovetskogo Soyuza* (USSR)
Vnesh. torg.: *Vneshnyaya torgovlya* (USSR)
Vnesh. trg.: *Vneshna trgovia* (Bulgaria)
Vopr. ekon.: *Voprosy ekonomiki* (USSR)
Vopr. ist.: *Voprosy istorii* (USSR)
Wirts.: *Wirtschaftswissenschaft* (GDR)
Wiss. Z.H.O.: *Wissenschaftliche Zeitung der Hochschule für Ökonomie* (GDR)
Wld Econ. Survey: *World Economic Survey* (UN)
Wld Marx. R.: *World Marxist Review* (Czechoslovakia)
Wld Pol.: *World Politics* (USA)
Yb. Internat. Trade Statist.: *Yearbook of International Trade Statistics* (UN)

Yb. Wld Aff.:	*Yearbook of World Affairs* (UK)
Zer. pop.:	*Zeri i popullit* (Albania)
Zyc. gos.:	*Zycie gospodarcze* (Poland)
Zyc. Part.:	*Zycie Partii* (Poland)
Zyc. War.:	*Zycie Warszawy* (Poland)

Note: Throughout the text diacritical marks have been omitted from eastern European names for typographical reasons.

Index

Organization chart of Comecon (excl

SE

EXECUTI

SEC

SECTOR COMMISSIONS	SECTOR DEPARTMENTS
CHEMICALS	CHEMICALS
FERROUS METALS	FERROUS METALS
NON-FERROUS METALS	NON-FERROUS METALS
OIL AND GAS	OIL AND GAS
COAL	COAL
ELECTRIC POWER	ELECTRIC POWER
ENGINEERING	ENGINEERING
RADIO-TECHNICAL AND ELECTRONIC INDUSTRY	RADIO-TECHNICAL AND ELECTRONIC INDUSTRY
LIGHT INDUSTRY	LIGHT INDUSTRY
FOOD INDUSTRY	FOOD INDUSTRY
AGRICULTURE	AGRICULTURE
CONSTRUCTION	CONSTRUCTION
TRANSPORT	TRANSPORT
USE OF ATOMIC ENERGY FOR PEACEFUL PURPOSES	USE OF ATOMIC ENERGY FOR PEACEFUL PURPOSES
GEOLOGY	GEOLOGY